Object-Oriented Reuse, Concurrency and Distribution

AN ADA-BASED APPROACH

SELECTED TITLES

Object-Oriented Reuse, Concurrency and Distribution

AN ADA-BASED APPROACH

Colin Atkinson

University of Houston-Clear Lake

ACM Press

New York, New York

Addison-Wesley Publishing Company

Wokingham, England · Reading, Massachusetts · Menlo Park, California · New York
Don Mills, Ontario · Amsterdam · Bonn · Sydney · Singapore
Tokyo · Madrid · San Juan · Milan · Paris · Mexico City · Seoul · Taipei

ACM Press Books

Copyright© 1991 by the ACM Press, A Division of the Association for Computing Machinery, Inc. (ACM).

Cover designed by Hybert Design and Type, Maidenhead
incorporating an artist's impression of the Freedom
space station, courtesy of NASA, and
printed by The Riverside Printing Co. (Reading) Ltd.
Printed in Great Britain by T.J. Press (Padstow) Ltd, Cornwall.

First printed 1991.

British Library Cataloguing in Publication Data
Atkinson, Colin
   Object-oriented reuse, concurrency and distribution :
   an Ada-based approach.
   I. Title
   005.113

   ISBN 0201565277

Library of Congress Cataloging in Publication Data
Atkinson, Colin.
     Object-oriented reuse, concurrency, and distribution : An Ada
   -based approach / Colin Atkinson.
        p.   cm.
     Includes bibliographical references and index.
     ISBN 0-201-56527-7
     1. Object-oriented programming.   2. Ada (Computer program
language)   3. DRAGOON (Computer program language)   I. Title.
QA76.64.A85   1991   91-22599
005. 1--dc20   CIP

Foreword

This book by Colin Atkinson describes in an eminently readable way the DRAGOON language which arose as part of the outcome of the Esprit DRAGON project. DRAGOON brings together within a single framework two important threads of development which emerged into practical use in the last decade, although their seeds were sown earlier. These developments are Ada and the Object-Oriented paradigm.

Ada is important because it addresses key problems of Software Engineering such as reliability, reuse, programming-in-the-large, parallelism, error recovery and portability. It is a fact that those who have used Ada for the development of serious systems have been well satisfied and shown reluctance to return to more primitive languages such as Fortran and C. Nevertheless, nothing is perfect and Ada's facilities for reuse are somewhat rigid.

The Object-Oriented paradigm is equally important because it has brought some structural help to the general problem of how to design systems. The general idea of designing a system around the objects being manipulated (rather than the manipulations themselves) seems to have borne fruit. However, it has equally appeared that there is a world of difference between Object-Oriented Design (OOD) and Object-Oriented Programing (OOP). OOD is generally acclaimed as a good thing and indeed Ada fits in well as an implementation language for OOD. The OOP languages on the other hand seem to have pros and cons; they appear to have excellent potential for reuse especially through rapid prototyping but equally need care in application if understandability of the resultant system is to be achieved – and this of course is very important for long-term maintenance.

The C++ language is currently a popular vehicle for OOP but appears to suffer from serious problems of reliability and readability. The Eiffel language, however, captures the principles of OOP within a much more elegant, understandable and coherent framework; but Eiffel does not have the extensive software engineering features of Ada nor is it widely available. What DRAGOON does is incorporate the ideas of Eiffel into an Ada extension which can be implemented by a translator which converts DRAGOON into normal Ada and which is therefore immediately available via the very large number of mature Ada implementations which now exist. One of the most exciting features of DRAGOON is its wide use of multiple inheritance as a general principle in areas as diverse as concurrency and distribution.

Colin is to be congratulated on an excellent book which is a must for all OOP enthusiasts and Ada engineers. It shows each community the key facilities of the technology of the other, including a chapter outlining the major concepts of OOP and an appendix outlining the major features of Ada, and thus is immediately accessible to a wide audience.

J G P Barnes
Reading, June 1991

Preface

Object-oriented languages have become popular in many different spheres of computing, but an important application domain in which they have failed to make a significant impact is that of embedded (real-time) systems. Such systems present problems of scale and complexity for which the reuse and modularity features of object-oriented languages would be invaluable, but also have special features, such as concurrency and distribution, that 'mainstream' object-oriented languages like C++ and Eiffel do not at present address.

In this application domain it is important to distinguish true object-oriented *languages* from object-oriented *design methods*. The latter have become very popular for modelling and imposing structure on the high-level architecture of embedded software systems, but lack the mechanisms of inheritance, polymorphism and dynamic binding that make object-oriented languages so powerful for supporting reuse. It is precisely these mechanisms which come into conflict with the requirements of concurrent and distributed systems.

This book describes some ideas developed in the European Esprit project DRAGON for exploiting the advantages of object-oriented programming in the development of embedded systems. These are embodied in the prototype language DRAGOON which provides most of the features of existing 'mainstream' object-oriented languages, but enhances the conventional inheritance model to support concurrency and distribution.

Because of the importance of Ada in the embedded systems industry and the desire to create a practical language, DRAGOON is heavily Ada-oriented. Most of its features for 'programming in the small' are borrowed from Ada, and all the object-oriented constructs were designed to fit in with Ada's style and ethos. In a sense, therefore, DRAGOON can be regarded as an Ada enhancement. Another principal design goal, however, was that DRAGOON source code be readily translatable into standard Ada, so DRAGOON can also be regarded as an Ada-oriented design notation.

Readership

The book is intended for software engineers and students who are interested in the techniques of object-oriented programming and how they may be applied to the construction of software for embedded systems. The ideas presented should be of particular interest to those involved in the development of Ada systems, since DRAGOON is very much intended to be accessible to people with Ada experience.

Several of the chapters do require a superficial knowledge of Ada, so for those unfamiliar with the language an overview of its main features is provided in Appendix A. However, a full understanding of the material in Chapter 9, which describes the DRAGOON-to-Ada translation, requires a much more detailed knowledge of Ada than that provided in Appendix A, and interested readers with a weak Ada background are referred to a standard Ada text such as Barnes (1989).

Organization

The material in the book is largely derived from the author's PhD thesis 'An Object-Oriented Language for Software Reuse and Distribution' completed towards the end of 1989. This has been extensively updated and reorganized into the present text of ten chapters.

The first three chapters are mainly introductory. Chapter 1 provides the general background to the book and describes the case study used throughout. A single, large case study was chosen in preference to many small examples to try to convey the unifying nature of the DRAGOON framework. This is a greatly simplified version of a computer system responsible for controlling a large supermarket or store. However, the basic architecture and communication patterns of the system are exhibited by many other embedded systems, so it serves as a general model for the development of DRAGOON software. Chapter 2 aims to describe the basic principles of object-oriented programming. Readers acquainted with these ideas may wish to move directly to one of the other specialized areas. Chapter 3 describes how the basic mechanisms of object-oriented languages described in Chapter 2 are realized in DRAGOON in an Ada-oriented fashion.

Chapters 4 and 5 address the issue of software reuse. Chapter 4 describes how the mechanisms of inheritance, polymorphism and dynamic binding combine to simplify the construction of component libraries and the construction of new applications. Chapter 5 compares the type of polymorphism offered by object-oriented languages with an alternative form known as genericity and describes how this is supported in DRAGOON.

Chapter 6 is concerned with the problems of concurrent systems and describes DRAGOON's new technique for handling the conflict between synchronization and inheritance-based reuse.

Chapters 7 and 8 deal with the other main problem addressed by DRAGOON – distribution. Chapter 7 describes the constraints that must be applied to the general object-model in order to produce objects appropriate for dispersal over the nodes of a network, leaving Chapter 8 to describe how a special form of inheritance is used to configure an executing distributed system.

Chapter 9 describes how the object-oriented features of DRAGOON are implemented by uniform translation into standard Ada. Finally, Chapter 10 describes other related research conducted in the DRAGON project and reviews the fundamental design principles embodied in DRAGOON.

Acknowledgments

Most of the ideas described in this book were developed as part of the European Esprit project, DRAGON (No. 1550), by members of the following three establishments: TXT S.p.A. (Milan), GSI-Tecsi (Paris) and Imperial College (London)[1]. I would like to express my gratitude to the Commission of the European Communities and the Imperial College of Science, Technology and Medicine for making the DRAGON project, and my participation in it, possible.

DRAGOON was created by the enthusiastic collaboration of people from several different countries, especially Andrea Di Maio (DRAGON project manager) and Stefano Genolini of TXT, Rami Bayan and Catherine Destombes of Tecsi, Stefano Crespi-Reghizzi of TXT and the Politecnico di Milano, and Stephen Goldsack and myself of Imperial College. Although it is difficult in a project of this nature to delineate each member's contribution, several people deserve a special mention. The original idea for behavioural inheritance is due to Stefano Crespi-Reghizzi, but its realization in DRAGOON is primarily due to Andrea Di Maio and Stephen Goldsack. The DRAGOON distribution model, on the other hand, is largely due to Rami Bayan.

In addition to the DRAGON project members, I would like to thank my colleagues in the Department of Computing at Imperial College for providing the support and environment necessary to work on a project of this kind. I am particularly grateful to the people who have read and commented on earlier versions of this work – David Auty, John Barnes, Andrew Davison, Stephen Goldsack, Sandra Holzbacher, Jeremy Pitt, Diana Protic, Charlie Randall, Cathy Rogers, Pat Rogers and Ian Sommerville.

At the time of writing there are several detailed aspects of DRA-GOON that have not yet been fully finalized. Consequently, the language

---

[1]The other participants in the project, who worked on related topics, were Dornier (Friedrichshafen), University College of Wales (Aberystwyth), University of Lancaster, University of Passau, University of Genoa and the Politecnico di Milano.

described in this book may not, in its entirety, represent the eventual language standard.

In order to distinguish between code written in the two languages, the keywords of Ada will be in **bold** while those of DRAGOON will appear in sans serif.

DRAGOON preprocessor

The DRAGOON-to-Ada preprocessor produced in the DRAGON project was developed by TXT S.p.A. in Milan. It may be used with any Ada compiler, and at the time of writing is supported on VAX and Sun workstation platforms under UNIX and VMS respectively. Certain aspects of DRAGOON, mainly in the area of distribution, are yet to be fully implemented by the preprocessor. Enquiries should be directed to:

> Andrea Di Maio,
> TXT Ingeneria Informatica S.p.A.,
> Via Socrate 41,
> 20128 Milano,
> ITALY.

Colin Atkinson
Houston, July 1991.

Contents

Foreword   v

Preface   vii

1 Introduction   1
   1.1 The role of Ada   2
   1.2 Object-oriented software development   2
   1.3 The DRAGON project   3
   1.4 Supermarket control system   4

2 Object-Oriented Programming   7
   2.1 Basic principles   7
        2.1.1 Objects   8
        2.1.2 Classes   9
        2.1.3 Object-oriented design   10
   2.2 Object-oriented languages   11
        2.2.1 'Pure' languages   11
        2.2.2 Clientship   13
        2.2.3 Polymorphism and dynamic binding   14
        2.2.4 Typing   15
        2.2.5 Inheritance   15
        2.2.6 Persistence   18
   2.3 Classification schemes   18

3 Introducing DRAGOON   23
   3.1 Programming philosophy   23
        3.1.1 A mixed paradigm   25
        3.1.2 Data abstraction   26
        3.1.3 Outline design of the supermarket control system . .   27
   3.2 Template packages   29
        3.2.1 Templates in the supermarket control system   29
   3.3 Objects and classes   30

                                                                         xi

	3.3.1	Clientship	32
	3.3.2	Class bodies	33
3.4	Inheritance		35
	3.4.1	Method modification	38
	3.4.2	Multiple inheritance	40
3.5	Typing scheme		41
	3.5.1	Class and data types	43
	3.5.2	Type compatibility	44
	3.5.3	Conformance	45
	3.5.4	Subtypes	45
	3.5.5	Terminology	46
	3.5.6	Type conversion	48

4 Inheritance-Based Reuse   53
4.1	Component engineering		53
	4.1.1	Component families	54
4.2	Component hierarchies		56
	4.2.1	Iterator queue	58
	4.2.2	Bounded queue	60
4.3	Abstract classes		62
	4.3.1	Pre/post conditions	63
	4.3.2	Completing methods	64
4.4	Dynamic binding		66
	4.4.1	Extensibility	67
4.5	Programming by difference		70

5 Genericity   73
5.1	Parametric polymorphism		73
5.2	Constrained and unconstrained genericity		74
5.3	Genericity versus inclusion polymorphism		77
	5.3.1	Declaration by association	79
5.4	Parameterization contract		81
5.5	Inheriting genericity		83
	5.5.1	Type compatibility and generic classes	84
	5.5.2	Method overloading	85

6 Concurrency   89
6.1	Approaches to concurrency		89
6.2	Concurrency in object-oriented languages		92
	6.2.1	Exclusion synchronization and inheritance	96
	6.2.2	Separating synchronization and functionality	97
6.3	Behavioural inheritance		98
	6.3.1	History functions	99
	6.3.2	Behavioural and behavioured classes	101
	6.3.3	The exclusion symbol	104
	6.3.4	Alternative readers/writers behaviours	104

  6.4 Behavioural class libraries 106
      6.4.1 Booch temporal forms 106
  6.5 Active objects 108
      6.5.1 Threads 108
  6.6 Agents 110
      6.6.1 Condition synchronization 111
  6.7 Forwarder objects 114
  6.8 Guarded permissions 117
      6.8.1 Guard evaluation semantics 118
  6.9 Future development 120
      6.9.1 Method families 122
  6.10 Building concurrent systems 123
      6.10.1 Reconfiguration 125

7 Distribution   **129**
  7.1 Loosely coupled distributed systems 129
      7.1.1 Object-orientation and distributed systems 130
  7.2 Programming distributed systems 131
      7.2.1 Separation of concerns 132
      7.2.2 Characteristics of virtual nodes 134
      7.2.3 Suitability of objects 135
      7.2.4 Reference-free communication 136
  7.3 Virtual node objects 137
      7.3.1 Instance variable categories 139
      7.3.2 Method categories 140
      7.3.3 Virtual node construction rules 140
  7.4 Virtual nodes in the supermarket control system 142
      7.4.1 Transferring object state 143
      7.4.2 Transferring attribute values 144

8 System Configuration   **149**
  8.1 Executing programs 149
      8.1.1 The 'main program' concept 150
      8.1.2 'Heavyweight' and 'lightweight' objects 152
  8.2 Execution support classes 152
  8.3 Physical node objects 155
  8.4 Software and hardware system components 157
      8.4.1 Corresponding system classes 159
  8.5 System calls and interrupts 161
      8.5.1 Device drivers 161
      8.5.2 Abstract hardware interfaces 164
      8.5.3 Interrupt methods 166
      8.5.4 Network specification 168
  8.6 Execution model 169
      8.6.1 Centralized reconfiguration 172
      8.6.2 Decentralized reconfiguration 177

9 Translation into Ada   **183**

9.1   Implementation strategies 183
    9.1.1   'Abstract state machine' packages 183
    9.1.2   Tasks 184
    9.1.3   Abstract data types 185
    9.1.4   DRAGOON translation strategy 188
9.2   Representation of object state 190
    9.2.1   The CREATE function 192
    9.2.2   The PART_OF function 194
    9.2.3   Linear inheritance 194
    9.2.4   Clientship 197
9.3   Dynamic binding 198
    9.3.1   Method selection shells 199
    9.3.2   Multiple offspring 202
    9.3.3   Abstract classes 204
9.4   Multiple inheritance 205
9.5   Generic classes 209
    9.5.1   Inheriting genericity 211
9.6   Concurrency 212
    9.6.1   Active objects 212
    9.6.2   Behavioured classes 214
    9.6.3   Guarded permissions 217
9.7   Executable objects 219
    9.7.1   Cross compilation 221
9.8   Distribution 221
    9.8.1   Supporting distributed execution 222

10 Conclusion   **229**

10.1 Other DRAGON research 229
10.2 DRAGOON design principles 231

A Overview of Ada   **235**

A.1   Background 235
A.2   Frames 236
A.3   Flow control 237
    A.3.1   Exceptions 238
A.4   Modularity 238
    A.4.1   Separate compilation 239
    A.4.2   Packages 240
A.5   Data abstraction 241
    A.5.1   Subtypes and derived types 242
    A.5.2   Private types 243
A.6   Generics 244
A.7   Concurrency 245
    A.7.1   The rendezvous 246
A.8   Real-time features 247

A.8.1 Representation clauses 247
A.9   Execution 248
A.10 The future 248

B Glossary   **251**

References   **255**

Program Unit Index   **265**

Index   **267**

Chapter 1
Introduction

Developing software for embedded systems, in which the computers to be
programmed are responsible for controlling encapsulating electromechani-
cal systems, is one of the most difficult and challenging fields of software
engineering. Not only is this type of software required to respond rapidly
and reliably – in 'real-time' – to events in the external environment, but
often has to execute under severe hardware and memory constraints. Moreover, embedded systems tend to be extremely large, and require sizeable
teams of people to program them. In this application domain, therefore,
the typical problems of software engineering are greatly complicated by
considerations of concurrency, reliability, efficiency and software integration.

Early techniques for handling these difficulties tended to be based
on a combination of ad hoc language modifications and operating system
'fixes'. However, this approach soon led to a proliferation of language
dialects, the fragmentation of the programming community, and ultimately
the erosion of prospects for sharing expertise and software between different
projects. This, in turn, lowered the productivity of programmers, and
the quality of software, while hardware became ever more powerful and
cheaper. Manufacturers and users of embedded systems have thus been
forced to place increasing emphasis on *reuse* at all stages in the software
lifecycle, in order to combat the escalating cost of software development,
and the typically poor quality of software delivered to the customer.

The advances in microprocessor and networking technology also fu-
elled a trend towards *distribution*, adding a whole new dimension to the
software construction problems. Distribution has a number of important
advantages over the traditional uniprocessor approach – it not only provides
a cheap, flexible source of processing power, but also offers significant reliability improvements because of its resilience to hardware failure. Moreover,
it introduces the possibility of *dynamic reconfiguration*, in which parts of
a system may be modified without recourse to a complete shutdown. Taking full advantage of these additional possibilities, however, creates extra
demands and difficulties for the software engineer.

The net result of these trends over the past two decades has been to

1

compound the traditional problems of developing software for embedded systems with the demands of software reuse and distribution. The developers of large-scale embedded software systems therefore urgently require a uniform design framework which not only addresses the traditional software engineering problems, but also encourages the reuse of existing software components in the development of new applications, and takes advantages of the prospects for dynamic reconfiguration and fault tolerance offered by distributed systems.

1.1   The role of Ada

By far the most ambitious response to the so-called 'software crisis' in the embedded systems industry was the development of Ada for the United States Department of Defense (DoD, 1983). The aim was to replace the vast number of languages and ad hoc techniques previously in use with a standard programming paradigm that could be used throughout the industry to promote software reuse and programmer productivity. Out of necessity, therefore, Ada is a large, 'broad-spectrum' language, embracing all the well established principles of software engineering as well as providing the special features needed for embedded systems (e.g. multi-tasking, exception handling). In addition, Ada is one of the first languages containing special facilities for overcoming the traditional incompatibility of strong typing and reuse (generics). However, by far the most important feature of the language is the fact that it is a strictly protected standard – no compiler can claim to provide a genuine implementation of the language without passing the rigorous validation tests.

Unfortunately, Ada was developed at a time when the full significance of distribution had not been fully appreciated. It is poorly designed for the purpose of programming such systems, although the need for distribution is acknowledged in the Ada Language Reference Manual (DoD, 1983). Furthermore, the introduction of Ada has not turned out to be the panacea for reuse that was originally hoped. While the language has certainly been the catalyst for significant improvements over the previous state of the art, the expected explosion in the practice of reuse, and emergence of 'software component factories' (McIlroy, 1969) has failed to materialize to any significant degree. Generics, in particular, have proved more difficult to use than was envisaged.

1.2   Object-oriented software development

One of the most promising vehicles for reuse to have emerged in recent years is the rapidly expanding discipline of 'object-oriented programming'. Meyer (1988) and Cox (1986), in particular, have shown how the features of inheritance, dynamic binding and polymorphism offered by this paradigm provide an extremely powerful and elegant approach to reuse, which differs fundamentally from other mechanisms. Certain features of this model can be helpful in the construction of Ada software, and there are now quite a number of 'design methods' that exploit its basic structuring concepts to impose a discipline on the use of Ada. The language does not, however, adequately support the inheritance, polymorphism and dynamic binding mechanisms needed to exploit fully the object-oriented approach.

Existing object-oriented programming languages have their drawbacks as well, however. No previous language has successfully extended this paradigm to handle both concurrency and distribution without sacrificing much of its support for reuse. Object-oriented languages that handle concurrency or distribution, such as POOL (America, 1987) or Emerald (Black *et al*, 1987), do not support an inheritance mechanism permitting the 'reuse' of implementations, while those designed to enhance the reuse advantages of the object-oriented approach, such as Eiffel (Meyer, 1988) and C++ (Stroustrup, 1986), do not tackle concurrency or distribution.

1.3   The DRAGON project

Despite its deficiencies in connection with software reuse and distribution, Ada is still of unique importance in the field of embedded systems. No comparable language has a chance of matching its stability, portability or scale of industrial backing, and without a high degree of standardization, strategies for supporting reuse are of little more than academic interest.

Although languages have been designed, therefore, which are much more powerful than Ada for the separate purposes of reuse (e.g. Eiffel, C++), or distribution (e.g. CONIC (Kramer and Magee, 1985), Argus (Liskov, 1982)), these do little to improve the *overall* prospects for software development in the embedded systems industry. Ada was introduced specifically to counteract the proliferation of specialized languages for particular applications, because this alone is a far stronger force *against* reuse than any features a particular language may provide to support it. What is urgently required is a language that combines the portability and stability advantages of Ada, the reuse mechanisms of object-oriented languages such as Eiffel or C++, and the support for software distribution provided by specialized languages such as CONIC or Argus – all within a unified framework.

To try to meet this need the European Esprit project DRAGON developed a language, called DRAGOON (Distributable, Reusable Ada Generated from an Object-Oriented Notation), which supports all the major features of the object-oriented paradigm, but extends this framework to handle concurrency, distribution and reconfiguration. DRAGOON can be translated into standard Ada for execution, and consequently can be regarded as a design language for Ada. However, since tools have been developed to perform the transformation automatically, DRAGOON can also be regarded as a language in its own right (Di Maio *et al*, 1989).

To make experienced Ada programmers comfortable with the language, all features of DRAGOON alien to Ada have been designed to fit in with the Ada spirit and philosophy. In one sense, therefore, DRAGOON perhaps indicates how Ada might have turned out had the importance of distribution and advantages of object-oriented programming been fully apparent when it was designed, and may provide ideas for the future development of Ada.

DRAGON is not the only project that has developed a preprocessor for translating an object-oriented language into Ada. Several others are described in the literature such as Classic Ada (Bach, 1989), Innovada (Simmonian and Crone, 1988) and Ada++ (Forestier *et al*, 1989). There is a big difference in scope between DRAGOON and these other systems, however, since DRAGOON is the only one that addresses the problems of concurrency and distribution. Moreover, of these systems, only Ada++ has attempted to *integrate* object-oriented concepts with Ada, rather than *superimpose* them at a higher level. The object-oriented features of Classic Ada, in contrast, are strongly tied to those of Smalltalk, while those of Innovada closely resemble Flavors (a Lisp-based language) (Moon, 1986). The programming paradigms adopted by these languages are thus primarily those of existing object-oriented languages alien to Ada.

The purpose of this book is to describe the main ideas embodied in DRAGOON, and the rationale behind them. It is therefore intended to be a supplement to the language reference manual (Di Maio *et al*, 1989), which gives a full description of the language syntax and semantics. In this book the features of DRAGOON will be introduced by means of a case study in which the development of the software for a simplified real-time system is studied.

1.4   Supermarket control system

The system considered is derived from the 'supermarket control system' described in the final report of the DIADEM project (Atkinson *et al*, 1988). This is a simplified version of the type of system used to control the flow of products through a large supermarket or department store. Its main function is to maintain a *database* describing all the products sold in the supermarket so that the *checkout points* distributed throughout the store can establish the prices of the items selected by the customers. These items are identified at the checkout points by means of a laser-readable bar-code.

Storing all product information in a single database, rather than distributing it around the supermarket, simplifies the problem of maintaining consistency, and enables it to be updated from a single *central control point*.

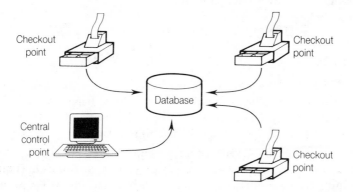

Figure 1.1   Components of the supermarket control system.

This provides the interface to the human managers of the system. As well as giving them access to the information stored in the database, such as the number of items of a given product type currently in stock, it allows them to modify, add or remove the *product descriptors* describing these attributes.

Each type of product sold in the supermarket has an associated product descriptor which stores at least the following four pieces of information:

- unique 'bar-code' number,
- price,
- number of items of the product type currently in stock,
- textual label storing such information as the product name, manufacturer and country of origin.

In addition to these attributes, perishable products, such as foods, have an associated 'sell-by-date' after which time they are no longer fit for sale, while electrical products have an associated fuse rating, describing the size of the fuse needed for their adequate protection.

A real system of this kind would naturally handle many more functions of the supermarket. The DIADEM version, for example, also dealt with aspects of security. However, the simplified view of the system described here is of sufficient complexity to illustrate all important aspects of the DRAGOON language. Any additional requirements will be added where necessary in later chapters.

In the form described, and illustrated in Figure 1.1, the system could be implemented using a single, centralized computer to house the database and control the other components (i.e. the central control and checkout points) as remote devices, or alternatively as a distributed system with a dedicated machine for each component.

Key points

The traditional software engineering challenges presented by the development of software for embedded systems have been compounded over recent years by the need to increase the reuse of software, and to exploit the facilities offered by distributed targets.

Ada is by far the most important language in the embedded systems industry because of the accompanying standardization effort and level of industrial support, but unfortunately is lacking in its support for both reuse and distribution.

Object-oriented languages offer one of the most promising approaches to software reuse to have emerged in recent years. However, 'mainstream' languages do not fully support inheritance-based reuse mechanisms in the domain of concurrent and distributed systems.

Standardization is far more important in the drive towards reuse than special mechanisms particular languages may offer.

DRAGOON attempts to combine the standardization advantages of Ada, the reuse benefits of object-oriented programming languages, and ideas embodied in languages specializing in distribution, within a single, unified object-oriented framework.

All features of DRAGOON have been designed according to the syntactic style and ethos of Ada. The language could therefore be regarded as an object-oriented enhancement of Ada, in the same way that C++ is an object-oriented enhancement of C.

All features of DRAGOON have been designed to be readily implementible by automatic translation into standard Ada. In this sense the language can be regarded as an object-oriented design notation for Ada software.

A single case study is used throughout the book, called the 'supermarket control system'. This is a highly idealized version of a system used to control the flow of goods through a supermarket.

Chapter 2
Object-Oriented Programming

The term 'object-oriented' is now so ubiquitous that no one is quite sure what it means any more, particularly in the field of software development where many widely differing languages, environments and design methods lay claim to this description. Although various attempts have been made to identify and classify the essential properties of the object-oriented philosophy (Wegner, 1987), (Blair *et al*, 1989), the provision of a broad, formal foundation for this model of computation is still some way from realization. It is impossible, therefore, to provide a precise and complete definition of object-oriented programming, but this chapter attempts to allay potential confusion by explaining the different contexts in which the term is used, and by identifying the concepts generally regarded as characterizing object-oriented systems.

2.1   Basic principles

Although new 'declarative' styles of programming have emerged in recent years to challenge the traditional 'imperative' view of software execution, the fundamental structuring concepts of software engineering are still pertinent and valuable tools for guiding the design process, and enabling humans to cope with the complexity of large applications. Chief among these are the principles of *modularity* – splitting a design up into smaller, more manageable components that can be tackled separately; *abstraction* - separating the concerns for what a particular component does from how it does it; and *information hiding* – concealing detail irrelevant at a particular level of abstraction.

Because of their importance, most modern languages directly support at least some of these principles, but often by means of distinct concepts. The modules of languages like Ada and Modula 2, for example, are distinct from the types which they encapsulate. Ada also introduces the additional concept of private types to provide information hiding. In these languages, therefore, the abstraction, modularity and information hiding boundaries within a program do not necessarily coincide.

Much of the current success of the 'object-oriented' view of software construction can be attributed to the fact that it is based on a simple, natural concept through which all these principles are unified – the *object*.

2.1.1   Objects

An object is a named entity that combines a data structure with its associated operations:

object = unique identifier + data + operations.

An object can thus be regarded as a state machine, with an internal state that remembers the effects of operations. Because the state can be manipulated only by those operations exported in the object's interface, the details of its internal implementation are shielded from external view[1]. This ensures that an object interacts with others only at the desired level of abstraction. The principles of data abstraction and information hiding are therefore united with the natural modularity of objects into a single, coherent concept.

Whereas traditional software design strategies focus on the procedural steps a program must perform to achieve the desired goal (i.e. on algorithms), and so tend to draw a distinction between passive data and active operations, the object-oriented approach views a program as a 'model' of the system composed of a set (or federation) of interacting 'objects'. Because these objects integrate data structures with the operations that act upon them, they give the data a much more significant role in determining the software architecture – an emphasis neatly captured in Meyer's (1988) 'motto' for the object-oriented approach:

'Ask not first what the system does, ask what it does it to'.

Organizing software in terms of objects is more than just an elegant technique for encouraging modularity and abstraction, however. It also tends to decentralize knowledge and data in a system, so confining implementation details to those parts that really need access to them. Conventional 'algorithm-oriented' methods, in contrast, tend to produce hierarchical 'master/slave' software structures assigning different levels of importance to different components. As a result, software components higher up in the hierarchy require knowledge of implementation details of

---

[1] But see Section 7.2.3.

those components they depend on. By confining these details to the operations that truly need to be aware of them, the object-oriented approach limits the impact of changes, and makes the resulting software much more flexible and extendible. This will be discussed in more detail in Chapter 4.

2.1.2   Classes

An important advantage of using objects as the basis of program decomposition is that systems are modelled in terms that more closely resemble the physical world. It is perhaps not surprising, therefore, that this idea first arose in the field of simulation. Simula 67[2] (Birtwistle *et al*, 1983), a language designed primarily for discrete event simulation, is generally credited with being the father of the object-oriented paradigm, introducing many of the key concepts. Perhaps the most fundamental of these is the idea of a *class*.

In most object-oriented languages the term class actually captures three distinct, but closely related, concepts. Firstly, a class is a *template*, or blueprint, for the generation of numerous structurally and behaviourally identical objects, or *instances*. The set of operations declared in such a template represent an 'interface' defining the outside appearance of instances. A class therefore also defines an abstract *type* which can be used to determine the compatibility of objects in a system. Finally, since a template can be instantiated many times to give a collection of structurally identical objects, a class also captures the notion of a *set* of objects. These different facets of classes become important when relationships are defined between them. The interpretation of the inheritance relationship, for example (described in Section 2.2.5), depends on the particular view of classes which is adopted.

As a consequence of the second (type) facet, classes are closely related to the concept of abstract data types as supported in most modern imperative languages and formalized using algebraic specification techniques. Object-oriented design is, in fact, often taken to mean simply the design of software using abstract data types – a class being viewed as an implementation of an abstract data type. However, a class is more than just an abstract data type. In the majority of object-oriented languages it is also a module. Therefore, as pointed out by Meyer (1988), classes unify the distinct concepts of separately compilable modules and abstract data types found in languages like Ada and Modula 2.

Another difference between classes and abstract data types is that, unlike abstract data types, certain classes of objects are characterized not merely by the services they provide, but also by services they require, at the same level of abstraction, from other 'peer' objects (Booch, 1987). This is particularly so in concurrent systems, where objects have the additional

---

[2] Renamed in 1986 to 'Simula'.

features of independent, concurrent 'threads of control' and synchronization constraints on the execution of their operations.

2.1.3   Object-oriented design

Although perhaps a natural evolutionary step in design methodology, the idea of basing the architecture of a program on the 'objects' manipulated in the application domain is a fundamentally different approach to software construction which transcends any particular programming paradigm or language. Consequently, the last few years have seen a surge in the popularity of 'object-oriented' design methods for use in conjunction with all kinds of languages (Ormsby, 1990). Many of the most recent methods, however, have been developed specifically for Ada as the target language, because its support for the software engineering principles mentioned earlier enables the advantages of object-oriented design to be fully exploited.

Although the use of classes and objects, or their equivalent, as the basis for system architecture is found in many earlier design strategies, such as MASCOT, one of the first people to advocate the use of 'object-oriented' techniques, as such, for the design of Ada programs was Booch (1983). His work has been extended by a number of other object-oriented design schemes such as that of EVB (Berard, 1985) and HOOD (1987).

Object-oriented analysis

In the traditional 'waterfall' model of software development (Sommerville, 1989) design methods are usually preceded by requirements elicitation and analysis phases. Some of the techniques employed in conventional analysis methods, such as the data-flow diagrams of JSD (Jackson, 1975) and CORE (Mullery, 1976), are useful in constructing object-oriented designs. However, for many years, object-oriented design methods suffered because there were no contemporary analysis techniques that fully embraced the object-oriented world view. Booch's original design method, for example, relied on Parnas's technique of underlining nouns and verbs in the informal requirements description to identify the objects and their operations.

Analysis techniques more sympathetic to object-oriented design methods have been developed over recent years (Coad and Yourdon, 1990). The introduction of such 'object-oriented analysis' techniques represents one step closer to the day when object-oriented concepts will pervade the software lifecycle. This book will describe several ideas for extending the object-oriented viewpoint in the opposite direction towards the system construction and execution phases of the lifecycle.

2.2 Object-oriented languages

Although emphasis can be placed on structuring in terms of objects without any special linguistic support, object-oriented programming in its full generality requires the use of specialized languages. Following the lead of Simula, there is now a large number of languages which are designed specifically to embrace this style of programming, and incorporate special constructs for modelling objects. In most cases these object-oriented facilities serve as high-level devices for imposing structure on software written according to some other programming paradigm. There are, consequently, examples of 'object-oriented' enhancements to all the major schools of programming. LOOPS (Bobrow and Stefik, 1982) and Flavors (Moon, 1986), for example, are languages enabling code written in the classic functional language LISP to be arranged and composed in terms of higher-level 'objects'. C++ (Stroustrup, 1986) and Object Pascal (Apple, 1989) are examples of languages performing similar roles for the imperative languages C and Pascal, and languages like ESP (Chikayana, 1984) and POLKA (Davison, 1989) superimpose the concept of objects on the logic programming languages Prolog and Parlog (Gregory, 1987) respectively.

At first sight, the notion of state-encapsulating objects might seem to conflict with the fundamental tenet of declarative languages, which is the avoidance of destructive assignments to memory locations. However, the notion of an object state can be attained without destructive assignment by the recursive invocation of predicates or functions. Changing the parameters of the recursive call after each operation mimics the effect of a state change on the processing of the next operation.

The common feature of these so-called 'hybrid' languages is that they allow objects to be treated as 'first-class citizens'. Thus, although objects are structuring units, encapsulating state and operations, they are also treated as basic data items which can be instantiated dynamically and passed as parameters to operations. In other words, objects serve both as the *operands* acted upon by operations, and as the *operators* performing operations on others. At first this duality is one of the most confusing aspects of object-oriented programming to newcomers, but is the basis of much of its power.

2.2.1 'Pure' languages

Taken to its logical conclusion the object-oriented approach is more than just a device for structuring code fragments written according to some conventional programming paradigm, but becomes a complete programming philosophy in its own right. Provided that a rich enough set of predefined primitive 'objects' is available, no other structuring concepts are needed to provide a fully general language capable of tackling most problems. Programmers are then truly only concerned with describing objects and the way in which they interact. The first language to adopt this philosophy wholeheartedly was Smalltalk-80 (Goldberg and Robson, 1983), which is consequently regarded as the archetypical object-oriented language, and is the origin of much general 'object-oriented' terminology. More recent examples of 'pure' languages adopting a uniform object model include BETA (Kristensen *et al*, 1985), Emerald (Black *et al*, 1986) and POOL (America, 1987).

Smalltalk refers to the operations exported by objects as *methods* and introduces the idea of objects interacting by exchanging *messages*. This should not be confused with the notion of messages in concurrent or distributed systems, which reflects a particular implementation strategy for inter-process communication (Chapter 6), but is used in this context to stress the independence of the request for the invocation of a method – the *invocation request* – from its actual execution.

Smalltalk, however, is also responsible for much of the confusion surrounding object-oriented programming, because it has a number of other unique features that are not really part of the object-oriented paradigm. The programming language is, in fact, only one part of a fully integrated programming and execution environment providing a high quality user interface, and for many years these equally innovative aspects of Smalltalk obscured the power of its object-oriented programming features.

The fact that Smalltalk is a combined development and execution environment allows it to treat classes and objects in a way that is impossible in 'compiled' object-oriented languages such as Simula, Eiffel or C++[3]. In Smalltalk, classes are not regarded as merely static templates defining the structure of the various objects that can exist at run-time, but also as objects which themselves have a run-time existence, and can respond to messages just like any other. Each Smalltalk class is regarded as being an instance of a corresponding *metaclass* which, in turn, is an instance of a special class called 'Metaclass'. The 'instance' hierarchy is terminated by making the metaclass of 'Metaclass' (called 'Metaclass Class') an instance of Metaclass. In other words, 'Metaclass' and 'Metaclass Class' are viewed as instances of each other.

Adopting a completely uniform view in this way, in which all classes are also objects, has a number of advantages as far as the consistency and power of the model is concerned. Since every object in the system is an instance of a class, which is itself a run-time object, the class may store shareable information common to all the instances. *Class variables* act as global data accessible to all instances of the class, while *class methods* enable operations such as instance creation and destruction to be defined as

---

[3]The term 'compiled language' is used in this book to describe languages whose normal (or only) implementation requires *explicit* compilation and linking steps to be performed before programs may be executed. Such steps are not normally necessary to execute Smalltalk code fragments in the Smalltalk environment.

normal methods. Creation of an object is thus modelled as sending a 'create' message to the object's class. In languages such as Simula, Eiffel and POOL, in which classes do not have a run-time existence, the creation and deletion of objects has to be handled by special predefined operations, or 'allocators', of the language, usually called 'create' or 'new'. Consequently, the definition of other class methods, or reimplementation of the 'create' operation, presents certain conceptual difficulties in such languages. In POOL, the equivalent of Smalltalk class methods are called *routines* to distinguish them from the normal methods which form the callable interface of instances.

While this uniform object-oriented model has a certain elegance, it is inappropriate for typical software development purposes in which the run-time environment must be regarded as distinct from the development environment. Most object-oriented languages, therefore, retain the traditional Simula view of classes as purely static entities. Objective C (Cox, 1986) has an interesting compromise which lies somewhere in between the purely static and purely dynamic view. Classes themselves are not regarded as existing at run-time, but give rise to special *factory objects* which act as their run-time surrogates capable of responding to the equivalent of class methods.

2.2.2 Clientship

Some languages, most notably C++, do not require all objects to be created dynamically, but under certain circumstances also allow them to be directly declared. In C++, for example, objects may be generated 'automatically' when the program execution enters a new block. In the majority of languages, however, objects have to be generated dynamically by the execution of some form of allocator. Since the number of objects is therefore unpredictable at compile time they have to be identified by indirect references (i.e. pointers) rather than static names. This use of *reference semantics* to identify objects is an important factor in the flexibility and power of object-oriented systems.

Object references are stored in program elements usually termed *instance variables*. Since several of them may contain references to the same object, they are also sometimes known as *aliases* for the object concerned. Instance variables are the mechanism by which objects, and classes, may make use of each other's operations. An object which calls the operations of (in Smalltalk sends messages to) another object via an instance variable is said to be a *client* or *user* of the object.

Clientship is the fundamental language-level relationship between objects and classes. It describes the situation in which one object uses (i.e. calls) the methods exported by another. Ultimately, object-oriented programming is concerned with the generation of a set of objects that are related by clientship and call one another's methods. Other concepts, even that of classes, merely offer a means of more concisely describing such systems.

Many subtly different relationships between objects may actually be realized as clientship at the language level. Both the 'component-of' and 'peer-of' relationships (called the 'use' and 'include' relationships in HOOD (1987)), for example, are programmed as clientship. In the former, the server object is completely encapsulated by the client and may therefore be regarded as its private resource. In the latter, the server object is regarded as a peer of the client, and may be 'shared' by several other objects. This corresponds to the classic client/server paradigm of software engineering, and is the origin of the name clientship. Clientship is therefore instrumental in permitting the sharing of server objects by multiple clients.

2.2.3   Polymorphism and dynamic binding

A single instance variable may refer to instances of several different classes during the life of a program. Instance variables are therefore polymorphic entities – they are able to denote several different forms of object. This is another key feature of object-oriented languages. The important difference between this form of polymorphism and that offered by conventional techniques, such as variant records, is that the set of classes whose instances an instance variable may refer to is not fixed at compile time. A class can be a client of classes added to the program library after it has been compiled.

Combined with the object-oriented view of method invocation, this form of polymorphism becomes even more useful. Because different classes may have different implementations of a given method, the particular version of the method which will be executed in response to a given request depends dynamically on the class of the object. In other words, the operation name appearing in the invocation request (i.e. call) is dynamically bound to the particular implementation provided by the object referenced by the instance variable. In most object-oriented languages all method invocation is by means of dynamic binding, but some languages offer the choice. In C++, for example, a method must be defined as 'virtual' to be open to redefinition in other classes, and thus amenable to dynamic binding.

The dynamic binding mechanism completes the logical separation of the act of requesting a service from that of deciding which method will be executed to satisfy it. The former is conceptually the responsibility of the client and the latter of the server. Conventional programming techniques usually require the client to perform both, and so unnecessarily spread implementation knowledge among components of a system.

2.2.4   Typing

Certain languages, particularly Smalltalk, support polymorphism and dynamic binding without constraint, allowing any object to be assigned to any instance variable. As a result, there is no guarantee that the method named in an invocation request will be possessed by the called object. If it does not possess a suitable method, the infamous 'message not understood' message is displayed and no operation is invoked.

Since it avoids the possibility of data corruption, so-called 'dynamic typing' of this kind is preferable to no typing at all, and is acceptable in the prototyping applications for which Smalltalk is primarily intended. It is not acceptable, however, for applications in which reliability is a major concern and in which it is desirable to have some assurance before run-time that objects will be able to service method calls directed to them. To provide more security, many object-oriented languages employ static typing mechanisms to constrain the assignments allowed on instance variables.

The idea of typing schemes in programming languages is to assign a 'type' to all values used in a program so that the set of contexts in which each value may be used is explicitly defined. Any attempt to use a value in a way that contradicts its declared type can thus be detected by the compilation system, and the program rejected as erroneous. The concept is usually extended to include the notion of subtypes which identify values that possess at least all the properties of the parent type, and which therefore may be used in contexts where a value of the parent type is expected.

The corresponding idea is applied to classes in the object-oriented programming paradigm by the general notion of *conformance*. One class is said to conform to another if it can be used in all contexts where the other is expected, that is, if it can understand and respond to all the method calls (i.e. messages) handled by the other. This essentially means that the protocol of a class – the number and profiles of the exported operations – subsumes that of any class to which it conforms. Conformance, therefore, depends only on the protocols of classes, defined by their interfaces, and is not in any way affected by details of their implementation. In many languages, such as Emerald and Trellis/Owl (Schaffert *et al*, 1986), conformance is used as the sole basis for defining *type compatibility* – the rules determining when an instance of one class may be assigned to an instance variable of another – but in other languages, such as Eiffel, if classes are to be type-compatible they must also have implementations related by *inheritance*.

2.2.5   Inheritance

Inheritance is another idea first introduced in Simula (but under the different name of concatenation) and is generally regarded as one of the most important features of object-oriented programming. Essentially, it is a mechanism for sharing knowledge in systems by enabling new classes to reuse parts of the declaration of others. Unlike clientship, inheritance is a relationship only between classes.

Inheritance defines three subtly different kinds of relationships depending on the interpretation of the classes involved. Taking the template view of classes, the inheritance relationship indicates that one class, the *heir*, reuses the *implementation* of another class, the *parent*. 'Reuse' here does not mean that the heir class merely gains visibility of the parent's implementation. Conceptually, the heir class receives a new copy of the entire structure of the parent. Taking the 'type' view of classes, however, the inheritance relationship defines a typing relationship, in which the heir is regarded as being a subtype of the parent. Finally, taking the 'set' interpretation of classes, inheritance implies a semantic relationship in which the heir class 'is-a' specialized version of the parent. This corresponds to the notion that instances of the heir class belong to the set of instances of the parent.

In languages without static typing, like Smalltalk, the subtype relationship is not present, while in other languages, such as Emerald, the subtyping and implementation relationships are distinct. In most cases, however, inheritance implies all three relationships. The implementation relationship is the most important from the point of view of software reuse, since it enables programmers to define new classes by explicitly stating how they differ from existing ones, rather than by specifying all their properties from scratch. In the remainder of this book, unless specifically stated otherwise, inheritance will imply all three relationships mentioned above.

Using inheritance, a new class, the heir (subclass or derived class), may be defined as a specialization of another class, the parent (superclass or base class), by inheriting its methods and instance variables, and adding to them. The heir class therefore usually conforms to its parent, since it normally inherits all the methods in its interface. This need not be the case, however, since many languages allow heirs to remove inherited methods from their interface and to redefine method parameter types.

Inheritance variations

There are several variations on the inheritance theme. Inheritance can be *single*, in which case a class has only one parent, or can be *multiple*, in which case it has many parents. This is useful not only as a quick way of combining the functionality of several classes, but since a class can be put into a subtype relationship with several other classes, instances of the class may be viewed through several different interfaces.

Depending on the role of classes in a system, inheritance may also be either *static* or *dynamic*. In compiled languages such as Simula, Eiffel and C++, inheritance is static since all information sharing is fixed at compile time. Systems such as Smalltalk, however, in which all objects in the system are accessible at run-time, provide a dynamic inheritance mechanism. The method which will be executed in response to an invocation request is located dynamically by the Smalltalk system. It first searches for a suitable method in the class of the object which received the request, and if unsuccessful looks in the superclass, and so on up the inheritance hierarchy. This allows the user to modify inherited methods while instances of inheriting classes are executing. The changes will become known to instances of the descendent classes on the next invocation of the method.

Deferred implementation

Straightforward inheritance enables the methods of new classes to reuse the implementation of methods of existing classes. However, in most object-oriented languages it is also possible for the reverse dependency to exist, in which the implementation of 'old' methods may be defined by 'new' classes. In other words, the designer of a class may entrust the implementation of its methods to classes yet to be defined. This is achieved in compiled languages such as Simula and Eiffel by the declaration of special methods whose implementation the compiler recognizes as being *deferred* (or virtual in Simula).

In dynamic languages such as Smalltalk, on the other hand, this effect is achieved by means of the special pseudo-variable *self*, which refers to the object that first receives a message. When a class implements a method by resending the message to 'self', it indicates that appropriate implementations should be provided by subclasses. The search for a method sent to 'self' starts from the subclass of the object which first receives the message.

The possibility of defining *abstract* classes, some of whose methods are yet to be implemented, enables systems designers to capture parts of their design in source code before the whole picture is complete. Object-oriented languages can therefore be used earlier in the development process than many other more traditional languages, and can therefore in some ways also be regarded as design notations (Meyer, 1988).

Delegation and prototypical objects

In Smalltalk the search for method code is performed 'invisibly' in the background by the environment. However, since classes are regarded as run-time objects it is possible to view this searching activity in terms of the normal object interaction mechanisms. This gives rise to the delegation model (Lieberman, 1986) (Borning, 1986), and essentially means that when an object (a class, in this case) receives an invocation request for a method that it does not itself directly implement, it *delegates* the servicing of this request to its parent. The locating of methods to service method calls is therefore viewed as communication between classes rather than the background work of the system. Delegation involves not only the forwarding of a message, but also the binding of any references to 'self' in the method to the delegating object.

When method searching is modelled using the concept of delegation, the notion of distinct classes and instances loses much of its value. It is more natural to combine the functionality originally separated into a class and instance into a single object, and model the creation of many identical clones as copying the original, rather than instantiation of a template. The delegation model is therefore usually combined with the notion of 'prototypical' objects (Lieberman, 1986) which represent both normal active components of the system (c.f. instances) and blueprints for the creation of others (c.f. classes). When an object is generated as an adaptation of a prototypical object, it delegates the servicing of the common ('inherited') methods to the prototype (its parent).

2.2.6   Persistence

Many object-oriented languages provide the notion of persistent objects. In their simplest form, these are objects that exist between executions of programs, and so can be thought of as 'files' storing the state of individual objects. This is not such a trivial matter as it might seem, however, since an object will usually contain references to other objects which in turn will contain references to other objects, and so on. The state of an object is often represented by the state of many other objects, therefore, and saving the state of one object may in some cases involve saving the state of the entire program.

The idea of object persistence leads naturally to the realm of databases and the longer term storage of objects. The object-oriented paradigm offers some powerful tools for describing structure and relationships, and these are exploited in so-called object-oriented databases. Databases open up the possibility of storing objects not only between different executions of a program, but also between different versions of a program, and even different applications. It then becomes necessary for classes, as well as objects, to become 'persistent' so that the representation of object state can be correctly interpreted in different programs. Ultimately, one arrives at fully fledged object-oriented environments like Smalltalk, which provide persistence for entire object libraries.

2.3   Classification schemes

Although 'object-orientation' became a recognized software structuring technique in its own right less than a decade ago, the ideas outlined in the previous sections are now finding application in almost all spheres of computing. To help categorize the different ways in which these ideas are employed, it is common practice to distinguish the term object-oriented *design*, which essentially implies an approach to program decomposition based on the notion of classes and objects, from object-oriented *programming*, which implies the use of a specialized language. Object-oriented analysis is a new term for a topic still in its infancy. It is essentially concerned with the introduction of object-oriented design concepts into the early part of the software lifecycle, traditionally termed the analysis phase.

Whatever linguistic facilities are available, however, both object-oriented design and programming are essentially concerned with employing object-oriented structuring techniques for the *development* of application software. The 'object-orientedness' of the eventual executing software is not of particular concern. Object-oriented *environments*, on the other hand, are not so much concerned with the language or methodology used to construct software components, as with employing the structuring techniques for organizing running systems. Many operating systems and databases (Banerjee *et al*, 1987), for example, exploit the notion of objects for handling the execution of software and storing data. As with the use of object-oriented design methods, the construction of object-oriented environments can be undertaken without a specialized language, but is greatly simplified if one is available.

The range of different language features captured under the umbrella of 'object-oriented programming' is enormous. Perhaps the simplest and best known scheme for classifying these various languages is that of Wegner (1987), which is based on the language mechanisms discussed in this chapter. To earn the title 'object-oriented' in Wegner's classification, a language must provide support for inheritance, as well as features supporting the definition of classes and objects. Languages that support the class/instance distinction but lack any form of inheritance mechanism are termed 'class-based' languages, while those that also lack the concept of classes, and merely provide support for encapsulated objects, are termed 'object-based' languages. Object-oriented design techniques therefore fall into the category of object or class based according to Wegner's classification. Wegner goes on to define further categories of languages depending on their support for strong typing, concurrency and distribution. These aspects will be considered in later chapters.

Blair *et al*(1989), on the other hand, have proposed an approach which concentrates more on the essential *properties* of object-oriented systems than on specific mechanisms, and thus incorporates alternative views of the same underlying concept, such as inheritance and delegation. The properties of object-oriented systems are, in fact, analyzed according to three criteria – encapsulation, abstraction and polymorphism.

None of the existing classification schemes, however, successfully captures one of the major differences between the various object-oriented languages – their view of classes at run-time. Smalltalk, for example, views classes as *dynamic* (i.e. run-time) objects, while most of the 'compiled' languages view them as *static* (i.e. compile time) templates. A comprehensive classification scheme needs to embrace all three aspects of 'object-orientation' outlined here (i.e. 'design', 'environments' and 'languages'), since Smalltalk's model of objects depends on the fact that it is both a language and an environment.

Key points

The idea of using objects as the focal point for software construction represents a natural evolution, and reinforcement, of established software engineering principles such as abstraction, modularity and information hiding.

Structuring software in terms of objects decentralizes knowledge and data, and leads to more understandable and maintainable programs.

Classes are a natural complement to objects which generally embody three closely related concepts – object templates, object types and object sets.

In object-oriented design, objects and classes form the basis of system decomposition. Object-oriented designs may be implemented in any language, but are most commonly used with Ada.

Object-oriented languages provide special linguistic support for objects and/or classes, making objects 'first-class citizens' which can be dynamically generated, and passed as operation parameters. Some object-oriented languages are 'pure', offering no other constructs but those related to classes and objects for building systems. Most are 'hybrid', however, and superimpose object-oriented mechanisms on an alternative programming paradigm.

Clientship is the fundamental relationship between classes and objects. It is used to provide a language-level realization of many different higher-level relationships, such as 'component-of' and 'client/server'.

'Polymorphism' permits instance variables and formal method parameters to refer to instances of different classes during the life of a program.

Since instance variables may refer to different objects with different implementations of a given method, a method call must be dynamically bound to an implementation.

Most object-oriented languages place constraints on polymorphism so that only objects with the appropriate interface can be assigned to instance variables, or be provided as an actual parameter matching a class.

Inheritance is a mechanism that permits parts of the definitions of classes to be reused in the definition of others. Depending on the view of classes, inheritance may be viewed as defining an implementation relationship, a subtype relationship or an 'is-a' (set inclusion) relationship.

Inheritance can either be single, in which case a class may only have one parent, or multiple, in which case a class may have multiple parents. Similarly, inheritance may be static, in which case all information sharing is fixed at compile time, or dynamic, in which changes to a class in the hierarchy take immediate effect.

Abstract classes defer all, or part, of their implementation to descendants.

Delegation and prototypical objects offer an alternative to the notions of inheritance and classes for creating objects and sharing information between them.

Persistence is a property of objects that permits them to exist between executions of programs.

Object-oriented design is normally distinguished from object-oriented programming. The former merely implies the uses of classes and objects in describing the architecture of a program, while the latter implies additional linguistic support for inheritance, polymorphism and dynamic binding.

Wegner classifies languages as object-based, class-based and object-oriented depending on whether they have features for describing objects, classes and inheritance, cumulatively.

Chapter 3
Introducing DRAGOON

This chapter introduces the language DRAGOON, and describes how it supports many of the object-oriented programming features outlined in the previous chapter. The language which has had the greatest influence on its features is Ada – one of the basic design goals of DRAGOON being to remain as faithful to Ada style and syntactic conventions as possible. In this sense DRAGOON is to Ada what C++ is to C – an object-oriented adaptation of the base language.

The language that has been the main influence on the non-concurrent object-oriented features of DRAGOON is Eiffel[1], developed by Bertrand Meyer (1988) also with the aim of exploiting the paradigm's power for reuse. Although heavily disguised in Ada-like syntax, DRAGOON adopts Eiffel's basic model of classes and objects, and its strategy for expressing method calls.

Another important design criterion for DRAGOON was that it should be translatable into straightforward, intelligible Ada. Consequently, it also has much in common with object-oriented design techniques targeted to Ada. Some of these, therefore, particularly HOOD (1987), and the work of Booch (1987), have also influenced several of DRAGOON's features.

3.1 Programming philosophy

As described in the previous chapter, the philosophy of 'object-orientation' is to base the architecture of software systems on tangible objects in the problem domain. The most fundamental feature a language designed to support this approach must provide, therefore, is some means of modelling the objects in a system. In common with most other object-oriented languages, DRAGOON adopts the 'class' as the mechanism for achieving this.

---

[1] Since the publication of Meyer (1988) several new versions of Eiffel have been released. Unless otherwise qualified, the term Eiffel in this book refers to version 2.1 of the language described in Meyer (1988).

Programming in class-based languages, such as DRAGOON, is largely concerned with the definition of new classes using instances of those defined previously, until ultimately the entire system is modelled by one or more classes. An extreme example of this object-oriented approach is provided by Smalltalk, in which *every* entity in the problem domain must be modelled as an 'object'.

Many of the concepts that need to be represented within computer programs, however, are not always naturally modelled as objects (MacLennan, 1982). Immutable abstractions without substance or location, such as colours and numbers, are much more intuitively thought of as 'values' than as objects. The quality of 'greenness', for example, which would probably feature heavily in a traffic-light simulation program, is not intuitively an object, since it can neither be copied nor counted. Greenness is a *quality* (or attribute) of objects, not an object in itself. The same is true of numbers. Although the number 'two', for example, can be represented physically by the strings 'two' or '2', the abstraction itself is a 'pure' mathematical concept without substance or location. Consequently, it can (and frequently does) exist solely in people's minds whenever they associate a pair of objects together.

For abstractions of this nature, it is important to distinguish between the pure concepts themselves and their various possible *representations*. A representation of a number in a computer, whether at the source or machine level, is certainly an object and can be shared where necessary for efficiency reasons, but this does not alter the fact that the abstraction itself is not intuitively an object. In spite of this, several languages, such as Smalltalk and Trellis/Owl, in their quest for a completely uniform object model, do attempt to treat value abstractions (not merely their representation) as objects. This is achieved by regarding such values (e.g. integers, characters and boolean values) as special 'immutable' objects which can never change their internal state. They consequently lack many of the fundamental properties usually associated with objects – they cannot be copied like normal objects, and instances cannot be dynamically created and destroyed. In Smalltalk the instances of the classes Character, SmallIntegers and Symbol are generated at system initialization time, and are assumed to remain in existence indefinitely.

The restrictions placed on immutable objects in Smalltalk essentially constrain them to behave as values. At best, therefore, attempting to describe such abstractions within a uniform object-based metaphor provides no tangible advantages over the value-oriented approach, and at worst greatly confuses and complicates their manipulation. It certainly places an uncomfortable asymmetry on simple arithmetic operations such as addition. Although conforming to the usual syntactic style, an arithmetic operation in Smalltalk is conceptually performed by sending a message containing the second operand to the first, so that the first can add itself to the second.

Because the traditional 'value-oriented' view of arithmetic operations is much closer to our arithmetic intuitions, many object-oriented languages do not follow the pure (Smalltalk-like) approach, but prefer instead to handle numerical values and characters as traditional data types.

3.1.1   A mixed paradigm

Instead of dogmatically pursuing a pure 'object-oriented' or a pure 'value-oriented' approach, software development becomes much more straightforward and manageable if the logical distinction between objects and values is explicitly recognized (MacLennan, 1982). Each approach provides important advantages in certain contexts, but is inappropriate in others. Consequently, one of the basic principles of DRAGOON is to provide a 'mixed' programming paradigm which allows a natural and complementary treatment of both 'values' and 'objects', and which is thus more powerful than either of these paradigms individually. DRAGOON, therefore, *supports* object-oriented programming but does not *enforce* it.

In conventional strongly typed languages such as Ada, abstractions that need to be treated as 'values' are often represented by simple enumeration types. For example:

```
type COLOUR is (RED, AMBER, GREEN);                          (3.1)
type PRODUCT_TYPE is (PERISHABLE, ELECTRICAL, BASIC);
```

Not all 'value abstractions', however, have such simple representations in computers. Consider, for example, how *dates* are handled. Although dates are essentially just natural numbers enumerating successive days, because humans like to organize their lives according to the motion of the Earth, the representation of a date in a computer is usually described by three components – the day, month and year. Nevertheless, conceptually, like numbers, dates are value abstractions, because a given date is a fixed and uncopyable notion[2]. To provide full flexibility in the representation of complex 'value abstractions' such as dates, DRAGOON permits the use of all Ada's typing facilities, rather than just primitive types.

DRAGOON is one of the few languages that recognizes and supports both the 'value-oriented' and 'object-oriented' paradigms in their full generality. Many object-oriented languages that support 'value-oriented' programming do so only for the primitive data types (e.g. INTEGER, CHARACTERS and REAL).

Conventional imperative languages like Ada tend to focus exclusively on the value-oriented view and therefore tend to use the term 'object' in a different way to object-oriented languages. In Ada, for example, any data structure brought into existence by the elaboration of a declaration, or

---

[2]Is it meaningful to have two copies of the *abstraction* '5th December 2010', for example?

the execution of an 'allocator' operation, is called an object. In class-based object-oriented languages, on the other hand, 'object' has the special meaning of an instance of a class. To avoid the obvious potential for confusion in DRAGOON, which has all these kinds of data structure, the 'object-oriented' meaning is adopted and other more specific terminology is used in place of the Ada meaning (e.g. array, integer, variable). In DRAGOON, therefore, *all* objects are instances of classes.

3.1.2 Data abstraction

Given a completely 'mixed' paradigm of this form, the programmer must not only identify the meaningful abstractions in the problem domain, but must also judge which of them are best regarded as objects and which as values. Selecting the objects in a system is often a non-trivial task, and is one of the weakest points of most object-oriented design methods. In the same way that one sometimes has to resort to using the nouns in an (informal) specification to identify the objects, and the verbs to identify the operations, the adjectives will often be a good indication of the 'qualities' or 'values'.

Not all the abstractions appearing in a problem will be so obviously recognizable as objects or values, however. Certain abstractions may have acceptable *representations* in either the value-oriented or object-oriented style. Dates are a good example. Although as a pure abstraction a date is a value, it may be represented in a program as an object which stores the three components (i.e. day, month and year) as more primitive values. Alternatively, in Ada, dates may be modelled as values by the definition of a package which exports a 'date' type and a set of associated subprograms. Because DRAGOON supports both ways of modelling such abstractions, it is important to distinguish carefully between the two, and assign special meanings to the usual terminology.

A concept such as a date, with a set of possible values and associated operations, is commonly termed an *abstract data type* and in its pure form is independent of any representation or implementation strategy. In the majority of object-oriented languages the *class* is the only mechanism available for modelling such an abstraction, and consequently classes are often described as 'implementations of abstract data types' (Meyer, 1988) (America, 1989). Since DRAGOON also allows such an abstraction to be modelled in the traditional value-oriented style using a package, to distinguish between these two possible implementation approaches, a class is *not* regarded as an implementation of an abstract data type. This term is reserved for the traditional Ada style representation in which a package exports a (data) type and a set of associated operations which manipulate values of that type. If it is necessary to distinguish the pure concept from one of its two possible representations (i.e. classes or abstract data types), the 'pure' abstraction will be referred to as a *data abstraction*, as illustrated

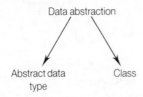

Figure 3.1   Alternative implementations of a 'data abstraction'.

in Figure 3.1.

The question as to whether to model a particular data abstraction as a class or an abstract data type is largely one of granularity. Most languages, including object-oriented languages such as Eiffel (version 2.1), Objective C, and C++, have a set of 'primitive' or 'simple' data types which are used so frequently that they have been built into the language. Even Ada, whose designers had a conscious policy of separating language-specific features from operations and types defined using them[3], permits these primitive values to be used in any program unit without the use of explicit 'with' clauses.

When the data abstraction being represented in DRAGOON can be regarded essentially as an addition to the basic set of 'primitive' values likely to be used frequently throughout the program, then it is better to define it as an abstract data type. If, on the other hand, it is a more substantial component of the system, which is not likely to be used as a primitive type in other parts, then it is better represented as a class. Classes, therefore, are more commonly used for larger components in the system, unlikely to recur frequently in other components, whereas abstract data types are used for smaller entities, such as dates, which will tend to be used for defining the structure of classes. In other words, classes tend to be used as a facility for programming 'in the large', while abstract data types tend to be used to provide additional types used for programming 'in the small'.

3.1.3   Outline design of the supermarket control system

DRAGOON is most effective when used in conjunction with a design method that recognizes and exploits inheritance. One such design method is DEMON developed in the DRAGON project. It is not the purpose of this current chapter, however, nor of the book in general, to describe DE-MON and other possible design strategies in detail (full details of DEMON

---

[3]In Ada, for example, the input/output routines are not regarded as an integral part of the language but as a set of predefined subprograms.

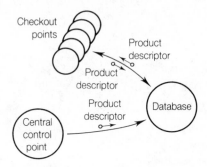

Figure 3.2   Data flow in the supermarket control system.

can be found in (Bott, 1989)). Rather, as stated in Chapter 1, the goal is to illustrate the main features of DRAGOON by demonstrating their use in the development of a small case study – the supermarket control system – described in the previous chapter. The difficult analysis and design issues likely to be faced at the early stages of developing such a system will therefore be avoided, and the following overall choice of objects and values in the system will be adopted as the starting point for development in DRAGOON.

The description of the system given in the previous chapter strongly suggests that the database, the checkout points and the central control point are the principal objects in the system. The other contenders for representation as objects are the product descriptors which hold the information about products in the system. Although they do not correspond directly to physical objects, there generally being many items (i.e. objects) of a given product type for each descriptor, they are not qualities or 'pure' abstractions such as 'greenness' or 'numbers', and can conceptually be shared and copied.

All of the information stored by the descriptors could be represented quite reasonably as values. However, since the purpose of the 'fuse rating' associated with an electrical item is to indicate which type of fuse it requires, and fuses are also presumably products sold in the supermarket, instead of recording the fuse rating as a simple numerical value, the information will be stored indirectly as a reference to a descriptor of the particular 'fuse' product actually required. As well as making it easier to provide the customer with information about the product, this strategy also has the commercial advantage to the supermarket that the fuse is more likely to be purchased along with the electrical item needing it.

The data flow between the various objects identified above is illustrated in Figure 3.2.

3.2   Template packages

If the product attributes are to be represented as values of a conventional Ada data type, the corresponding type definitions must be contained in shareable modules which can be made visible to any classes that need to see them. The obvious candidate for such a module is the Ada package, since one of its main purposes in Ada is to provide a convenient repository for grouping together logically related declarations. The package, therefore, has been adopted as one of the main structural elements of DRAGOON. Whereas normal Ada packages may declare state variables, however, and thus model abstract state machines, this is not desirable in DRAGOON because state is to be encapsulated by 'objects' in the way described in the next section. It is important that packages used in DRAGOON have no associated state whatsoever.

Packages with precisely this property were found to be useful in the DIADEM project (Atkinson et al, 1988) for housing declarations shared by potentially distributed units. Such packages were termed *template units* since they mainly contain declarations acting as 'templates' for the subsequent generation of variables. In fact, in DIADEM, any Ada library unit not possessing a persistent state, and which therefore could be shared with impunity between distributed Ada software, was termed a template unit. The concept therefore also admits all generic units and subprograms without side effects.

Although 'template unit' is perhaps not the best name, particularly for library subprograms, it is retained in DRAGOON for continuity. Moreover, DRAGOON also permits the use of all other library units conforming to the rules for template units defined in DIADEM. This facilitates the direct reuse of large libraries of reusable subprograms and also of the libraries of commercially developed 'abstract data type' packages. Template packages in DRAGOON may contain the definition of types, subprograms, constants and exceptions, but not variables or tasks.

3.2.1   Templates in the supermarket control system

Since the type definitions used to represent product attributes need to be visible to a number of the classes in the system, they need to be defined in template packages. The bar-code and stock-level attributes (Section 1.4), being simple natural numbers, are clearly best represented by variables of the Ada type NATURAL. By storing prices in terms of pence (hundredths of a pound), this also becomes the most straightforward representation for the price attribute. However, rather than use the type NATURAL directly, it is safer to define separate derived types for each, since this ensures that the attributes will never be mixed. The textual label, on the other hand, clearly needs to be represented as a character string. Since a string subtype in Ada must be of a certain specified length, a size of 100 is chosen arbitrarily.

These four types are defined together in a single template package:

```
package PRODUCT is                                              (3.2)

    type CODE_NUMBER is new NATURAL;
    type VALUE is new NATURAL;
    type STOCK_NUMBER is new NATURAL;
    subtype LABEL is STRING(1 .. 100);

end PRODUCT;
```

In view of the earlier discussion, the 'sell-by-date' attribute of perishable products will also be represented as values of an abstract data type, but not as a single number like the others. In fact, it is tempting to reuse the type definitions in the standard Ada package, CALENDAR, (DoD, 1983) for this purpose, but this is not a legal DRAGOON program unit since it is not a template package. Although it contains no obvious variable declarations, CALENDAR has a state by virtue of the function, CLOCK, which returns the current time (including the date) as measured by the system clock. This facility is not required for the purposes of recording a product sell-by-date. Only three subprograms are really necessary: a constructor function, MAKE_DATE say, a function to check for the equality of two dates, and a function to determine whether one date is earlier than another. Provided the type is defined to be 'limited private' the infix operators '=' and '<' may be overloaded to designate these last two functions.

Another template package, therefore, is required which provides similar type definitions to CALENDAR, but without provision for the time, and without a CLOCK function:

```
package SIMPLE_CALENDAR is                                      (3.3)

    type DATE is limited private;

    subtype YEAR_NUMBER is INTEGER range 1901 .. 2099;
    subtype MONTH_NUMBER is INTEGER range 1 .. 12;
    subtype DAY_NUMBER is INTEGER range 1 .. 31;

    function MAKE_DATE (YEAR : YEAR_NUMBER;
             MONTH : MONTH_NUMBER;  DAY : DAY_NUMBER) return DATE;
    function "=" (D1, D2 : DATE) return BOOLEAN;
    function "<" (D1, D2 : DATE) return BOOLEAN;
private

    :                                        -- implementation dependent

end SIMPLE_CALENDAR;
```

3.3 Objects and classes

Having defined the Ada types used to represent the attributes of products, it is now possible to consider the product descriptors themselves, and how they would be modelled in DRAGOON as objects. As mentioned earlier, this is achieved by the definition of a *class*, which is a 'blueprint' describing the properties that all objects or *instances* of this class will possess.

DRAGOON classes consist of two separate parts – the *specification part* and the *body part*. These are separately compilable units, and like their Ada package counterparts, the specification must be compiled before the body. Unlike packages, however, it is not possible to nest one class definition within another. *All* DRAGOON classes are library units, therefore.

The class specification defines the *interface* that instances of the class present to other objects, while the body defines their *implementation*, and hides all aspects that should not be externally visible. Since the private variables of an object should not be directly manipulated by other objects, these must be defined in the body of the class. DRAGOON, therefore, allows only *methods* and *exceptions* to appear in class interfaces. This means that specific *access* functions must be defined to determine the values of internal state variables, and *update* operations to change their values.

In the case of the objects representing product descriptors, therefore, methods are required for accessing and updating all four attributes. In addition, a method, DECREMENT_STOCK_NUMBER, will be provided for the use of checkout points so that when items are purchased and removed from the store they can decrement the stock level recorded in the corresponding product descriptor. The specification of a DRAGOON class defining product descriptors is thus of the form:

```
with PRODUCT;                                                   (3.4)
class PRODUCT_DESCRIPTOR is
    introduces

        function PRICE return PRODUCT.VALUE;
        procedure SET_PRICE_TO (PRICE : in PRODUCT.VALUE);

        function BAR_CODE return PRODUCT.CODE_NUMBER;
        procedure SET_BAR_CODE_TO
                            (BAR_CODE : in PRODUCT.CODE_NUMBER);

        function STOCK_LEVEL return PRODUCT.STOCK_NUMBER;
        procedure DECREMENT_STOCK_NUMBER;
        procedure SET_STOCK_TO
                            (STOCK_LEVEL : in PRODUCT.STOCK_NUMBER);

        function LABEL return PRODUCT.LABEL;
        procedure SET_LABEL_TO (LABEL : in PRODUCT.LABEL);

    end PRODUCT_DESCRIPTOR;
```

This illustrates how closely the syntax of DRAGOON follows the style of Ada. The 'with' clause is used to give the class visibility of the type definitions in the template package PRODUCT (3.2). DRAGOON does not allow use clauses to be used in classes, however, although they can be used as normal in template packages.

The method specifications in the interface define the *protocol* of the class, and represent the operations that instances of the class can perform.

They have precisely the same syntactic form as Ada subprograms, and differ semantically only in that *conceptually* new copies of the methods are generated along with each new instance of the class.

3.3.1   Clientship

There are two principal mechanisms by which DRAGOON classes can depend on each other – *inheritance* and *clientship*. In the clientship relationship, one class, the *client*, is implemented using the services offered by instances of another, the *server*. As far as clients are concerned, a server class is completely defined by the interface exported in the specification part, since this defines the set of methods that instances of the class offer for invocation. Once the specification of a class has been compiled, therefore, it is possible to define client classes that employ the services of its instances.

The implementation of a class through clientship determines the communication pattern of its instances at run-time. Clientship, therefore, is also a relationship between objects, defining a *dependency* hierarchy which may vary dynamically according to which instances of a class are serving a particular client.

To generate instances of a class it is necessary to declare an *instance variable* of the appropriate type. An instance variable is analogous to an access variable in Ada in that it stores an indirect reference to (or internal name for) a dynamically generated entity. Whereas normal access variables point to data structures, instance variables always refer to class instances – that is, objects. In this context, therefore, the adjective 'instance' is not used in the sense of Smalltalk to distinguish variables in a class object (class variables) from those in instances (instance variables) or in methods (temporary variables), but merely to distinguish variables pointing to class instances from those that denote conventional data structures. As mentioned earlier, DRAGOON permits the use of both static and dynamically allocated data types, as well as classes.

A new object is brought into existence by invoking the special predefined operation, CREATE, through an instance variable. It is convenient to think of this operation as a method (Meyer, 1988), since it is invoked in the same manner as other methods, but strictly speaking it is not a method because no object exists to receive and execute the CREATE request before it is performed. In fact, in pure object-oriented languages such as Smalltalk, in which classes are regarded also as objects with a run-time existence, the CREATE operation is elegantly handled as a method of the class object. In DRAGOON, which has a static view of classes, it is more closely analogous to the '**new**' operation of Ada which generates dynamically allocated data structures. However, provided that the very special nature of the CREATE operation is recognized, there is no difficulty in referring to it as a method. In particular, it is important to note that although every class possesses a

CREATE 'method' (except special abstract classes described in Section 4.3) it is not part of the protocol of instances.

Consider the class modelling the central control point in the supermarket control system, for example. This is responsible for generating new product descriptor objects when new product types are introduced into the supermarket. To achieve this, an instance variable of class PRODUCT_DESCRIPTOR (3.4) would be defined in the body of the class:

```
NEW_DESCRIPTOR : PRODUCT_DESCRIPTOR;
```

Elaboration of this declaration does not bring a new object into existence, but merely an instance variable capable of holding a reference to one. Until an existing object is assigned to it, or a new one generated, the value of the reference denoted by this variable is 'null', just as with newly elaborated access variables in Ada.

As in Eiffel and Simula, the invocation of a method in DRAGOON has a similar form to a subprogram call, but is prefixed, in the Ada dot notation style, with the name of the object to which the invocation request is directed. Therefore, the invocation of the CREATE 'method' bringing an object into existence has the form:

```
NEW_DESCRIPTOR.CREATE;
```

and causes the instance variable to refer to a new instance of class PRODUCT_DESCRIPTOR. Similarly, the price attribute of the object just created can be set to the value 50, say, by invoking its SET_PRICE_TO method:

```
NEW_DESCRIPTOR.SET_PRICE_TO (50);
```

If the method invoked is a function, then the method call is an expression, otherwise it is a statement. Invocation of a method in this style corresponds to the transmission of a message in Smalltalk terminology.

3.3.2 Class bodies

The clients of a class can be defined and compiled as soon as the specification is available, but as with Ada packages, nothing can actually be executed until the body part is also compiled. Each method defined in the class specification (except those that are deferred (Section 4.3)) must be implemented in the body of the class. The body is also responsible for declaring the variables that hold the state of instances of the class. In the case of the PRODUCT_DESCRIPTOR objects, four variables are needed to store their state:

```
class body PRODUCT_DESCRIPTOR is                                    (3.5)
    INTERNAL_BAR_CODE : PRODUCT.CODE_NUMBER;
    INTERNAL_PRICE : PRODUCT.VALUE;
    INTERNAL_STOCK_LEVEL : PRODUCT.STOCK_NUMBER;
    INTERNAL_LABEL : PRODUCT.LABEL;

    function PRICE return PRODUCT.VALUE is
    begin
        return INTERNAL_PRICE;
    end;

    procedure SET_PRICE_TO (PRICE : in PRODUCT.VALUE) is
    begin
        INTERNAL_PRICE := PRICE;
    end;

    :                                     -- similarly for other methods

end PRODUCT_DESCRIPTOR;
```

Only two method bodies are illustrated in this example since the others are also simple accessor and update functions implemented in an analogous fashion. Not only do methods have the same syntactic form as Ada subprogram bodies, but within the class body they have the same semantics since the visibility rules are identical to those of a package body; the variables declared in the body are directly visible in the following method bodies. While there can only be one instance of a package, however, it is possible to generate many instances of a class. Conceptually, each new instance possesses a separate copy of the class body, so that the methods, as well as the state variables upon which they operate, are replicated. In this respect, classes are very similar to Ada generics, the only difference being that generics have to be instantiated at compile time with a fixed name, whereas classes can be instantiated dynamically with an indirect reference. As is often the case with Ada generics, although 'methods' are conceptually replicated for each instance of a class, the code for their implementation is shared.

It is possible to define subprograms in the body of a class that do not appear in the specification. These can be thought of as *internal methods*, similar to other methods in every way except for the fact that they are not made visible in the interface. However, since they are essentially nothing more than Ada subprograms defined internally, it is convenient in DRAGOON to refer to them as such, and to reserve the word 'method' for subprograms that are exported in the interface. Thus, within the body of a class, internal operations of this kind can be invoked as normal Ada subprograms instead of using some clumsy notation for introspective method invocations such as the pseudo-variable SELF of Smalltalk.

DRAGOON does not permit the (externally visible) methods of a class to be invoked directly from within the body, since this can easily lead to erroneous programs, particularly in a concurrent environment (Chapter 6). The same effect can easily be achieved by defining an internal subprogram to implement the body of the method (i.e. arranging for the method to invoke the internal procedure), since this subprogram can be called from anywhere within the body of the class.

3.4   Inheritance

The last few sections have described the facilities available in DRAGOON for defining completely new classes. However, the inheritance mechanism of object-oriented languages such as DRAGOON also makes it possible to define new classes simply by specifying how they differ from existing ones. In other words, a class can *inherit* the properties of another, and extend or adapt them to meet new requirements. The inheriting class, or the *heir*, therefore, becomes a specialization of the inherited class, or *parent*.

In the case of the supermarket control system, for example, certain categories of products have additional attributes – perishable products have an extra 'sell-by-date', while electrical products have an extra 'fuse rating'. In a conventional language such as Ada, a new descriptor type would have to be defined for such products, involving the redefinition of all the common methods, not just those that are affected by the change. In DRAGOON, on the other hand, it is only necessary to define an heir of PRODUCT_DESCRIPTOR (3.4) which inherits all the common attributes and introduces the additional ones needed. Thus, a specialization of the class PRODUCT_DESCRIPTOR to represent perishable items would have the following form:

```
with SIMPLE_CALENDAR;                                        (3.6)
class PERISHABLE_DESCRIPTOR is
    inherits PRODUCT_DESCRIPTOR;
    introduces
        function SELL_BY_DATE return SIMPLE_CALENDAR.DATE;
        procedure SET_SELL_BY_DATE_TO
                        (SELL_BY_DATE : in SIMPLE_CALENDAR.DATE);
end PERISHABLE_DESCRIPTOR;
```

This indicates why the keyword 'introduces' appears before the list of new methods in a DRAGOON class specification. The methods SELL_BY_DATE and SET_SELL_BY_DATE_TO are introduced (i.e. added) to the set of methods offered by instances of class PRODUCT_DESCRIPTOR (3.4). The protocol of PERISHABLE_DESCRIPTOR objects is thus a union of the methods inherited from the parent, and those 'introduced' by the class specification. Since the parent class may, in turn, have inherited methods from its parent, in general, the protocol of a class is the union of the methods of all its ancestors in the inheritance hierarchy. The inheritance relation is transitive, therefore, so that if a class X inherits from another Y, and Y inherits from Z, then X also inherits the properties of Z. However, X is not said to be the heir of Z, or Z the parent of X, because these terms are reserved for classes immediately related by inheritance. In other words, the parent(s) of a class are those appearing in its inherits clause, while the heirs of a class are those that name it in their inheritance clauses. To describe classes indirectly related by inheritance the terms *ancestor* and *descendant* are introduced. The ancestors of a class are all those classes from which it directly or indirectly inherits its features, while the descendants are all those classes that directly or indirectly inherit its features.

Although the specification of an heir class can be compiled before the body of its parent, the same is not true for the body. Inheritance is essentially a mechanism for sharing the implementation of classes, and unlike the clientship relationship, therefore, in general requires the heir class to have access to the 'hidden' information in the bodies. Consequently, the code in the body of a class is not hidden from its heirs as it is from its clients.

The body of PERISHABLE_DESCRIPTOR is of the form:

```
class body PERISHABLE_DESCRIPTOR is                                    (3.7)

      INTERNAL_DATE : SIMPLE_CALENDAR.DATE;

      function SELL_BY_DATE return SIMPLE_CALENDAR.DATE is
      begin
          return INTERNAL_DATE;
      end;

      procedure SET_SELL_BY_DATE_TO
                          (SELL_BY_DATE : in SIMPLE_CALENDAR.DATE) is
      begin
          INTERNAL_DATE := SELL_BY_DATE;
      end;

  end PERISHABLE_DESCRIPTOR;
```

In the same way that new methods 'introduced' in the specification extend the interface of class instances, the variables defined in the body extend their set of state variables. PERISHABLE_DESCRIPTOR objects, therefore, have five variables, four inherited from PRODUCT_DESCRIPTOR (3.4) and one declared directly in the class body. Although in this case the methods introduced by PERISHABLE_DESCRIPTOR do not have cause to manipulate the inherited variables, they could easily have done so. All declarations contained in the bodies of ancestors of a class are effectively replicated in its body. Any method implementation may therefore reference inherited variables directly, as if they had been defined explicitly in the same body part. This implies also that 'with' clauses are inherited. It is not possible, however, to invoke the inherited methods from within the bodies of introduced methods, because as mentioned earlier, no class is allowed to call its own methods directly.

A class can be both a descendant and client of another class. Consider the descriptor for electrical products as an example. As mentioned in Chapter 1, rather than simply record the associated fuse rating as a numerical value, this information is stored by reference to the product descriptor for the appropriate fuse. Just like PERISHABLE_DESCRIPTOR, therefore, electrical product descriptors need to be an heir of the class PRODUCT_DESCRIPTOR (3.4), but they also need to be a client so that they may contain a reference to the product descriptor for the appropriate fuse:

```
with PRODUCT_DESCRIPTOR;                                        (3.8)
class ELECTRICAL_DESCRIPTOR is
    inherits PRODUCT_DESCRIPTOR;
    introduces
        function REQUIRED_FUSE return PRODUCT_DESCRIPTOR;
        procedure SET_FUSE_TO (FUSE : in PRODUCT_DESCRIPTOR);
end ELECTRICAL_DESCRIPTOR;


class body ELECTRICAL_DESCRIPTOR is

    INTERNAL_FUSE : PRODUCT_DESCRIPTOR;

    function REQUIRED_FUSE return PRODUCT_DESCRIPTOR is
    begin
        return INTERNAL_FUSE;
    end;

    procedure SET_FUSE_TO (FUSE : in PRODUCT_DESCRIPTOR) is
    begin
        INTERNAL_FUSE := FUSE;
    end;

end ELECTRICAL_DESCRIPTOR;
```

The previous classes have had only variables of static data types. This class, however, also possesses an instance variable of the class PRODUCT_DESCRIPTOR (3.4), containing a reference to an instance of a class, rather than a data value. In general, there are three different kinds of variables (sometimes also called *fields*) which may appear in the body of a class: instance variables for holding references to objects (i.e. class instances), access variables for holding references to dynamically generated data structures (but not objects) and *data* variables for holding values of *static* data types. In DRAGOON, variables of the last kind, and/or the values they contain, are termed the *attributes* of the object. This is a different usage of the term to that found in some other languages, where it is the instance variables that are referred to as attributes. The DRAGOON interpretation, however, corresponds more closely to the intuitive meaning of the word, because as discussed in Section 3.1, (static) data types are used to model qualities (i.e. attributes) of objects, rather than objects themselves. In DRAGOON, therefore, the attributes of a class are its variable *qualities*, not the objects of which it may be a client, or the variables referring to them.

3.4.1   Method modification

In the previous examples of inheritance, the heir classes have merely extended their parents by adding new properties to those they inherited. Specialization, therefore, has been achieved by *enrichment*. However, it is also possible to specialize a class by *modification* of the inherited properties. More specifically, it is possible to modify the methods inherited in the following ways.

Method redefinition

Probably one of the most important ways in which an heir can modify the inherited properties is by *redefining* one or more of the inherited methods. DRAGOON permits an heir class to replace the *body* of an inherited method by a new implementation, but does not allow the specification of the method to be changed. 'Reimplementation', therefore, is probably a more accurate description of this facility. In circumstances where the 're-definition' of a method involves merely extending the inherited definition with extra steps immediately before and after, it is possible to 'reuse' the inherited version in the definition of the new one.

Eiffel, in contrast, permits the types of the parameters to be changed in the redefinition of a method, but this complicates the typing scheme of the language, as discussed in the next section. Since DRAGOON does not permit such redefinition, and the specifications of inherited methods remain unchanged, the fact that a method is reimplemented in an heir is made known to clients by means of a 'redefines' clause in the heir's interface. The specification of the following class, for example, indicates that it redefines the method SELL_BY_DATE. In its body, therefore, it must provide a new implementation (i.e. body) for the method:

```
class REDEFINED_DESCRIPTOR is                              (3.9)
    inherits PERISHABLE_DESCRIPTOR;
    redefines SELL_BY_DATE;
end;
```

It is important to note that reimplementation can be used for two different purposes. The new version of a method defined in an heir can stay faithful to the semantics of the original version and merely adopt another implementation strategy, or alternatively, can provide a different service to the original, perhaps bearing no relationship whatsoever.

Method renaming

As well as redefining the body of an inherited method, it is also possible to change the name associated with it. This is achieved using a 'renames' clause in the specification, which indicates to a client that the specified inherited method is to be known by a new name. In the case of single inheritance this is merely a convenient facility for improving program understandability, but in the case of multiple inheritance (introduced in the next subsection) it is sometimes essential for overcoming name clashes. It is, in fact, possible both to rename and redefine an inherited method.

The renaming of methods in the specification of a class does not actually alter the interfaces of its instances, but rather the set of methods callable through instance variables of the class. Consider the following heir of PERISHABLE_DESCRIPTOR, for example:

```
class RENAMED_DESCRIPTOR is                                  (3.10)
    inherits PERISHABLE_DESCRIPTOR;
    function PERISHED_BY return SIMPLE_CALENDAR.DATE
                                        renames SELL_BY_DATE;
end;
```

An attempt to call this renamed method via an instance variable of class RENAMED_DESCRIPTOR using the old name (SELL_BY_DATE) will be rejected by the compiler, since it can only be called from such an instance variable using the new name (PERISHED_BY). If the object concerned is assigned to an instance variable of class PERISHABLE_DESCRIPTOR (3.6), however, the reverse is true. From such an instance variable the method is known by its old name. Renaming, therefore, affects the interfaces associated with instance variables, rather than objects.

Method restriction

Perhaps the most drastic modification that can be made to inherited methods is their complete removal from the interface of the heir. This is sometimes necessary when the heir models a specialization of the parent in which it would be an error to call certain of its methods. It is achieved by a special 'removes' clause in the specification of a class similar to that for renaming and redefining:

```
class RESTRICTED_DESCRIPTOR is                               (3.11)
    inherits PERISHABLE_DESCRIPTOR;
    removes SELL_BY_DATE;
end;
```

These method modification facilities not only have an important part to play in the use of DRAGOON for concurrent and distributed systems, and the power of object-oriented languages generally for promoting reuse, but also have an important impact on the typing scheme of the language. These issues will be discussed as they arise in the following chapters.

3.4.2 Multiple inheritance

Another important extension of the basic inheritance mechanism is multiple inheritance – the possibility for a class to inherit the properties of more than one parent. This is exhibited by a number of languages, including Eiffel (Meyer, 1988), Flavors (Moon, 1986) and CLOS (Bobrow *et al*, 1988). Suppose, for example, that a class called DATED_ITEM was available in the DRAGOON library which simply possessed an attribute of type SIMPLE_CALENDAR.DATE (3.3) and associated accessor and update methods. When instantiated directly such a class, with a specification of the form:

```
with SIMPLE_CALENDAR;                                    (3.12)
class DATED_ITEM is
    introduces
        function DATE return SIMPLE_CALENDAR.DATE;
        procedure SET_DATE_TO (DATE : in SIMPLE_CALENDAR.DATE);
end DATED_ITEM;
```

would be of little value, since instances would simply encapsulate a single 'date' attribute, and in most circumstances, therefore, would be no more useful than the attribute itself. However, when combined with other objects using multiple inheritance the class is extremely useful, since it enables any kind of object requiring a date attribute (but others also) to be modelled cleanly and efficiently. There are many examples of classes which need such a 'time-stamp', such as people with birthdays, students with exam dates and products with sell-by dates.

Given the availability of DATED_ITEM, a class with identical properties to PERISHABLE_DESCRIPTOR (3.6) could have been generated from PRODUCT_DESCRIPTOR (3.4) simply by also inheriting the properties of the class DATED_ITEM (3.12) rather than by explicitly introducing extra methods and attributes:

```
class DATED_DESCRIPTOR is                                (3.13)
    inherits PRODUCT_DESCRIPTOR, DATED_ITEM;
end DATED_DESCRIPTOR;
```

When the effort required to define the DATED_ITEM (3.12) class in the first place is taken into consideration, there is little difference to choose between the PERISHABLE_DESCRIPTOR 'route' for generating 'perishable-food' descriptors, and the DATED_DESCRIPTOR (3.6) 'route' using multiple inheritance. The point is, however, that the properties of DATED_ITEM can also be inherited by any other class which needs to have an additional date attribute.

In a simulation of a library, for example, classes will be required to model the books handled by the library. Independently of its status in a library, a book is a well defined abstraction with fixed attributes such as author, title and publisher, and so it is likely that a class will be defined, LIBRARY_BOOK say, to model the basic book abstraction. As soon as a book is borrowed from the library, however, it assumes an extra set of attributes, one of which will be the return date (other possibilities are the borrower's name, address etc.). Using multiple inheritance, the required date attribute can be added to the new version of the class simply by inheriting the class DATED_ITEM along with LIBRARY_BOOK:

```
class DATED_LIBRARY_BOOK is                                    (3.14)
    inherits LIBRARY_BOOK, DATED_ITEM;
end DATED_LIBRARY_BOOK;
```

Multiple inheritance, therefore, provides a mechanism for factorizing common information into inherited classes and increases the range of relationships that can exist between classes. Whereas single inheritance enables objects to be arranged into subsets, instances of an heir class belonging to a subset of those of the parent, multiple inheritance permits them to be arranged into set intersections. Instances of DATED_LIBRARY_BOOK (3.14), for example, belong to the intersection of the set of DATED_ITEM (3.12) instances and LIBRARY_BOOK instances.

In order to overcome the name clashes that arise when the parents of a class have identical method specifications or variable names, DRAGOON permits the inherited identifiers to be qualified by the name of the parent class in the Ada 'dot notation' style. This is sufficient to overcome any ambiguities when the clashing identifiers are declared in the body of the parent classes. For example, if the LIBRARY_BOOK and DATED_ITEM parents of DATED_LIBRARY_BOOK each had a variable called COUNTER, code in the body of DATED_LIBRARY_BOOK could distinguish these variables by using the identifiers LIBRARY_BOOK.COUNTER and DATED_ITEM.COUNTER respectively.

When the clashing identifiers appear in the specifications of the parents, however, this technique alone is not sufficient, since clients of a class should not require knowledge of the ancestry of a class in order to unambiguously call methods of its instances. In such circumstances, the programmer is required to use the renaming facilities of the language to rename one, or both, of the clashing methods.

3.5   Typing scheme

Most languages intended for the development of non-trivial programs employ some form of typing scheme to help minimize logical errors and improve program reliability. This shortens the debugging stage of program development, which is often one of the most costly parts, and also reduces the likelihood of undetected software errors occurring at a later stage when the software has been supplied to the client. These are particularly important requirements in the field of embedded systems where software is often the critical part of a system and the consequences of a software failure could be disastrous. Consequently, languages such as Ada, which are intended primarily for this application domain, usually adopt a *strong typing* scheme in which *every* value in a program has an associated type and all operations are checked to ensure the logical compatibility of the operands.

It is possible to perform type checking dynamically by tagging each data structure with a type label, and checking that the labels of operands are consistent before operations are performed[4]. Dynamic typing of this form, however, generally carries an unacceptably high run-time overhead for real-time applications. It is preferable in such applications for as much of the type checking as possible to be performed *statically* by the compiler before the program is executed.

Most statically typed languages require the programmer to provide supplementary type declarations that explicitly define the type of every data structure employed in the program. Much of this information is actually redundant, as demonstrated by languages such as ML (Milner, 1984) which ensure the type consistency of programs with only minimal type declarations. Nevertheless, providing explicit types for every operand significantly reduces the work that has to be carried out by the compiler and improves the readability and correctness of source code.

The benefits of static typing have to be carefully balanced against the constraints on the flexibility of the language. This is particularly so in object-oriented languages, one of the most important features of which is polymorphism. Since any object may be assigned to any instance variable in languages like Smalltalk, a method call may be directed to, and serviced by, many different objects during the course of a program. This property is largely responsible for Smalltalk's power for rapid prototyping, but at the same time accounts for most of the run-time problems that occur as a result of inappropriate assignments.

Too rigid a typing scheme also directly conflicts with the interests of reuse because it restricts a program component to operating on exactly one set of types. This often makes it necessary to define components that are identical in every way apart from the types they operate on, even though these types may have identical representations in the computer. Even Ada, therefore, has a number of mechanisms for ameliorating the undesirable restrictions of strong typing. Ada's typing scheme is not completely static, but allows the programmer to define *subtypes* by specifying dynamic constraints on the values a variable may assume. The set of values defined by a subtype is a proper subset of that of the type itself. In addition, Ada supports generic components which are parameterized with respect to one or more types.

Because DRAGOON is intended to be an enhancement of Ada in the domain of embedded systems, DRAGOON shares the same basic goal of using strong typing to improve program correctness and reliability. Like other object-oriented languages with strong typing, however, such as Emerald,

---

[4]In fact, variant records in languages like Ada and Pascal are just such structures, with the discriminant acting as a dynamically checkable type label.

Trellis/Owl and Eiffel, DRAGOON aims to strike a fine balance between the safety advantages of typing and the flexibility and reuse advantages of object-oriented languages, especially those resulting from polymorphism.

3.5.1   Class and data types

DRAGOON differs from the majority of object-oriented languages in that it deliberately incorporates the full power of Ada's typing and encapsulation mechanisms. In discussing the typing rules, therefore, it is important to distinguish carefully between the various possible representations of data in the language.

A 'type' is associated with every entity in the program upon which operations may be performed, including simple assignments from one variable to another. Given the 'hybrid' nature of DRAGOON, therefore, there are two different kinds of entities to which types may be attributed: objects, whose types are defined by the classes of which they are instances, and data elements, whose types are defined by type declarations in the traditional Ada style. In other words, there are two different kinds of type in DRAGOON: *class types* and *data types*. Every DRAGOON class is a type, but not every type is a class.

Following the normal Ada terminology, it is convenient to further subdivide data types into *static* data types which are allocated on the stack as part of the elaboration of the program unit in which they are defined, and *dynamic* or *access* data types which are allocated on the heap whenever the corresponding allocator operation is invoked. The distinction between static and dynamic types will be useful in the discussion of distribution later in the book.

Dynamic data types behave in many ways similar to class types in that elements of the type may be generated dynamically at any point in the program, and are referenced indirectly. Nevertheless, it is important to be aware of the conceptual difference between them. An element of a dynamic type is merely a data structure referenced indirectly by an access variable, whereas an instance of a class is an object encapsulating both data and associated operations. These principal categories of types in DRAGOON are illustrated in Figure 3.3.

Distinguishing between these different types in DRAGOON reinforces the terminology introduced earlier to distinguish between the alternative representations of 'data abstractions' either as 'abstract data types' or 'classes'. Pure data abstractions in DRAGOON may, thus, be represented in either one of the two principal categories of types. Similarly, the term 'instance variable' distinguishes variables intended to refer to *instances* of a class type (i.e. objects) from 'data variables' or 'attributes' intended to contain values of a data type.

Because classes are types they can be used in the construction of compound data structures. It is possible for the elements of an array and

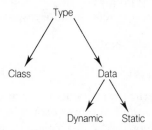

Figure 3.3   Type categories in DRAGOON.

the fields of a record to be of a class type (i.e. objects). Classes, therefore, are fully integrated into the typing rules 'inherited' from Ada. Naturally, as far as data types are concerned, the associated typing rules are precisely those of Ada. Similarly, the rules for compound data structures are the same as those of Ada except in so far as the elements or fields are objects of class types. In this case, it is the rules related to class types discussed below that apply.

3.5.2   Type compatibility

The basic goal of typing is to ensure that every entity in a program is used in a manner consistent with its declared type. In the context of object-oriented programming, in which client objects make use of server objects by invoking their methods, this transposes into the goal of ensuring that every attempted method invocation is meaningful for the object to which it is directed. In other words, static typing in object-oriented languages is intended to ensure at compile time that no attempted method invocation fails because the method is not part of the server's interface.

The methods of an object are actually invoked by issuing a method call through a reference (or internal names) stored in either:

- an instance variable, or
- a formal method parameter

which are *statically* declared to be of a particular class type. During execution of the program, however, references to different classes of objects may be assigned to these entities – in the first case by means of direct assignment statements, and in the second when actual parameters are mapped on to formal parameters during a method call. The *static* type of an instance variable or formal method parameter – the class type with which it is statically associated – may not be the same as its *dynamic* type – the class type of the object to which it is dynamically made to refer.

To protect against the invocation of unrecognized methods, therefore, it is necessary to define typing rules which ensure that no instance variable or formal method parameter is ever made to refer to an object that is not able to respond to all the method calls that instances of the *static* class type can. Moreover, if these rules are to be statically checkable from the program text, it is necessary to check the compatibility of classes at the point of assignment, rather than at the point when the method call is made. In other words, the type of the *source* of an assignment must be able to respond to at least all the method invocations (messages) to which the static type of the *target* (i.e. an instance variable or formal method parameter) may respond.

If the typing rules of the language permit an instance of a class S to be assigned to an instance variable or formal method parameter of class T, then S is said to be *type compatible* with, or a *subtype* of, T. Type compatibility is a transitive relationship, so that if S is a subtype of T, and T is a subtype of U, then S is a subtype of (i.e. type compatible with) U.

3.5.3   Conformance

The simplest way of deciding whether two classes are type compatible is by the set of methods exported in their interfaces – that is, their *protocols*. If the interface of the source class S indicates that its instances are able to respond to all method calls that instances of the target class T can, then, adopting the terminology of Emerald (Black *et al*, 1986) which was one of the first languages to adopt this approach, S is said to *conform* to T. Conformance, therefore, is not in any way related to the implementation of classes, but is determined solely by their protocols.

Informally, for a source class S to conform to a target class T, S must export at least all the methods of T, and the (formal) results (i.e. the 'out' parameters) of any methods in S common to T must conform to the corresponding argument in T. On the other hand, the (formal) arguments (i.e. the 'in' parameters) of the methods of T common to S must conform to the corresponding arguments in S. Not only is this definition recursive, therefore, but the last condition (known as contravariance) requires that conformance of the arguments holds in the opposite direction to that of the classes. This is because instances of S may be treated as (i.e. sent the parameters expected by) instances of T, so that the protocols of the parameters must export all the methods expected by instances of S.

3.5.4   Subtypes

Conformance is sufficient to serve as the basis for type compatibility rules, since it guarantees that the target of a method call will always be able to respond in some way or another. However, because it is only based on the forms of class interfaces, classes may conform that bear no logical relationship to one another whatsoever. For this reason, languages such as DRAGOON and Eiffel, which possess an inheritance mechanism, have an additional requirement for one class to be type compatible with another – it must also be its ancestor. Type compatibility is no longer determined by the form of the interface alone, therefore, but also by the relationship of the implementations. Although it is *necessary* for a class to be an ancestor of another class to be type compatible with it, this is not *sufficient* because of the method modification possibilities. It is clearly also necessary that the heir class conforms to the parent.

Some languages, like Eiffel, permit an heir class not only to change the body of inherited methods, but also to change the class types of their formal parameters. Unfortunately, despite elaborate rules, this meant that the typing mechanisms of early versions of Eiffel (including version 2.1) were not completely watertight (Cook, 1989). Moreover, it is questionable how necessary the ability to redefine the parameter types of inherited methods really is, because most of its uses can be catered for by generic classes (Chapter 5).

To ensure the consistency of the typing scheme, DRAGOON adopts a very simple strategy for defining when descendent classes are type compatible with their parents. In DRAGOON:

- an heir class that removes from its interface one or more methods inherited from a parent is not a subtype of (i.e. type compatible with) that parent.

- an heir class may only redefine the body of an inherited method; the interface must remain unchanged (except for parameters with default values (see below)).

- an heir class is *not* permitted to change the class type of inherited instance variables.

Although DRAGOON does not permit the types of existing method parameters to be changed in descendent classes, it does permit additional parameters to be added, provided they are given a default value. Like the corresponding Ada mechanism for subprogram parameters, when invoking a method it is not necessary to provide actual parameters for the formal parameters with default values, since the formal parameters take the value of the default if no other value is supplied. The redefinition of methods by adding default parameters does not destroy their ability to respond to method calls directed to instances of the parent class, therefore.

3.5.5   Terminology

Before proceeding further it is important to clarify the different ways in which the terminology associated with typing in object-oriented languages is used in DRAGOON. In some languages, such as Eiffel, the term conformant is taken as synonymous with 'type compatible'. In other words, if a class S is conformant with a class T in Eiffel, then it is also type compatible, and vice versa. This is not the case in DRAGOON, however, which adopts the original meaning as defined in Emerald (Black *et al*, 1989). As described earlier, a class S is conformant to another class T if its *interface* satisfies certain rules in relation to T's. This does not guarantee, however, that the typing rules will permit an instance of S to be assigned to an instance variable of class T, and hence it is not necessarily type compatible.

Another source of ambiguity is the use of the terms subclass and superclass. Many object-oriented languages regard the term 'subclass' as synonymous with 'heir' and 'superclass' with 'parent'. In other words a subclass is an immediate descendant of its superclass. This terminology presents no problem in languages like Smalltalk which do not have a static typing scheme, but in languages which do, such as DRAGOON and Eiffel, it clashes unfortunately with the subtyping relationship between classes. If the term 'subclass' was used synonymously with 'heir' in DRAGOON, the typing rules outlined in the previous subsection would mean that a sub-'*class*' would not always be a sub-'*type*', even though a class is supposed to be a type. There is, moreover, no need to use this terminology to describe inheritance relationships, because perfectly adequate terminology already exists ('heir/parent', 'descendant/ancestor'). In DRAGOON, therefore, the term subclass is not regarded as synonymous with 'heir' but rather with 'subtype'. A class S is a subclass of a type T if, and only if, it is a subtype – that is, type compatible. Naturally, T is then termed a superclass of S.

Inheritance, subclassing and conformance in DRAGOON are therefore three closely related but distinct concepts. A subclass relationship implies both conformance and inheritance, but not vice versa. To illustrate these differences, consider the various classes introduced so far during the course of this chapter, and illustrated in Figure 3.4.

The class PERISHABLE_DESCRIPTOR (3.6), for example, conforms with DATED_ITEM (3.12), since it exports all its methods (i.e. DATE, SET_DATE_TO), but is not a subclass (i.e. type compatible) because it is not an heir. Conversely, the class RESTRICTED_DESCRIPTOR (3.11) is an heir of PERISHABLE_DESCRIPTOR (3.6), but is not a subclass because it does conform with it. For a class to be a subclass of another it must be both an heir and conformant. PERISHABLE_DESCRIPTOR (3.6) is therefore a subclass of PRODUCT_DESCRIPTOR (3.4).

It is important to be aware of the difference between the Ada and DRAGOON view of subtypes. The basic concept is the same: a subtype representing a subset of entities in the parent type. The difference is that DRAGOON's subtyping scheme for classes is static, whereas Ada's is dynamic. This means that subtyping errors cannot, in general, be statically detected by Ada compilers, whereas they form the basis of the static assignment rules in DRAGOON.

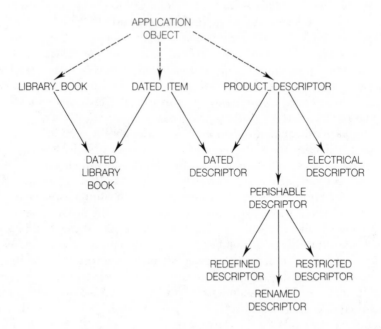

Figure 3.4 Inheritance hierarchy.

3.5.6 Type conversion

The formulation of type compatibility rules is a careful balancing act between the need to prohibit potentially dangerous assignments likely to cause run-time errors, and the need to allow a certain degree of flexibility in the structuring of programs. Nevertheless, however carefully the typing rules are designed, it is impossible to formulate purely static rules that will not be either too restrictive in some situations or too liberal in others. In other words, these two goals are essentially incompatible. Therefore, many languages with strong typing schemes, including Ada, provide mechanisms which the programmer may use explicitly to override the typing rules of the language in contexts where these are too restrictive.

Such facilities are also needed in DRAGOON because the static typing rules described in Section 3.5.4 may, in certain circumstances, drastically undermine the usefulness of polymorphism for the purposes of reuse. To see why this is so, consider a class STACK which implements a stack of PRODUCT_DESCRIPTOR (3.4) objects:

```
with PRODUCT_DESCRIPTOR;                                    (3.15)
class STACK is
    introduces
        procedure PUSH (ITEM : in PRODUCT_DESCRIPTOR);
        function POP return PRODUCT_DESCRIPTOR;
end;
```

where PUSH and POP are the usual methods for adding and removing objects
to and from the top of the stack respectively.

Since the classes PERISHABLE_DESCRIPTOR (3.6) and ELECTRICAL_DES-
CRIPTOR (3.8) are subclasses of PRODUCT_DESCRIPTOR (3.4), the typing rules
of DRAGOON allow the programmer to take advantage of type compatibility of classes and PUSH instances of both these subclasses on to a STACK
object, as well as instances of PRODUCT_DESCRIPTOR itself. All the following
PUSH operations are legal, therefore:

```
                    ⋮

    S : STACK;

    PRODUCT : PRODUCT_DESCRIPTOR;
    PERISHABLE : PERISHABLE_DESCRIPTOR;
    ELECTRICAL : ELECTRICAL_DESCRIPTOR;

                    ⋮

    PRODUCT.CREATE;
    PERISHABLE.CREATE;
    ELECTRICAL.CREATE;

                    ⋮

    S.PUSH(PRODUCT);
    S.PUSH(PERISHABLE);
    S.PUSH(ELECTRICAL);

                    ⋮
```

The problem is that once instances of the subclasses of PROD-
UCT_DESCRIPTOR – PERISHABLE_DESCRIPTOR and ELECTRICAL_DESCRIPTOR –
have been 'pushed' on to S they lose their independent identity, and are
essentially transformed into instances of PRODUCT_DESCRIPTOR. Although
the additional information associated with PERISHABLE and ELECTRICAL is
stored in the stack, this can never be accessed again, because the static
typing rules of DRAGOON forbid anything 'popped' off S from being assigned to a subclass of PRODUCT_DESCRIPTOR. The following statements are
therefore illegal:

⋮

```
PERISHABLE := S.POP;
ELECTRICAL := S.POP;
```

⋮

even when the object on the top of S is, in fact, an instance of PERISH-ABLE_DESCRIPTOR or ELECTRICAL_DESCRIPTOR, as appropriate.

This is a very serious constraint on the language's support for reuse, and a situation in which the static typing rules are clearly too restrictive. It is not possible to assign an object 'popped' off S to a PERISH-ABLE_DESCRIPTOR instance variable, for example, even if the programmer ensures that nothing is pushed on to it other than PERISHABLE_DESCRIPTOR objects.

To overcome this unhappy state of affairs, DRAGOON provides a mechanism for ascertaining which class an object is an instance of, and for converting objects between classes in the same branch of an inheritance tree. So, for example, if the programmer was sure that the object on the top of S was an instance of PERISHABLE_DESCRIPTOR, he/she can explicitly convert the class type of the object returned by the POP method into PERISHABLE_DESCRIPTOR:

⋮

```
PERISHABLE := PERISHABLE_DESCRIPTOR'(S.POP);
```

⋮

The notation chosen for type conversion is not the same as that used in Ada because it was felt that there may be confusion with method calls. The expression providing the value to be converted is prefixed by the name of the target type followed by a 'tick'. This corresponds to the Ada notation for expression qualification rather than type conversion but as long as this is understood there should be no confusion.

If the programmer was not certain of the type of the object at the top of S, on the other hand, he/she may establish whether it is a particular subclass of the static (i.e. apparent) type using the 'in' operation:

⋮

```
PRODUCT := S.POP;
if PRODUCT in PERISHABLE_DESCRIPTOR then
    PERISHABLE := PERISHABLE_DESCRIPTOR'(PRODUCT);
end if;
```

⋮

This does correspond to the Ada notation for determining the subtype membership of values – 'in' being a binary operation returning true if the class of the object referenced by the left argument is a subclass of that of the right argument (in other words, if the dynamic type of the left argument is a subclass of the static type of the right). As in this illustration, this facility is most commonly used to check the class type of an object before an attempted type conversion. If a conversion is attempted in which the source is not a subclass of the target, a run-time error results.

These two facilities are extremely useful for overcoming the constraints of the static typing rules of the language in situations where they are too restrictive. They are used entirely at the programmer's risk, however, since they also clearly permit the construction of erroneous programs that would otherwise be prohibited by the static typing rules.

Key points

Many abstractions that need to be represented within computer programs, such as numbers and colours, are more naturally modelled as 'values' than 'objects'.

DRAGOON is a 'mixed' paradigm language that supports both 'value-oriented' programming in terms of Ada-style types and object-oriented programming in terms of classes and objects.

There are two ways of modelling a given *data abstraction* in DRAGOON – either as an Ada-style *abstract data type* or as a *class.*

Stateless packages, called *template packages*, are used in DRAGOON to declare types, subprograms and exceptions which need to be shared by more than one task.

DRAGOON classes are composed of two separate compilation units – the specification and the body.

One of the principal relationships between classes is clientship which exists when one class – the client – calls the methods of an instance of another – the server. The clientship relationship also holds between instances of the classes at run-time.

The other principal relationship which exists only between classes is inheritance. This permits one class to 'inherit' all the properties of another, including its interface and implementation. The *heir* class becomes a specialization of its *parent.*

Three possible modifications may be applied to inherited methods – they may be *redefined*, they may be *renamed* or they may be completely *removed* from the interface of the heir. In the third case the heir is no longer regarded as a subclass (i.e. subtype) of the parent.

Multiple inheritance permits a class to have more than one parent. This is useful for enabling an object to be viewed through two distinct interfaces, but can lead to name clashes.

DRAGOON classes are full types in the language and may be used as the type of the elements of an array or the components of a record.

For one DRAGOON class to be a subtype of (i.e. type compatible with) another it must be an heir which removes none of the inherited methods.

DRAGOON permits the type of an object to be converted between classes in the same branch of an inheritance tree, so that it is possible to regain the true type of an object after it has been treated as an object of the parent type through polymorphism.

Chapter 4
Inheritance-Based Reuse

Having introduced the basic features of DRAGOON, and illustrated how classes and objects are modelled in the language, this chapter focuses on the issue of software reuse, and describes why the inheritance, polymorphism and dynamic binding mechanisms of object-oriented languages such as DRAGOON provide such a powerful vehicle for reuse.

4.1 Component engineering

As the costs of software development have soared, 'reuse' has become a more and more important requirement, and now affects virtually all aspects of modern software engineering from requirements and design specification through to documentation and testing. Its basic goal is to minimize the amount of new application software that has to be developed from scratch for each new system. Reusing design and requirements information enables consideration of reuse to be introduced at much earlier stages in the development process, thereby facilitating the reuse of larger bodies of software.

Traditional techniques for supporting reuse are based on the concept of what may be called 'component engineering', in which new software systems are developed by assembling 'reusable components' chosen from a large, carefully designed and tested library. This approach essentially divides the problems of promoting software reuse into two distinct considerations (Sommerville; 1989a): how to produce software components with maximum potential for reuse – design *for* reuse – and how to design new systems making the most effective use of such components – design *with* reuse.

Although it is fairly easy to state in general terms what attributes a 'good' reusable component should possess (commonly accepted requirements include efficiency, simplicity, functional independence and maintainability (Booch, 1987) (Matsumoto, 1984)) it is much more difficult to define how one should go about designing components to exhibit these properties (Gautier *et al*, 1989). Object-oriented design is in fact one of the most helpful approaches since it not only encourages good programming practice, but also leads to modular, 'well structured' designs in which the object forms a natural unit of reuse. Many of the recent reuse methodologies targeted to Ada are consequently based on the ideas of object-oriented design (Booch, 1987).

Modularity and independence alone, however, do not ensure that a component will be reusable. One of the most critical factors affecting 'reusability' is the 'generality' of a component, because this determines the range of different applications and contexts in which it may be employed. A component tailored specifically to one particular application is less likely to be reusable in different contexts than one designed with generality in mind.

The most important techniques for increasing the generality of components is *parameterization* – each parameter that can be selected by the 'reuser' at the time of reuse provides an extra degree of freedom that increases the component's range of potential uses. One of the oldest and simplest examples is the parameterization of subprograms by data values, which was supported in the earliest high-level languages such as FOR-TRAN, and is the basis for the success of reusable mathematical routines. More recent languages have introduced new parameterization facilities such as the parameterization of components by types (e.g. genericity) and subprograms (e.g. procedure variables in Modula, generics in Ada). Genericity is a particularly useful tool for obviating the replication of essentially identical code in languages with strong typing, and is discussed further in Chapter 5.

While increasing the degree of parameterization (i.e. the number of parameters) of a component may increase its 'generality' it also significantly increases its complexity and thus the obscurity of its function. Therefore, the 'reusability' of a component is not necessarily maximized by identifying every conceivable operation that it may perform, and introducing as many parameters as possible. On the contrary, there is a practical limit to the extent to which a component can be parameterized without making it prohibitively complex and obtuse. A delicate balance needs to be achieved, therefore, between a component's *generality* and its *intelligibility* – a balance which is obviously harder to achieve for larger components with more scope for parameterization.

4.1.1 Component families

An important alternative to explicit parameterization as a way of providing additional degrees of freedom in the use of a component is to define a 'family' of distinct, but related components, each member representing either a variant of the basic component abstraction or providing a different implementation policy. Booch has been one of the main proponents of this approach for constructing reusable components, and has done much influential work on defining a detailed taxonomy.

All the principal 'collection' components[1] considered by Booch have at least two variants – the iterator and non-iterator. Most have quite a few more, however. An *iterator*, popularized in the language CLU (Liskov *et al*, 1981), is a version of a component that provides operations enabling every encapsulated data item to be 'visited' (i.e. have operations performed upon it) without destroying the structure itself. This facility is useful in a large variety of contexts where clients need to obtain information about the elements stored in a component without actually consuming any elements.

Depending on whether it provides support for iteration, therefore, a component may be classified as either an:

- **iterator** – with iterator facilities included, or a

- **non-iterator** – with no such facilities.

Members of the family which differ only by their implementation policy rather than their interface are known as different *forms*. These, in turn, are divided into *spatial* and *temporal* characteristics. Temporal characteristics relate to the component's behaviour in a concurrent environment with multiple execution threads, and will be considered further in Chapter 6. Spatial characteristics, on the other hand, relate to the component's memory requirements and are therefore essentially orthogonal to the temporal ones. Components may either be:

- **bounded** – with fixed or limited size, or

- **unbounded** – with an unlimited size.

Unbounded forms of a component must clearly be implemented using dynamic data structures (e.g. linked lists), whereas the bounded form can be implemented using either static or dynamic data structures.

The final spatial categorization identified by Booch relates to the memory management policy of the component, which may either be:

- **managed** – reclaiming redundant memory resources, or

- **unmanaged** – performing no explicit memory reclamation.

Managed forms of a component take explicit steps to ensure that unused memory is reclaimed – that is, garbage collection is performed explicitly – while unmanaged forms provide no such guarantee.

---

[1] Objects that store other objects according to certain access rules.

Implementation in Ada

Although this taxonomy is essentially independent of any particular language, Booch primarily had Ada in mind during its development. Ada is undoubtedly more suitable than most conventional languages for implementing this approach to reuse, since it supports modularity and information hiding by means of packages, concurrency in terms of tasks, and powerful parameterization facilities in terms of generics. These facilities notwithstanding, however, it suffers from the same basic shortcoming as other languages without inheritance – each different variant and form of component has to be implemented independently as a separate package, despite the fact that large parts of them may be identical. Not only does this vast replication of code significantly increase the effort required to produce the components in the first place, but it also greatly increases the amount of space needed to store the components, the problems of organizing and cataloguing them, and ultimately, therefore, the ease with which they can be retrieved and reused.

Consider, for example, all the variations and forms of a simple 'queue' abstraction. In its most abstract form, a queue is simply an ordered set of elements arranged according to the rule that elements can only be added at one end and removed from the other. In other words, queues impose a FIFO (first in first out) discipline on the addition and removal of elements from the set. As with other component families considered by Booch, queues can exist in all the different variants and forms mentioned in this section, that is, iterator/non-iterator, bounded/unbounded and managed/unmanaged. In addition, Booch identifies two other variants of the basic queue abstraction that allow element removal and addition to break the strict FIFO rules. A *balking* queue allows items to be removed from an arbitrary position, while a *priority* queue allows items to be added to the queue at places other than the rear. With these additional variants the total number of meaningful versions of the queue abstraction is 104, each of which needs to be implemented separately as an independent package.

4.2   Component hierarchies

The inheritance mechanism of object-oriented languages such as DRAGOON provides a much more elegant and efficient way of creating such a component family. Instead of representing the various possible forms of an abstraction as unrelated members of a family of components, the inheritance mechanism allows the relationship between them to be modelled explicitly in an inheritance hierarchy. This not only improves the organization of information in the library, but also significantly reduces the work required to produce the family, since common parts of their implementation can be factored out into a single class which they all inherit.

This can be seen by considering how a simplified queue component family could be created in DRAGOON using the various facilities offered by inheritance. The problem of generalizing the type of the elements in the queue (i.e. defining a queue component applicable to different types) will be considered further in the following chapter. For the moment it is assumed that all the elements of the queue are instances of some as yet unknown class type ELEMENT. The following is a DRAGOON class representing the conceptually simplest variant of this component abstraction – the unbounded, unmanaged, non-iterator variant:

```
with ELEMENT;                                                    (4.1)
class SIMPLE_QUEUE is
    introduces
        function POP return ELEMENT;        -- adopting Booch's 'method' names
        procedure ADD (ITEM : in ELEMENT);
        function IS_EMPTY return BOOLEAN;
        UNDERFLOW : exception;
end SIMPLE_QUEUE;

class body SIMPLE_QUEUE is

    type QUEUE_POINTER;
    type QUEUE_NODE is record
        ITEM : ELEMENT;
        NEXT : QUEUE_POINTER;
    end record;

    type QUEUE_POINTER is access QUEUE_NODE;

    FRONT, LAST : QUEUE_POINTER;

    function POP return ELEMENT is
        FRONT_NODE : QUEUE_POINTER := FRONT;
    begin
        if FRONT = null then
            raise UNDERFLOW;
        else
            FRONT := FRONT.NEXT;
            return FRONT_NODE;
        end if;
    end;

    procedure ADD (ITEM : in ELEMENT) is
    begin
        if FRONT = null then
            FRONT := new QUEUE_NODE;
            LAST := FRONT;
        else
            LAST.NEXT := new QUEUE_NODE;
            LAST := LAST.NEXT;
        end if;
        LAST.ITEM := ITEM;
    end;

    function IS_EMPTY return BOOLEAN is
    begin
        return FRONT = null;
    end;

end SIMPLE_QUEUE;
```

It is an error to attempt to POP an element off an empty queue, so the class provides a boolean method IS_EMPTY to check whether an instance is empty, and defines the exception UNDERFLOW which is raised by POP if it is invoked under such circumstances. Since this class models an unbounded version of the queue abstraction, however, conceptually there is no limit to the number of items that can be added to the queue, and so no corresponding IS_FULL method and OVERFLOW exception are needed at this stage. The only practical constraint on the size of the queue is the amount of memory available on the heap. If this should be exhausted, the exception STORAGE_ERROR will be raised by the run-time system when the ADD method requests the allocation of a new QUEUE_NODE.

Notice how records and incomplete type definitions are used in the normal Ada style to define the dynamic 'linked list'. This fits in simply and naturally with the class/object concept, and so avoids the unnecessary complication of recursive class definitions which would have to be employed in other languages such as Eiffel and Smalltalk.

4.2.1 Iterator queue

As mentioned earlier, one of the common variations on basic component abstractions is the inclusion of an iterator which enables each of the elements currently stored in a compound data structure to be 'visited' – that is, to have some operation performed on it. Two ways of implementing iterators are considered by Booch: the passive form, in which the client (or user) supplies the required operation as a parameter, and when so instructed the component ensures that this operation is performed on each element; and the active form, in which another object is provided (as part of the overall component) which can access the elements of the queue and return them successively to the user for manipulation. The main difference is that in the first approach the user does not gain access to the encapsulated data elements but merely supplies the operation that needs to be performed upon them, whereas in the second approach the user gains unrestricted access.

It is in the simulation of the active form that the advantages of object-oriented programming and inheritance are most powerfully displayed. In Booch's formulation an active iterator is a distinct 'object' in the component with four characteristic operations:

- **Initialize** – prepare the component,
- **Get_Next** – advance the iterator to the next item,
- **Value_Of** – return the current item,
- **Is_Done** – return true if every item has been 'visited'.

Using inheritance, an iterator version of the component can be generated simply by creating a subclass of SIMPLE_QUEUE which adds the necessary operations to those already provided.

```
class SIMPLE_ITERATOR_QUEUE is                                    (4.2)
    inherits SIMPLE_QUEUE;
    introduces
        procedure INITIALIZE;
        procedure GET_NEXT;
        function VALUE_OF return ELEMENT;
        function IS_DONE return BOOLEAN;
        ITERATOR_ERROR : exception;
end SIMPLE_ITERATOR_QUEUE;


class body SIMPLE_ITERATOR_QUEUE is

    NEXT : QUEUE_POINTER;

    procedure INITIALIZE is
    begin
        NEXT := FRONT;
    end;

    procedure GET_NEXT is
    begin
        if NEXT = LAST then
            raise ITERATOR_ERROR;
        else
            NEXT := NEXT.LAST;
        end if;
    end;

    function VALUE_OF return ELEMENT is
    begin
        return NEXT.ITEM;
    end;

    function IS_DONE return BOOLEAN is
    begin
        return NEXT = LAST;
    end;

end SIMPLE_ITERATOR_QUEUE;
```

In this class the iteration operations have been added to those of the SIMPLE_QUEUE (4.1), so there is no need for a separate 'iterator' object as in Booch's implementation. This maintains the notion of classes as the unit of reuse, and has been achieved without reimplementation or modification of the existing SIMPLE_QUEUE code, as would be necessary in Ada.

The problem with active iterator classes of this kind is that they are unsafe when used in a concurrent environment. There is no protection against concurrent invocation of the component's non-iterator methods while the iteration is being performed, with the consequent danger of the component's state being rendered inconsistent. Nor is there any guarantee that a single client will perform the iteration. It is possible that one object may interfere with another's use of the active iterator operations.

Techniques for overcoming these problems using DRAGOON's concurrency features are discussed by Ben-Gershon (1990).

4.2.2   Bounded queue

In order to generate different *forms* of the abstraction, however, a certain amount of reimplementation is unavoidable, since by definition these embody different implementation policies. Nevertheless, inheritance permits the amount of reimplementation required to be restricted to those parts that are truly affected by the change. The following class, for example, represents a bounded version of the class SIMPLE_QUEUE (4.1):

```
class BOUNDED_SIMPLE_QUEUE is                                    (4.3)
    inherits SIMPLE_QUEUE;
    redefines
        ADD, POP;
        CREATE (SIZE : in POSITIVE);
    introduces
        function IS_FULL return BOOLEAN;
        OVERFLOW : exception;
end BOUNDED_SIMPLE_QUEUE;
```

```
class body BOUNDED_SIMPLE_QUEUE is

MAX_NUMBER, CURRENT_NUMBER : POSITIVE;

procedure CREATE (SIZE : in POSITIVE) is
begin
    MAX_NUMBER := SIZE;
    CURRENT_NUMBER := 0;
end;

function POP return ELEMENT is
    FRONT_NODE : QUEUE_POINTER := FRONT;
begin
    SIMPLE_QUEUE'POP;
    CURRENT_NUMBER := CURRENT_NUMBER − 1;
end;

procedure ADD (ITEM : in ELEMENT) is
begin
    if CURRENT_NUMBER < MAX_NUMBER then
        SIMPLE_QUEUE'ADD;
        CURRENT_NUMBER := CURRENT_NUMBER + 1;
    else
        raise OVERFLOW;
    end if;
end;

function IS_FULL return BOOLEAN is
begin
    return CURRENT_NUMBER = MAX_NUMBER;
end;

end BOUNDED_SIMPLE_QUEUE;
```

This class illustrates the benefits of being able to redefine the CREATE 'method' of an inherited class to specify new initialization conditions. Although BOUNDED_SIMPLE_QUEUE implements queues with a fixed capacity[2], to increase the 'generality' of the component it is clearly desirable for this number to be a parameter selectable by the reuser. This is achieved by redefining the class's CREATE method to receive the necessary arguments and perform the appropriate initialization.

As pointed out in the previous chapter, the CREATE operation is the mechanism by which new objects are generated in DRAGOON, and although activated in the same way as a method, it is not really one. The 'redefinition' of CREATE, therefore, conforms to different rules to that of normal methods, and is perhaps better thought of as *adding* initialization actions performed at object creation time. Firstly, a 'redefined' CREATE method may only have 'in' parameters, since these may serve only as initialization values. Secondly, a class inheriting from a parent whose CREATE operation has already been redefined must preserve the 'inherited' parameters in any further redefinition. In other words, the redefinition of CREATE is cumulative, because it is essential that all initialization values expected by the code inherited from the parent be supplied also by its descendants. Note that since CREATE does not form part of the interface of a class, any redefinition does not affect the conformance of the class to others. In the current example, the CREATE operation is redefined to receive the required buffer size and assign this value to the internal variable MAX_NUMBER.

BOUNDED_SIMPLE_QUEUE also demonstrates how it is possible to reuse the 'old', inherited version of a method in the redefinition of its body. The 'new' versions of POP and ADD in BOUNDED_SIMPLE_QUEUE do not actually change the way in which the inherited operations are performed in the heir class, but merely add additional steps before and/or after the inherited part. Rather than replicate the code of the inherited method in the body of the redefined version, therefore, it is possible to incorporate the 'old' version directly. For example, the old version of the method POP in SIMPLE_QUEUE is incorporated into the redefined version in BOUNDED_SIMPLE_QUEUE by the statement SIMPLE_QUEUE'POP. This should not be thought of as a method call, but as a direct substitution of the text of the parent method into the heir. Note that it is only possible to do this for the methods of heirs, not indirect ancestors.

Since this version of the queue is 'bounded', and cannot expand indefinitely, it is an error to attempt to add an item to an instance of the class which is full. The exception OVERFLOW is introduced to indicate such an error, and is raised by the new version of the ADD method when it detects that the number of items in the buffer has reached its upper bound.

---

[2]In fact, it is not a particularly efficient component, since although the size of the structure is bounded at any one time, it generates a new list node for each new element added to the queue. In other words, it is 'unmanaged'. Nevertheless, it serves to illustrate how inheritance can be used to change the functionality of classes.

4.3   Abstract classes

Although use of the inheritance mechanism enables the class BOUN-DED_SIMPLE_QUEUE (4.3) to be implemented more succinctly than would otherwise have been possible, it is still necessary to redefine most of the inherited methods. This should not really be surprising, since the bounded and unbounded forms of a queue demand substantially different implementation strategies, particularly in the case of the 'static' form based on static data structures. If such an implementation had been adopted for the bounded queue, there would have been little point in inheriting the implementation of SIMPLE_QUEUE (4.1) since its body would have had to be completely redefined. Irrespective of the implementation strategy, however, it remains true that the methods offered in the interface of a bounded queue are *logically* a superset of those offered by the unbounded form (e.g. SIMPLE_QUEUE). This suggests that BOUNDED_SIMPLE_QUEUE should indeed be an heir of SIMPLE_QUEUE despite the fact that the inherited code may have to be completely redefined.

This apparent contradiction is a symptom of the fact that in DRA-GOON, as in many other object-oriented languages, the inheritance hierarchy is used both to represent logical 'is-a' (i.e. subset) relationships and practical 'implementation' relationships for reusing code (Chapter 2). It is not possible to express the fact that two classes logically exist in a subclass/superclass relationship without the heir also inheriting the complete implementation of the parent. Like most other object-oriented languages, however, DRAGOON provides a facility for overcoming this particular difficulty.

The basic problem is that the bounded and unbounded forms of a queue are not genuinely in a subclass/superclass relationship, but actually represent alternative implementation strategies for a single, higher-level abstraction – a queue. To permit this relationship to be expressed more naturally, DRAGOON supports the concept of *abstract classes*, which define the interface of a particular abstraction but leave descendent classes to provide the specific implementations. Just such a class is needed to define the basic abstraction of a queue without carrying any implementation commitments:

```
class QUEUE is                                              (4.4)
    introduces
        function POP return ELEMENT is deferred;
        procedure ADD (ITEM : in ELEMENT) is deferred;
        function IS_EMPTY return BOOLEAN is deferred;
        UNDERFLOW : exception;
end QUEUE;
```

The keyword 'deferred' after a method specification indicates that this class does not provide an implementation for the method. However, this does not necessarily mean that abstract classes such as QUEUE possess no body. Quite the contrary, even if a class defers all its methods – which is not obligatory – it may still define instance variables and data types in its body. In fact, it may also provide a special kind of 'degenerate' body for each of the deferred methods. Such a body does not actually 'implement' the method as such, but defines *pre* and *post conditions* that should be satisfied before and after its execution.

4.3.1   Pre/post conditions

The pre and post conditions of DRAGOON are similar in style to those of Eiffel – enhanced boolean expressions specifying conditions that should be valid before and after the execution of a method. As in Eiffel, a predefined exception (CONDITION_ERROR) is raised if the precondition is not satisfied on invocation of the method, or the postcondition is not satisfied on its completion. However, pre/post conditions perform a completely different role in DRAGOON to that in Eiffel, where their main purpose is to define the 'contract' between the *client* of a class and its implementor. The idea is that if the client ensures that the precondition is satisfied before calling a method, its implementor will guarantee that the postcondition is satisfied on its completion.

While this view of 'programming as contracting' certainly has important benefits for reuse and program correctness in a sequential environment, it runs into difficulties in concurrent systems. This is because the preconditions that need to be satisfied generally depend on the state of the server object, and the client can only obtain the required information by calling a method of the object concerned. A typical precondition of a queue's POP operation, for example, is that the queue should not be empty, and since this assertion depends directly on the state of the queue, a client can only ascertain this information by calling the IS_EMPTY method beforehand. This presents no problem in a system with only one execution thread, but in a concurrent system, where there may be many concurrently executing clients, there is no guarantee that the state of the object will not alter in the time between the calls to IS_EMPTY and POP.

The 'programming as contracting' approach is not appropriate for concurrent environments, therefore. Nor is it compatible with the DRA-GOON philosophy of separating the specification and body parts of a class, since an assertion placed in the specification cannot refer to the state variables, while an assertion placed in the body cannot be seen by a client and serves as the basis of a 'contract'.

Although assertions are of no value in DRAGOON for specifying a contract between the client and implementor of a class, they are useful for specifying a 'contract' between the 'deferrer' of a method and its implementor in a descendent class. If an abstract class specifies certain pre and post conditions on the body of a method that it defers, then these will apply to all subsequent implementations of the method. The designer of the abstract class is therefore conveying information about the intended semantics of the deferred methods to future implementors.

In common with Eiffel, DRAGOON supports the definition of 'class invariants' in the body of a class, which specify conditions that must be satisfied at all times, particularly after the execution of any of its methods.

4.3.2   Completing methods

Since by definition an abstract class is not equipped with a full implementation (at least one method must be deferred), it is not possible to generate instances of the class within other DRAGOON objects. This does not rule out the possibility of defining *instance variables* of an abstract class, however, since the polymorphism facilities of DRAGOON enable the variables to refer to instances of descendent classes.

Having defined QUEUE (4.4) as an abstract class, it is now possible to model the true relationship between the bounded and unbounded forms of the abstraction as separate subclasses providing alternative implementations. However, bounded and unbounded are not the only forms of queues that need to be represented somewhere in the hierarchy. As mentioned earlier, bounded forms may be implemented by either dynamic or static data structures, while unbounded queues may either be managed or unmanaged. To cater for these additional forms, it is sensible to introduce two more abstract classes to distinguish between the bounded and unbounded forms, while leaving open the other implementation alternatives:

```
class UNBOUNDED_QUEUE is                                        (4.5)
    inherits QUEUE;
end UNBOUNDED_QUEUE;
```

```
class BOUNDED_QUEUE is                                          (4.6)
    inherits QUEUE;
    introduces
        function IS_FULL return BOOLEAN is deferred;
        OVERFLOW : exception;
end BOUNDED_QUEUE;
```

Although it may not be immediately apparent from the specification of the first class, BOUNDED_QUEUE, both these classes are abstract because they do not provide implementations for the deferred methods they inherited from QUEUE. The class BOUNDED_QUEUE introduces a new deferred method and so is clearly abstract. It is the descendent classes at the next level in the hierarchy that provide the required implementations, for example:

```
class UNMANAGED_QUEUE is                                        (4.7)
    inherits UNBOUNDED_QUEUE;
    completes
        POP, ADD, IS_EMPTY;
end UNMANAGED_QUEUE;
```

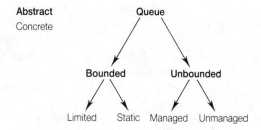

Figure 4.1   Inheritance hierarchy for the 'queue' forms.

The keyword 'completes' is used in the interface to indicate that the class provides complete bodies for the methods listed. In this case, the class implements the unmanaged, unbounded form of the component just like the original class SIMPLE_QUEUE (4.1). In fact the body of SIMPLE_QUEUE, would be perfectly satisfactory as the body of UNMANAGED_QUEUE. The advantage of using abstract classes in this way is that other implementations can now be defined with the proper relationship to this form, rather than having to inherit from SIMPLE_QUEUE and then redefine most of the implementation. For example, a bounded form implemented using dynamic data structures (e.g. BOUNDED_SIMPLE_QUEUE (4.3)) is now defined as a subclass of the abstract class BOUNDED_QUEUE:

```
class DYNAMIC_QUEUE is                                    (4.8)
    inherits BOUNDED_QUEUE;
    completes
        POP, ADD, IS_EMPTY;
end DYNAMIC_QUEUE;
```

Similarly, the other two forms – 'static' and 'managed' – are defined as subclasses of BOUNDED and UNBOUNDED with specifications that are identical to DYNAMIC_QUEUE and UNMANAGED_QUEUE respectively. The inheritance hierarchy containing all these different spatial forms of the queue abstraction is illustrated in Figure 4.1. Common properties have been factored out and represented by abstract classes.

One of the effects of deferring methods is to decouple the specification of a method from its implementation. In languages like Eiffel, therefore, in which classes must be defined completely in a single module, abstract classes are used as a way of separating the specification part of a class from its implementation. This is not the case in DRAGOON, however, because the specification and implementation of classes are already contained in separate program modules – the specification part and body part. The role of abstract classes in DRAGOON is only to allow the correct logical relationship between classes to be expressed in the inheritance hierarchy, permitting genuinely alternative implementations to be defined as independent peers.

Separation of the implementation and specification parts of a class or method should not be confused with the facility for defining separate subunits either. DRAGOON adopts Ada's approach of permitting the implementation of methods (i.e. subprograms) to be defined in a different program module to the encapsulating unit by replacing the method body with a *stub*. The implementation must eventually be provided in a distinct subunit of the main unit. However, as in Ada, this facility merely serves as a mechanism for simplifying the textual complexity of a program unit, and does not alter the logical structure of the program.

A comprehensive family of queue components would naturally contain many more versions and forms of components than those mentioned here and illustrated in Figure 4.1. This is a highly idealized family, designed to avoid obscuring the important concepts with unnecessary detail. A more complete library of Booch-like DRAGOON components, including a hierarchy of queue components, has been developed at Imperial College, London (Ben-Gershon, 1990).

4.4   Dynamic binding

The previous sections of this chapter have described how inheritance together with the notion of abstract classes can be used to minimize the quantity of replication involved in the generation of families of reusable components. This simplifies the design and *construction* of reusable classes – that is, design *for* reuse. Object-oriented programming languages, however, also have some very powerful facilities for supporting programming *with* reuse.

In the 'component engineering' approach to reuse considered so far, the mechanism by which components are reused is *clientship*. If a class in a new system wishes to employ the services of a reusable component, such as the QUEUE (4.4) component developed in this chapter, it defines an instance variable of the component class and generates the required instance. The services of the component are therefore exploited by method calls.

As pointed out in the previous section, one of the key ideas of the object-oriented approach is to decouple the act of invoking a method from that of executing it. When combined with the polymorphism properties of object-oriented languages, and the facility for redefining methods in descendent classes, this separation of concerns gives rise to another extremely powerful feature for reuse known as *dynamic binding*.

Consider, for example, an object that needs to use a queue component in its implementation. As described earlier, there is a whole family of variants and forms of the basic queue abstraction, of which those discussed in Section 4.1.1 and illustrated in Figure 4.1 are but a small number. With a conventional Ada implementation of the component family, the designer of the client software must select one particular implementing package to use, and must explicitly name that package in a 'with' clause. This is fine if the context does in fact require one particular variant or form of the component and the designer is able to identify the form at the coding stage, but in many cases this is not the case. The client software is often not concerned which particular form of queue is used, and even if it is, at the coding stage the designer may not know precisely which form is required.

The dynamic binding properties of object-oriented languages, such as DRAGOON, overcome this problem because the client software can be completely decoupled from any consideration about the implementation of the reused component. Although a client object may invoke the services of a queue through an instance variable of class type BOUNDED_QUEUE (4.6), therefore, the polymorphism rules permit any subclasses of BOUN-DED_QUEUE to service the method calls at run-time. The form of the queue component to which the instance variable refers, and hence the specific way in which the methods accessible through the variable are implemented, is determined dynamically by the previous assignments. In other words, the particular version of a method that services a method call is dynamically 'bound' to the method name.

This feature is particularly powerful in connection with abstract classes, since as described earlier, they enable common, implementation-independent features of classes to be factored out and modelled at a higher level of abstraction. Thus if a client object were not concerned with which particular form or variant of queue it used, but simply wished to use a queue of any kind, it would be a client of the abstract class QUEUE (4.4). Although this is an abstract class, it is possible for the client software to define an instance variable of the class and invoke its methods, because at run-time the instance variables will refer to instances of its concrete subclasses. The class QUEUE, therefore, would be used by client software with no particular implementation requirements, while clients with more specific implementation needs would use other classes at a lower level of abstraction. For example, a class requiring a bounded queue would be a client of BOUNDED_QUEUE (4.6). Augmented by abstract classes, therefore, dynamic binding permits client software to use components of precisely the desired level of abstraction and be completely unaware of the particular object that actually services the method class. Moreover, as new implementations of the component are added to the library, the type of the object implementing the methods can be changed without affecting the client.

4.4.1   Extensibility

As pointed out by Cox (1986) and Meyer (1988), and demonstrated by the above example, the main advantage of this feature from the reuse point of view is the extensibility of software systems – the ease with which they can be adapted to satisfy new requirements. In conventional procedure-oriented languages, such as Pascal and Ada, implementation-dependent aspects of design are dispersed widely among the components of a system, even when an object-oriented design method is adopted. This means that the consequences of a change or extension to one part of the system have an impact throughout. In object-oriented languages, on the other hand, the decoupling of method invocation from execution, together with polymorphism, localizes the implementation details and stops them spreading beyond those components that actually require the information.

Consider, for example, a client of the class PRODUCT_DESCRIPTOR (3.4) defined in the previous chapter. This may declare an instance variable of the class:

$$\vdots$$

```
P : PRODUCT_DESCRIPTOR;
D : SIMPLE_CALENDAR.DATE;
```

$$\vdots$$

and may invoke any of the methods exported in its interface:

$$\vdots$$

```
D := P.SELL_BY_DATE;
```

$$\vdots$$

Instances of any subclass of PRODUCT_DESCRIPTOR, such as ELECTRICAL_DESCRIPTOR (3.8), PERISHABLE_DESCRIPTOR (3.6) and REDEFINED_DESCRIPTOR (3.9), may be assigned to the instance variable P. Moreover, any method calls expressed using P are unaffected by such an assignment because the body that will service any request is dynamically bound to the call. Since the class REDEFINED_DESCRIPTOR redefines the method SELL_BY_DATE, the version of the method executed by the above method call depends dynamically on the type of the object to which the instance variable refers.

This contrasts sharply with the way such a scenario would have to be programmed in Ada. It is possible to achieve a certain degree of polymorphism using variant records – the different sets of attributes of the various kinds of descriptors being represented as different variants of a single record type:

$$\vdots$$

```
type DESCRIPTOR_STATE (FORM : PRODUCT_TYPE) is record              (4.9)
                                    -- type PRODUCT_TYPE defined in (3.1)
        BAR_CODE : PRODUCT.CODE_NUMBER;
```

```
PRICE : PRODUCT.VALUE;
STOCK_LEVEL : PRODUCT.STOCK_NUMBER;
LABEL : PRODUCT.LABEL;
case FORM is
    when PERISHABLE =>
        DATE : SIMPLE_CALENDAR.DATE;
    when ELECTRICAL =>
        LABEL : PRODUCT_DESCRIPTOR;
    when others =>
        null;
    end case;
end record;
```

$$\vdots$$

However, once the type has been fixed, it is not possible to add a new kind of descriptor to the system without changing this type definition, and all the procedures (methods) that use it – a process at least involving the recompilation of all the client software.

The situation with respect to dynamic binding is even worse. In order for the client software to select dynamically one of these implementations depending on the particular descriptor variant assigned to the access variable, it would have to explicitly select the version required using a case statement controlled by an appropriate enumeration type, VERSION_ENUMERATION, say:

$$\vdots$$

```
case VERSION_ENUMERATION is                                      (4.10)
    when BASIC =>
                                            -- call the original version
    when REDEFINED =>
                                            -- call the redefined version
    when ...
    end case;
```

$$\vdots$$

This results in details about the various implementations being embedded throughout the system in all client software. It is not possible to add a new product descriptor to the system, therefore, without modifying large segments of the client code. Clearly, by minimizing the extent to which client software is coupled to implementation details of components, object-oriented programming significantly improves the prospects for the incremental modification and extension of software.

4.5   Programming by difference

So far this chapter has been concerned with the basic 'component engineering' or 'compositional' approach to reuse, in which the process of software development is at least implicitly divided into two parts: programming *for* reuse and programming *with* reuse (Sommerville *et al*, 1989). It has been shown how the features of object-oriented languages in general, and of DRAGOON in particular, greatly enhance both these facets of reuse.

Although the 'component engineering' approach is an important tool in the quest for reuse, it is by no means a panacea. In spite of the significant advantages of inheritance for developing component families, there is still a practical limit to the number of variants and forms of components that can be defined and stored in a library and the degree to which these can be generalized. Situations are bound to arise, therefore, in which the basic abstraction represented by a family of components would be useful in a particular application, but none of the existing components provides precisely the required mix of properties, or is parameterized in precisely the right way to be used. It is impossible for a component designer to predict and cater for *all* the possible contexts in which the abstraction may be potentially applicable. This is more so for complex objects with a large number of potential variants and applications.

The component engineering philosophy works well, therefore, for simple, well understood program abstractions, but is difficult to extend to larger, more complex components without making them extremely difficult and unattractive to use. The inheritance mechanism of object-oriented languages also has something to offer here, however, by facilitating a fundamentally different approach to reuse commonly termed 'programming by difference'. Although inheritance plays an important role in in the 'component engineering' approach by reducing the replication of code involved in the *production* of component families, clientship is the mechanism that is employed to use the components. New objects are thus constructed by *combining* existing components in different ways. In the alternative approach, however, inheritance is employed as the mechanism of reuse, and new objects are generated by adopting or extending old ones.

In the 'programming by difference' approach it is not necessary for a component designer to try to predict all the potential uses of a component and provide it with large numbers of parameters or component forms to make it adaptable for each of the scenarios anticipated. Instead, objects are tailored to new applications *at the time of reuse* rather than generalized *at the time of definition*. If an object is *almost* suitable for a given application but does not have exactly the right properties, inheritance allows the programmer to generate a new version of the component with the necessary additions and modifications.

Since any class can be modified or extended by inheritance, and is thus potentially reusable, 'programming by difference' blurs the traditional distinction between the process of designing components – programming for reuse – and the process of reusing them in new systems – programming with reuse. This feature is termed the 'open and closed' principle by Meyer (1988), and describes the fact that a class represents both a concrete ('closed') component that can be directly instantiated for use in a system, and at the same time a modifiable ('open') component that can be adapted for reuse in different contexts. In fact, 'programming by difference' is a technique that has been applied on an informal basis by individual programmers for many years. Inheritance is essentially nothing more than a formal linguistic mechanism for an informal mode of reuse which is probably the most commonly performed – the editing of existing code to fit a new application.

Key points

Traditional reuse techniques are based on the notion of 'component engineering' in which new applications are constructed from a library of carefully designed and tested reusable components.

The 'component engineering' philosophy splits the problem of reuse into two distinct considerations – how to design components with maximum reuse potential (i.e. design for reuse) – and how to design new applications deriving maximum benefit from a component-rich environment (i.e. design with reuse).

Up to a certain threshold the reusability of a component is increased by increasing its generality through parameterization. Beyond this point, however, it is clearer to define different variations of a component abstraction as different members of a component family.

Grady Booch has created a very successful library of components in Ada based on a comprehensive taxonomy of component variants.

An *iterator* is a component variant that enables a given operation to be performed on each element stored in a collection component without altering its state.

A *bounded* component is a variant with limited memory usage, while a *managed* component is a variant that takes steps to reclaim unused memory.

The large quantity of code replication that arises in an Ada implementation of the components can be significantly reduced using inheritance as provided in DRAGOON.

Abstract classes defer the implementation of at least one of their methods to subclasses. Consequently, it is not possible to instantiate an abstract class, although it is possible to define instance variables of the class type.

An abstract class may possess a body that defines pre and post conditions on the implementation of the deferred methods in subclasses, and class invariants that must also be satisfied by subclasses.

Polymorphism and dynamic binding complement abstract classes by enabling a class to be a client of the component variant of precisely the required level of abstraction. A satisfactory concrete subclass can be provided at run-time to implement the desired services.

Inheritance supports a fundamentally different reuse philosophy known as *programming by difference*. This makes it possible to reuse any class, whether or not it was designed with reuse in mind, by modifying it for the new purpose in hand.

Inheritance supports what Meyer terms the 'open and closed' principle in which a class represents both a concrete ('closed') component which can be instantiated for reuse in a system, and an ('open') component capable of being reused for new applications.

Chapter 5
Genericity

In discussing the advantages of inheritance for implementing component families the previous chapter avoided the question of generalizing the types of the elements they store or manipulate by basing the examples on the undefined class type ELEMENT. It is clearly unsatisfactory, however, for a strongly typed language such as DRAGOON to have supposedly 'reusable' components which are only able to operate on a single type. This would make it necessary to define a new component for each different type, even though the implementation of the components would be the same.

This chapter describes Ada's strategy for overcoming this problem – the notion of generic units – and compares the various manifestations of genericity with the 'inclusion' polymorphism inherent in object-oriented languages. It then describes the particular form of genericity supported in DRAGOON.

5.1 Parametric polymorphism

The polymorphism supported in object-oriented languages (Chapter 2) is known as *inclusion* polymorphism (Cardelli and Wegner, 1985), since it is based on the set view of classes in which the set of instances of a subclass is regarded as being a subset of (i.e. included in) the set of instances of the parent. Using this type of polymorphism it is possible to define queue components applicable to *any* class type by defining them to be clients of the class at the root of the inheritance hierarchy, which in DRAGOON is APPLI-CATION_OBJECT (i.e. by substituting APPLICATION_OBJECT in the previously defined components for ELEMENT). Since it is the root of the DRAGOON class hierarchy, every object is a subclass of APPLICATION_OBJECT and could therefore be added to a queue of such objects.

This approach, however, undermines the typing system of the language, since no constraints are imposed on the types of objects manipulated by instances of the component. While this may be desirable in certain circumstances, in the majority of applications it is important to have some

73

guarantee that the objects manipulated by a component are consistent with its intended usage. The associated reduction in the likelihood of run-time errors and improvements in software reliability is the basis for the inclusion of strong typing in most modern languages.

What is required is a mechanism that supports the definition of general components capable of being used with a large number of different types (possibly all), but which also ensures that instances of the component manipulate only certain mutually consistent subsets of these types. In other words, it is desirable to maintain type distinctions when a component is being *used*, but to 'factor out' dependencies on particular types in its *definition* (Ichbiah *et al*, 1986).

This facility is sometimes termed parametric polymorphism (Cardelli and Wegner, 1985) and is supported in its full generality by languages such as ML (Milner, 1984). ML allows functions to be defined with formal arguments of an unspecified type, but when they are invoked checks the mutual consistency of the actual parameters. Typing of this form not only depends on a fairly sophisticated inference system, however, but also makes typing errors less obvious and easy to understand for the programmer.

The Ada generic mechanism, on the other hand, provides a static form of parametric polymorphism in which generalized, generic templates have to be explicitly 'instantiated' at compile time with the particular type they are to operate on. In one sense, generics are simply a convenient syntactic device for generating different versions of a component tailored to different types. However, because it enables compilers to arrange for the different versions to share the same implementation, it is none-the-less an effective method for increasing the generality of components. Ada allows generic components to be parameterized not only with respect to types, but also subprograms and values.

5.2   Constrained and unconstrained genericity

Inclusion polymorphism and genericity are two distinct language solutions to the problem of generalizing components. It is not immediately obvious how they compare and interact, and whether adding genericity to a language which already possesses inclusion polymorphism would be beneficial. Meyer considers this question in detail in his seminal paper (Meyer, 1986) and book (Meyer, 1988), which explicitly compare Ada-style genericity with inheritance as found in Eiffel. To provide a basis for the comparison, Meyer identifies two principal forms of 'type' genericity in Ada: constrained and unconstrained.

Unconstrained genericity

In the unconstrained form the generic component makes no assumption about the type with respect to which it is parameterized. A queue is a good

example of such a component since it performs no operations, other than
basic assignments, on the elements it stores. It is possible to have queues
of any (non-limited) type, therefore, although it is likely that particular
instances of the queue should only contain elements of a single type. This
form of genericity is represented in Ada by parameterizing the component
with respect to a single *private* data type. For example, an Ada package
defining such a queue would have a generic formal part of the form:

```
generic                                                          (5.1)
    type T is private;
package QUEUE is
```

$$\vdots$$

Specifying the type as private means that the body of the package is only
able to perform 'basic' operations on it, such as assignments, and membership and equality tests. The component can thus be instantiated with any
type providing these facilities (i.e. any data type not defined to be 'limited
private'):

```
package INTEGER_QUEUE is new QUEUE (T => INTEGER);          (5.2)
package COLOUR_QUEUE is new QUEUE (T => COLOUR);            (5.3)
```

These generic instantiations generate new queues specialized to operate on
one particular type. Although they are generated from the same template,
the strong typing rules of Ada will not allow an inappropriate type to be
added to such a queue.

Constrained genericity

In the case of constrained genericity the component makes some additional
assumptions about the operations that can be performed on the type. In
Ada, these 'constraints' on the type are specified as additional subprogram
parameters in the generic formal part of the component. These indicate
that the component can only be instantiated with a type for which operations of the required form have been defined. When the instantiation is
performed, the associated subprograms must be provided as actual parameters along with the type on which they operate.

Suppose, for example, that a variant of the queue component defined
in the previous chapter was required to store 'dated items' of the kind introduced in Section 3.4.2 in chronological order, so that the item 'popped'
off such a queue would be the one with the 'lowest' date. Only if several
items have the same 'date' are they arranged in FIFO order. As mentioned
in Section 3.4.2, the term 'dated item' refers to any abstraction which
possesses at least one SIMPLE_CALENDAR.DATE attribute, and associated accessor and update operations, but will usually, of course, possess many
more attributes and operations. Since Ada does not support classes, such

a 'dated item' abstraction would have to be represented as a conventional abstract data type of the following form:

```
with SIMPLE_CALENDAR;                                      (5.4)
package DATED is
    type ITEM is private;
    function DATE (I : in ITEM) return SIMPLE_CALENDAR.DATE;
    procedure SET_DATE_TO (I : in out ITEM;
                                DATE : in SIMPLE_CALENDAR.DATE);

        ⋮
                                              -- other subprograms

private

        ⋮                   -- type ITEM defined as a record with at least

        ⋮                   -- one field of type SIMPLE_CALENDAR.DATE

end;
```

Since the SIMPLE_CALENDAR.DATE field is only one of many possible fields the (private) type DATED.ITEM could possess, there is no limit to the different 'dated item' abstractions that could be modelled by packages of this basic form. The special 'chronological queue' component mentioned earlier can be made generic to all these different abstractions, and only these, by a generic formal part of the form:

```
with SIMPLE_CALENDAR;                                      (5.5)
generic
    type T is private;
    with function F (I : in T) return SIMPLE_CALENDAR.DATE;
    with procedure P (I : in out T;  DATE : in SIMPLE_CALENDAR.DATE);
package CHRONO_QUEUE is
        ⋮
```

The formal part of this package indicates that, at instantiation time, it expects to be provided with a type, and associated subprograms, with the specified signature. In contrast with the unconstrained case, therefore, in which the body of the generic package could only perform the basic (private type) operations on T, in this case the body is able to use the additional operations F and P. Hence this component is 'constrained' to being instantiated only with types possessing the required kind of associated operations, such as DATED.ITEM:

```
with DATED;                                                (5.6)
package DATED_QUEUE is new CHRONO_QUEUE (T => DATED.ITEM;
                    F => DATED.DATE;  P => DATED.SET_DATE_TO);
```

The essential difference between these two forms of genericity is that in the unconstrained form no special assumptions are made about the generic formal type, while in the constrained form the component is parameterized with respect to a type intimately associated with certain kinds of operations – in other words, an abstract data type. Constrained genericity, therefore, can be seen as a way of supporting parametric polymorphism with respect to *abstract data types*. Unconstrained genericity is merely a limiting case in which the type has no special user-defined operations.

5.3   Genericity versus inclusion polymorphism

As described in Chapter 3, object-oriented languages provide classes as an alternative means of representing data abstractions such as 'dated item'[1]. In terms of the class-based representation of data abstractions, therefore, genericity can be regarded as providing parametric polymorphism with respect to classes.

Classes, however, are also the source of inclusion polymorphism of object-oriented languages. Making a component generic with respect to a class, therefore, combines the mechanisms of parametric and inclusion polymorphism (the two *universal* forms identified by Cardelli and Wegner (1985)) in the same component. Is this desirable, or indeed even safe, however? To answer this question, consider the alternative ways in which the 'chronological queue' component of the previous section could be generalized with respect to the 'dated item' abstraction using these two forms of polymorphism.

Inclusion polymorphism is achieved simply by making the component (i.e. the class) a direct *client* of the class DATED_ITEM (3.12):

```
with DATED_ITEM;                                          (5.7)
class INC_CHRONO_QUEUE is
    function POP return DATED_ITEM;
    procedure ADD (ITEM : in DATED_ITEM);
end INC_CHRONO_QUEUE;
```

As a consequence of inclusion polymorphism, any instance of INC_CHR-ONO_QUEUE can manipulate instances of any subclass of DATED_ITEM (3.12), such as DATED_DESCRIPTOR (3.13) and DATED_LIBRARY_BOOK (3.14). INC_CHRONO_QUEUE is therefore generalized with respect to the 'data abstraction', DATED_ITEM, as required.

To achieve parametric polymorphism, on the other hand, the class modelling the 'chronological queue' component must have the 'dated item' abstraction as a formal generic parameter:

---

[1]DRAGOON, of course, permits data abstractions to be represented as classes or abstract data types.

```
generic                                                              (5.8)
    DATED_ITEM;
class PAR_CHRONO_QUEUE is
    function POP return DATED_ITEM;
    procedure ADD (ITEM : in DATED_ITEM);
end PAR_CHRONO_QUEUE;
```

Once again the queue component PAR_CHRONO_QUEUE is generalized with respect to DATED_ITEM, but this time it is necessary first to instantiate the generic component with the desired version of DATED_ITEM. The result is a class specially tailored to a particular version of the abstraction. Functioning components (i.e. objects) are generated by further instantiating the resulting classes in the normal way.

There are, therefore, two 'instantiation' steps involved in the parametric form: instantiation of the generic component class with the class(es) being manipulated, and instantiation of the resulting class to produce instances. To avoid potential confusion between the two operations, the term *actualization* is used in DRAGOON to describe the 'instantiation' of a generic, leaving the term 'instantiation' to have its usual meaning with respect to classes. To generate a working chronological queue using parametric polymorphism, therefore, the class PAR_CHRONO_QUEUE must first be actualized with a particular version of DATED_ITEM (3.12) and the resulting class instantiated.

Since constrained genericity, at least as provided by Ada, only requires that the signatures of the formal and actual operations match, there is no reason why the class provided as the actual parameters of an actualization of PAR_CHRONO_QUEUE should be a subclass of the formal parameter DATED_ITEM. PERISHABLE_DESCRIPTOR (3.6), for example, possesses precisely the kind of methods expected by the component PAR_CHRONO_QUEUE and therefore could be supplied as an actual parameter of an actualization, even though it is not a subclass of DATED_ITEM. However, for compatibility with the general assignment rules, DRAGOON restricts the actual parameter to be a subclass of the formal.

The main difference between the two approaches is that in the first *any* subclass of DATED_ITEM can be manipulated by *any* instance of the component INC_CHRONO_QUEUE. With the second, however, depending on the particular generic actualization from which they are generated, different instances of the component can be constrained to manipulate one particular version of the abstraction DATED_ITEM.

Consider the following actualizations of PAR_CHRONO_QUEUE:

```
class LIBRARY_CHRONO_QUEUE is new PAR_CHRONO_QUEUE              (5.9)
                (DATED_ITEM => DATED_LIBRARY_BOOK);
```

```
class DESCRIPTOR_CHRONO_QUEUE is new PAR_CHRONO_QUEUE           (5.10)
                (DATED_ITEM => DATED_DESCRIPTOR);
```

LIBRARY_CHRONO_QUEUE and DESCRIPTOR_CHRONO_QUEUE are actualizations of the basic PAR_CHRONO_QUEUE component tailored to different versions (i.e. subclasses) of the DATED_ITEM abstraction. Consequently, it is not possible to 'ADD' a DATED_LIBRARY_BOOK (3.14) object to an instance of the former, and a DATED_DESCRIPTOR (3.13) object to an instance of the latter, despite the fact that they are both subclasses of DATED_ITEM. It is possible, however, to 'ADD' descendants of DATED_LIBRARY_BOOK and DATED_DESCRIPTOR to the respective PAR_CHRONO_QUEUE actualizations.

With inclusion polymorphism, any instance of INC_CHRONO_QUEUE can be treated as a queue of DATED_LIBRARY_BOOK objects or DATED_DESCRIPTOR objects, since both these classes are descendants of DATED_ITEM. Precisely because of this, however, there is nothing to stop a DATED_LIBRARY_BOOK object being added to a queue supposed to contain only DATED_DESCRIPTOR objects, and vice versa. Although this may in fact be what is required in a small number of applications, in the vast majority of cases this is likely to be a logical error.

Parametric polymorphism allows the logical distinction between the different types of queue elements to be made explicit and enforced by strong typing rules, while at the same time allowing their common structure to be modelled in a single component. In such circumstances, therefore, it provides the same advantages of strongly typed languages over untyped ones.

Inclusion polymorphism and parametric polymorphism in the form of genericity are therefore distinct, but complementary, mechanisms providing different facilities to the programmer.

5.3.1   Declaration by association

Much of the original work in comparing genericity and inheritance was carried out by Bertrand Meyer – the designer of Eiffel. It is perhaps not surprising, therefore, that this language has some of the most advanced facilities for combining genericity and inclusion polymorphism. In fact, Eiffel supports genericity in two distinct ways. *Unconstrained* genericity is supported through the concept of generic classes, which are parameterized with respect to an 'unconstrained' class type. The implementor of the component is therefore unable to make any assumptions about the methods of the formal parameter.

Constrained genericity, on the other hand, is supported in a completely different way through the mechanisms of 'declaration by association' and 'type redefinition'[2]. Type redefinition permits a subclass to change the types of instance variables and formal method arguments to a conformant type (i.e. a subclass). An Eiffel class using these facilities to model the 'generic' class PAR_CHRONO_QUEUE (5.8) would be of the form:

---

[2] Recent versions of Eiffel also provide more direct facilities for constrained genericity.

```
class EIFFEL_CHRONO_QUEUE export                                    (5.11)

    ADD, POP              -- indicates which 'features' are exported by the class

feature

    ANCHOR : DATED_ITEM;                                    -- the anchor
    DATA_STORE : ARRAY (like ANCHOR);              -- using the Eiffel library
                                                               -- class ARRAY

      .
      .
      .

    POP : like ANCHOR is
    do

          .
          .
          .

    end;

    ADD (ITEM : like ANCHOR) is
    do

          .
          .
          .

    end;

end;
```

The main difference between DRAGOON and Eiffel classes is that the latter
do not have a separate specification and body. Instead, the class name is
followed by an 'export' part which identifies those 'features' (methods or
instance variables) that are visible to clients. The other differences are
largely syntactic. The 'body' of an Eiffel class, which describes how it
is implemented, follows the keyword 'feature', while methods possess no
keyword 'function' or 'procedure', but are distinguished merely by their
profiles. Also, the body of a method is initiated by the keyword 'do' rather
than 'begin'.

Because an Eiffel class is defined as a single module, its methods are
declared in the scope of its state variables, such as DATA_STORE above. This
is an important prerequisite for declaration by association since it allows
variables and method parameters to be declared in relationship to other
variables.

In the above class, for example, the elements of the array DATA_STORE
and the formal parameters of the 'ADD' and 'PUT' methods are defined to be
'like' (i.e. of the same type as) the variable ANCHOR, which is provisionally
defined to be of class type DATED_ITEM (3.12). This variable is called the
'anchor' for the associated declarations, and may be used by the methods
of the class just like any other object of class DATED_ITEM. The same is true
of the objects declared to be 'like' it. In fact, in this particular class, the
variable ANCHOR plays no role other than as an 'anchor' for the associated
declarations. It is the array object DATA_STORE that actually stores the
queue.

EIFFEL_CHRONO_QUEUE is a normal class which behaves just like
INC_CHRONO_QUEUE (5.7). Instances of the class may store objects of class

DATED_ITEM (3.12) and any of its subclasses. The difference arises when subclasses of EIFFEL_CHRONO_QUEUE are defined. Eiffel permits an heir class to redefine the type of inherited variables to be of any type compatible class. For example, the variable ANCHOR can be redefined to be of class type DATED_LIBRARY_BOOK in a subclass of EIFFEL_CHRONO_QUEUE, since this is a subclass of DATED_ITEM (3.12):

```
class EIFFEL_BOOK_QUEUE export                                    (5.12)

    ADD, POP

inherit                                        -- using EIFFEL syntax
    EIFFEL_CHRONO_QUEUE
        redefine ANCHOR

feature

    ANCHOR : DATED_LIBRARY_BOOK;               -- redefined to a subclass

end;
```

Thanks to the 'declaration by association' mechanism, however, this not only has the effect of changing the class type of the variable ANCHOR, but also of all the other variables and parameters declared to be 'like' ANCHOR. This, in turn, has the effect of altering the signature of the inherited methods, since the formal parameters were declared by association with ANCHOR. The class EIFFEL_BOOK_QUEUE, therefore, is a version of its parent specialized to handle objects of class DATED_LIBRARY_BOOK (3.14), and thus corresponds to the generic actualization LIBRARY_CHRONO_QUEUE (5.9) of PAR_CHRONO_QUEUE (5.8).

One of the advantages of this approach is that different actualizations of a particular generalized component are handled as subclasses in the inheritance hierarchy. No extra typing rules are therefore required to describe the type compatibility of such classes. However, this is gained at the expense of additional complexity, unconstrained genericity being supported by generic classes, while constrained genericity is handled by the additional notions of 'declaration by association' and 'type redefinition'. One consequence of this complexity was that, in early versions of Eiffel, these constrained genericity features 'inherited' the typing problems arising from 'type redefinition' (Cook, 1989). More recent versions of the language provide a more straightforward mechanism for constrained genericity similar to that described in the next section.

5.4   Parameterization contract

Rather than the 'declaration by association' approach just outlined, DRAGOON adopts a uniform generic-based mechanism in the style of Ada to support all forms of parametric polymorphism. DRAGOON consequently introduces the notion of *generic classes* which are parameterized with respect to one or more types, and must be *actualized* with an appropriate actual type to give rise to a normal class.

As pointed out earlier, the constraints specified in the formal part of a generic component define a contract between the component implementor and the component user who 'actualizes' it for a specific purpose. If the actual generic parameters with which the component is actualized satisfy the contract by providing the services expected in the implementation, the component will be 'guaranteed' to function correctly.

Constrained and unconstrained genericity as defined in Section 5.2 are in fact just two examples of a range of different 'contracts' that can be expressed between the implementor of a generic component and its user. Quite apart from constrained genericity, in which subprograms are specified explicitly as part of the contract, Ada provides direct syntactic support for a number of other constraints on generic parameter types (DoD, 1983), such as:

type T is private – specifies that only basic operations may be used by the component implementor, such as assignment, equality and inequality comparisons.

type T is limited private – more strict than the above in that it also forbids the use of assignment and comparison operations by the implementor. Since these are available with every declared type, including classes, any DRAGOON type can be supplied as an actual parameter.

type T is (<>) – in this context the box '<>' denotes a discrete type. Unlike the above, therefore, this constrains the set of types that can be used as actual parameters to discrete (data) types (i.e. enumeration and integer types).

type T is range (<>) – more strict than the above in that it denotes an INTEGER range.

type T is delta (<>) – denotes a fixed-point type.

type T is digits (<>) – similarly, a floating-point range.

As DRAGOON incorporates the full typing scheme of Ada, it naturally permits all these syntactic constructs to be used as the formal parts of generic classes. This permits a full range of constraints to be placed on the data types used as generic parameters. DRAGOON supplements the range of constraints possible in 'constrained genericity' by permitting classes to be named as generic formal parameters. In DRAGOON, for example, the precise form of the class PAR_CHRONO_QUEUE (5.8) would be:

```
generic                                              (5.13)
    type T is DATED_ITEM;
class PAR_CHRONO_QUEUE is
    introduces
```

```
      function POP return T;
      procedure ADD (ITEM : in T);
  end PAR_CHRONO_QUEUE;
```

with particular 'actualizations', such as LIBRARY_CHRONO_QUEUE and DESC-RIPTOR_CHRONO_QUEUE, having a similar form as in (5.9) and (5.10), but with 'DATED_ITEM' replaced by 'T'.

A class that is generic with respect to another class type is permitted to call all the methods of the formal class type, because it can only be actualized with classes that are type compatible with (i.e. subclasses of) the formal parameter. If the body makes no assumptions about operations associated with a type, the generic parameter is defined to be private or limited private depending on whether assignment or equality tests are required. Such a formal parameter can be matched with either a class type or data type at actualization time. If a class is required which is generic with respect to some anonymous class type (i.e. which should not be actualized with a data type) it should be defined with a formal parameter of class APPLICATION_OBJECT. This class possesses no methods (other than the special CREATE operation) and so when used as a generic formal parameter in a sense represents a 'private' class. Since this is also the ancestor of all (non-generic) classes in the library, however, it can be matched by any of them.

5.5   Inheriting genericity

Using genericity alone to support parametric polymorphism in the way described above has the advantages of simplicity and uniformity. There is, however, one major difference between DRAGOON's support for 'constrained' parameterization by means of generic formal class types and the approach using declaration by association. Classes parameterized using declaration by association are amenable to incremental development by means of the inheritance mechanism, but this is not so with the DRAGOON generic classes presented so far.

There is no fundamental reason, however, why generic classes should not be enriched by the mechanisms of inheritance just like any other class type. Adding new methods to the interface of a generic class by inheritance does not alter the fact that certain parameters of the class are formal, and therefore must be associated with an actual parameter before an executable version is generated. In DRAGOON, therefore, it is possible to define heirs of generic classes which inherit the 'genericity' of their parent.

Suppose, for example, that a new version of the generic PAR_CHRONO-_QUEUE (5.8) component was required with an additional method NUM-BER_WITH_DATE returning the number of stored objects with a given date. This can be generated in DRAGOON by defining an heir of PAR_CHRONO_QUEUE which extends its interface with the required method:

```
class EXTENDED_CHRONO_QUEUE is                                    (5.14)
    inherits PAR_CHRONO_QUEUE;
    introduces
        function NUMBER_WITH_DATE (D : in SIMPLE_CALENDAR.DATE)
                                                    return NATURAL;
    end EXTENDED_CHRONO_QUEUE;
```

Although this class has no explicit generic formal part like other generic classes, it is nevertheless generic by virtue of the fact that its parent is generic. In other words, the class has inherited the generic formal part of its parent, and therefore needs to be actualized with precisely the same number and type of actual parameters. Not all the generic parameters have to be inherited, however. A generic subclass may have its own generic formal part which extends the set of generic parameters.

There is no reason why multiple inheritance of generic classes (or a mixture of generic and non-generic classes) should not also be allowed. Genericity and inheritance can thus be made completely orthogonal concepts. However, the current version of DRAGOON only provides linear inheritance of generic classes (i.e. if a class has a generic parent, this is its only parent).

5.5.1   Type compatibility and generic classes

The remaining question that has to be addressed concerning generics is how they fit into the typing scheme of the language. Firstly, it is important to note that generic classes themselves are not 'first-class' types of the language; they cannot be directly instantiated, they cannot act as method parameters, and it is not possible to declare an instance variable of a generic class. Actualizations of generic classes, however, are normal classes for which all these operations are possible.

There are essentially two approaches for defining the type compatibility of generic actualizations. In one approach, which is adopted by Eiffel, generic actualizations are regarded as type compatible if they conform. Formulating rules to ensure that this is so, however, is even more complicated than in the non-generic case, since it not only depends on the reverse conformance of generic parameters defining method argument types (i.e. 'in' parameters), and the forward conformance of generic parameters defining result parameter types and instance variables, but also requires that no parameter is used for both (Cook, 1989).

Once again, however, it is questionable whether the flexibility provided by such a definition of type compatibility justifies its complexity. This is particularly so in the case of generic classes, where the reason for choosing genericity (i.e. parametric polymorphism) rather than the usual inclusion polymorphism for generalizing a component is to distinguish statically between the types of elements assigned to them. This advantage is largely lost, however, if the different actualizations of a generic component are regarded as type compatible, because there is no way of ensuring that an instance of one actualization will not be assigned to an instance variable on which operations only suitable for instances of the other are performed.

As before, therefore, DRAGOON typing rules for generic actualizations are much more straightforward than those of Eiffel. In DRAGOON, a class that is generated by actualization is *not* type compatible with any other class.

5.5.2   Method overloading

The two forms of polymorphism discussed here, inclusion and parametric, are termed the universal forms of polymorphism by Cardelli and Wegner 1985). DRAGOON also supports the other category, *ad hoc* polymorphism, in the form of method overloading. Like subprograms in Ada, methods may be given the same name provided they are distinguishable by the types of their formal parameters.

A good example of where this facility comes in useful is provided by the database object in the supermarket control system. The job of this object is simply to store PRODUCT_DESCRIPTOR (3.4) objects generated by the central controller, and to enable the checkout points, as well as the central controller, to retrieve product descriptors by means of their attributes. The most common attribute used for retrieving product descriptors is their bar-code, since this is the only attribute guaranteed to be unique, and is recognized by the laser reading facilities of the checkout points. However, there will be occasions when it is desirable to retrieve product descriptors by other attributes, such as the label. To cater for these different retrieval possibilities it is necessary to provide a different method for each different attribute key. However, since all the attributes are of different types (partly because of the use of derived INTEGER types) and calls to the different methods can be distingushed by their profile, it is not necessary to provide each method with a different name. The overloading facilities of DRAGOON allow them to have the same, overloaded, name. The class modelling the database, therefore, may have an interface of the form:

```
with PRODUCT_DESCRIPTOR, PRODUCT;                                (5.15)
class DATA_BASE is
    introduces
        procedure ADD (P : in PRODUCT_DESCRIPTOR);
        function RETRIEVE (PRICE : in PRODUCT.VALUE)
                                    return PRODUCT_DESCRIPTOR;
        function RETRIEVE (BAR_CODE : in PRODUCT.CODE_NUMBER)
                                    return PRODUCT_DESCRIPTOR;
        function RETRIEVE (STOCK_LEVEL : in PRODUCT.STOCK_NUMBER)
                                    return PRODUCT_DESCRIPTOR;
        function RETRIEVE (LABEL : in PRODUCT.LABEL)
                                    return PRODUCT_DESCRIPTOR;
end DATA_BASE;
```

The ADD method is used by the central controller to add new PRO-DUCT_DESCRIPTOR (3.4) objects to the database, while the purpose of the RETRIEVE methods is to return a product descriptor with an attribute of the specified value. It is not specified which object is returned if there is more than one with the appropriate attributes, but if there are none, the null reference is returned.

It is important to note the difference between method overloading and dynamic binding. When an identifier is overloaded because it is used to denote several methods of a given class, these methods must have distinct parameter profiles. This permits the compiler to resolve statically the overloading and select which of the methods should be invoked in response to a call. With dynamic binding, on the other hand, several method bodies exist for the same specification (i.e. the same method profile) so it is not possible for the compiler to select one statically. Instead the selection is performed dynamically according to the class type of the object referenced by the instance variable through which the call is made. The crucial point is that whereas a single class (or object) may possess several methods with the same name (but different profiles) it may not possess several implementations for a given profile. The various method implementations that may be selected dynamically in response to a call must belong to different classes in an inheritance hierarchy.

Key points

Object-oriented languages provide a form of polymorphism known as *inclusion polymorphism* since it is based on the set view of classes in which the set of instances of a subclass is regarded as being a subset of (i.e. included in) the set of instances of the parent.

An alternative form of polymorphism is *parametric polymorphism* in which a component is parameterized with respect to one or more types.

Genericity is a static form of parametric polymorphism supported by Ada. Generic program units may possess formal type parameters, but must be statically instantiated with actual types.

Two forms of genericity can be identified – *unconstrained genericity* in which the generic component makes no assumptions about the type with respect to which it is parameterized, and *constrained genericity* in which the component assumes the existence of certain user-defined operations on the type.

In a language that supports classes, constrained genericity corresponds to parameterization with respect to a class type.

Genericity and inclusion polymorphism are two distinct but complementary mechanisms. The latter provides more control than the former on the types that instances of a component may manipulate.

The generic classes of DRAGOON support both constrained and unconstrained genericity in terms of generic formal parameters.

To avoid potential confusion with the *instantiation* of a class, DRAGOON uses the term *actualization* to describe the 'instantiation' of a generic class with actual parameters to yield a non-generic class.

Eiffel provides an alternative way of supporting constrained genericity using the mechanisms of *declaration by association* and *type redefinition*. These make generic classes amenable to specialization using inheritance, but also mean that the single concept of genericity is supported in several distinct ways.

DRAGOON permits several parameterization contracts to be specified between the user and implementor of a generic class. These range from *limited private* types in which the generic class makes no assumption whatsoever about the operations applicable to the values of a type, to contained genericity in which a generic class is parameterized with respect to a class type and may therefore assume the operations of the class.

It is possible to define subclasses of generic classes, which inherit the generic formal parameters of their parent. The subclass is therefore also generic, and must be actualized with the appropriate actual parameters before instances can be executed.

Classes that are actualizations of generic classes are not type compatible with any other class. Instances of such classes may only be referenced by instance variables of the same type.

Method overloading is an alternative form of polymorphism known as *ad hoc* polymorphism. A given class may have several methods with the same name provided they have different parameter profiles.

Because the methods identified by an overloaded name have different parameter profiles the compiler is able to establish which method should be invoked to service a call (i.e. resolve the overloading) statically. This contrasts with the dynamic binding of calls to methods with identical profiles which belong to different classes in an inheritance tree.

Chapter 6
Concurrency

The 'sequential' features of DRAGOON outlined in the previous chapters are fairly conventional. It is in its support for concurrency and distribution that DRAGOON differs more radically from other object-oriented languages. In order to provide a framework for a discussion of concurrency in the context of object-oriented programming, this chapter first provides a general overview of the main techniques used to support concurrency in conventional languages and then reviews how these techniques have been employed in various other object-oriented languages supporting concurrency. The particular approach adopted in DRAGOON is then described.

6.1 Approaches to concurrency

In concurrent systems, computations are performed by the cooperation of several independent (asynchronous) *execution threads*, assumed to have indeterminate (or unrelated) execution speeds. It is this indeterminacy that provides the opportunities for parallel execution in multi-processor systems, with all the attendant performance advantages, but which also makes it necessary to provide well-defined synchronization and communication mechanisms to ensure safe and useful interaction.

In principle, it is possible for intelligent compilers to spot potential parallelism in normal (i.e. sequential) programs, and to generate concurrent execution threads transparently, but in practice this has proved feasible only for certain limited kinds of numerical applications. For more general applications, where it is necessary to model coexisting activities in the problem domain, the programmer must be aware of the scope for concurrency in a given context, and design the software accordingly. Languages intended to support the explicit specification of concurrency in such applications must facilitate the description of:

- concurrent execution threads,
- inter-thread communication,

- inter-thread synchronization.

Concurrent execution threads

The imperative (Von-Neumann) model of software execution is inherently sequential – a computation being performed as a linear sequence of atomic machine instructions. Imperative languages wishing to support explicit concurrency must consequently allow the programmer to identify program segments that may execute in parallel. This can either be achieved by mechanisms for the splitting, and subsequent joining, of otherwise sequential execution threads, such as cobegin/coend (Dijkstra, 1968) and fork/join (Conway, 1963), or by identifying sequences of statements, often termed *sequential processes* or *tasks*, that will execute in parallel with each other. Some languages permit only a predefined number of such sequential processes to be activated at the start of a program (static process model), while others permit the dynamic generation of new processes at arbitrary points (dynamic process model).

Communication

Mechanisms for supporting communication between separate execution threads have traditionally been placed into two categories: those based on the use of shared memory and those based on the concept of message passing. In the first approach, execution threads communicate by updating shared data structures, and consequently rely on some accompanying synchronization mechanism to ensure that the shared resource is not corrupted by simultaneous access. This approach incurs significant implementation overheads in environments where the communicating processes do not actually have access to shared memory, such as a loosely coupled distributed system.

In the message passing approach, on the other hand, processes communicate by transferring data values. This approach, therefore, requires no shared storage and is practical in both distributed and non-distributed environments, although it usually implies greater overhead than the first approach in environments possessing shared memory.

The notion of message passing in concurrent systems should not be confused with the terminology commonly used in object-oriented languages (but avoided in DRAGOON). In the former, 'message passing' usually implies simply the unidirectional transfer of data, whereas in the latter 'message passing' denotes the invocation of a procedure, and thus usually involves bidirectional data exchange as well as the execution of the servicing code.

There are many detailed variants of the basic message passing communication scheme, depending on such things as the naming conventions for identifying the communicating parties and the accompanying synchronization policies. In a fully *synchronous* message scheme, such as that employed by CSP (Hoare, 1978) or Occam (May and Shepherd, 1985), both parties must reach a predetermined synchronization point before communication may take place – in other words, they must *rendezvous*. The first correspondent to arrive at the point is blocked until the other reaches its corresponding synchronization point. At the other end of the spectrum are fully *asynchronous* schemes in which either correspondent may perform a 'send' or 'receive' operation at any time, irrespective of the execution state of the other. In its pure form this approach therefore requires unbounded buffer space to store all the messages that could be sent before being processed. In between these two extremes are schemes with limited buffering capacity in which one of the primitives (usually the receiving) is always blocking (i.e. synchronous) while the other (usually the sending) is non-blocking (i.e. asynchronous) so long as there is free space in the buffer.

Synchronization

Closely related to the communication issue is that of synchronization. The most fundamental form of synchronization needed in concurrent systems is *condition synchronization* where one process is suspended until some condition, or event, is detected or caused by another. With a message passing communication scheme, this can be achieved quite straightforwardly by arranging for the process to be suspended on a 'receive' primitive, waiting for the arrival of the appropriate message (usually called a *signal* if no data is transferred). Shared variable schemes, on the other hand, have the additional problem of *exclusion synchronization* in which the shared resources used for communication must be protected from erroneous concurrent access. The basic aim of this form of synchronization is to define 'critical regions' of code that behave like indivisible operations so far as concurrent execution threads are concerned.

It is possible, in the shared variable approach, to realize both forms of synchronization using complex access protocols such as Dekker's algorithm (Burns, 1985), but an efficient and natural implementation of exclusion synchronization ultimately relies on hardware support for indivisible 'test-and-set' operations. One of the first linguistic concepts to reflect such a facility was the *semaphore* introduced by Dijkstra (1968), but many variations have since emerged, such as conditional critical regions (Brinch Hansen, 1973). A semaphore provides indivisible operations for reading and modifying its integer value and an associated queuing mechanism to block processes until a particular value is reached. In their general form they are powerful enough to tackle all synchronization scenarios, but because the processes wishing to access a shared resource are responsible for calling the semaphores in the correct order, they are tricky and cumbersome to use for all but the most trivial problems. Moreover, the erroneous use of a semaphore by just one of the client processes cannot only compromise the integrity of the shared resource, but also the freedom from deadlock of the entire system.

To remove the responsibility for handling exclusion synchronization from the clients of a resource, the concept of a *monitor* was introduced by Hoare (1974). A monitor tightly encapsulates a shared data structure so that it can only be accessed by the official procedures guaranteed to provide safe access. Communicating processes, therefore, are no longer concerned with ensuring exclusion synchronization, but simply request the service they require and are suspended on a queue of calls until execution of the corresponding operation is permitted.

Using monitors to encapsulate and protect shared resources is a much safer way of achieving exclusion synchronization than semaphores, but unfortunately is not totally compatible with condition synchronization (Andrews and Schneider, 1983). The exclusion protocols necessary to ensure safe access to a variable often tend to conflict with those needed to use it as a flag for signalling a condition. Consequently, languages that have adopted the monitor concept as a means of resource protection usually have to incorporate an additional mechanism for handling condition synchronization.

One approach uses the concept of *condition variables* (Wirth, 1982), which have a syntactic similarity to semaphores, but serve to override the queuing policy of the monitor when it conflicts with the requirements of condition synchronization. An alternative solution is to generalize the monitor concept by the introduction of *guards*. These permit the selection of calls to be determined by the state of the monitor, rather than simply by the mutual exclusion criteria. This state, in turn, reflects the previous access history of the resource.

Guards have found application in languages as disparate as Occam, Ada and Parlog, but have the drawback that they typically require an independent execution thread to exist within the 'monitor' in order to evaluate them repeatedly. Such monitors, therefore, must be active processes, and hence are often combined with the mechanisms for generating threads of control into a generalized process model, such as that of Ada.

6.2   Concurrency in object-oriented languages

There are essentially two basic strategies for introducing concurrency features such as those just described into the 'sequential' object-oriented programming paradigm described in the last few chapters. One approach is to superimpose the concurrency constructs as an extra layer *orthogonal* to the object-oriented programming features, while the other approach attempts to achieve full *integration* at the same level.

As pointed out by America (1989), the 'orthogonal' approach is usually adopted by languages such as Smalltalk and Trellis/Owl (Schaffert *et al*, 1986) which were originally intended to be sequential. This strategy is certainly effective, but because the concurrency constructs are completely independent of the encapsulation and communication mechanisms of the (normal) objects in a system, it has the major disadvantage that programmers are required to work at two different levels of abstraction (Yokote and Tokoro, 1986).

The 'integration' approach is much more in keeping with the general goal of unifying different concerns through the notion of objects, and is adopted by the many object-oriented languages designed for the purpose of supporting concurrency. As might be expected from the large number of traditional concurrency strategies outlined in the previous section, however, there are also quite a number of different ways in which this goal can be achieved. These are best considered in relation to the three main aspects of concurrency outlined in the previous section.

Concurrent execution threads

Smalltalk provides the classic example of the 'orthogonal' approach, and employs one of the earliest techniques for generating multiple execution threads – forking. An otherwise sequential 'block' is split into two threads by sending it a 'fork' message, resulting in the generation of a new 'process' object.

For languages in the 'integration' camp, on the other hand, there are essentially two basic techniques for generating multiple execution threads in a way that is compatible with the sequential object structure of a system (America, 1989).

Asynchronous method execution. In the first approach, a new execution thread is generated to execute the body of a method in response to an invocation request (message). The client object, therefore, is free to proceed (asynchronously) with the execution of the method as soon as the call is accepted. This approach is employed by a number of languages, such as Hybrid, but its most notable application is in the Actor languages (Agha, 1986).

The actor model of concurrency combines asynchronous method execution with the functional style of generating persistent objects by recursive *behaviour replacement*. Whereas in the sequential object-oriented model the precise functionality of a method changes according to the *state* of the associated object, in the actor model this effect is achieved by changing the 'behaviour' (i.e. the way in which messages are processed) in response to method calls. Each actor has a mailbox and a behaviour. Messages directed to a particular actor (i.e. sent to the mailbox associated with the actor) are stored in the order of arrival until they can be processed. Before the execution of a behaviour is complete, it must identify the behaviour that will be used to process the next message (which may be the same behaviour) using the 'become' primitive. Different messages, therefore, are processed by different behaviours depending on the previous history of message arrival. As well as specifying its 'replacement', a behaviour may generate new actors, using the 'create' primitive, and send messages to others (including itself), using the 'send to' primitive.

Active objects In the other approach, instead of generating a separate execution thread for each method invocation, a permanent thread is associated with the whole object. In other words, as well as being a unit of modularity and encapsulation, an object is also regarded as an *active* process. This approach, therefore, combines the notion of 'sequential processes' as found in traditional concurrent languages with the concept of 'objects' from the object-oriented world.

The difference between these two approaches is essentially one of 'granularity'. The first approach, characteristic of the Actor languages, offers much 'finer grained' concurrency than the second, since it provides parallelism at the level of individual operations rather than for a set of operations associated with a given object, and the processing of the next queued call may begin as soon as the replacement behaviour has been specified. Actor languages, therefore, are very popular in systems where maximum concurrency is important. The active object model, on the other hand, is more appropriate for embedded systems and simulation purposes, where the objects model or control physical devices with a limited capacity for performing parallel actions (Kaiser *et al*, 1989). Concurrency in such systems, therefore, is of a larger 'granularity' and much more naturally expressed at the level of objects. This approach is adopted by a significant number of languages including Emerald, POOL, Concurrent Smalltalk (Yokote and Tokoro, 1986)[1], Orient84/K (Ishikawa and Tokoro, 1987), ABCL/1 (Yonezawa *et al*, 1986), as well as DRAGOON.

Communication

Languages adopting the 'orthogonal' approach like Smalltalk usually rely on the sharing of objects as the means of supporting communication between separate execution threads. This, in itself, combines fairly naturally with the object model, but the associated synchronization techniques are more difficult to integrate successfully.

In the 'asynchronous method execution' technique for generating concurrent threads, because a client proceeds asynchronously with the execution of a method, it is not possible, in a single transaction, to transfer information from the server to the client on completion of the method body. Such transactions, therefore, reduce to the simple unidirectional message passing model described earlier – any required data exchange from the server to the client having to be programmed as a separate transaction.

---

[1] An attempt to *integrate* concurrency features with Smalltalk, rather than *superimpose* them.

Asynchronous message passing of this kind can also be adopted in the 'active object' model of concurrency – messages being queued until they can be executed within the thread of control of the *active* receiving object.

'Message passing' in the object-oriented sense actually conforms much more closely to the traditional 'remote procedure call' model of distributed systems, involving two-way communication and interposed code execution. Most object-oriented languages adopting the 'active object' approach to concurrency (including DRAGOON), therefore, view the method call as a form of 'remote procedure call' mechanism. Some, such as POOL, Concurrent Smalltalk and MELD (Kaiser *et al*, 1989), offer both the synchronous remote procedure call and asynchronous message passing forms of communication.

Synchronization

The most difficult aspect of concurrency to handle satisfactorily in object-oriented languages is synchronization. In those languages following the 'orthogonal' philosophy, such as Smalltalk and Trellis/Owl, separate execution threads communicate by means of shared objects. These languages, therefore, have to employ traditional exclusion synchronization techniques for handling access to the shared resources. Smalltalk, for example, introduces the concept of semaphore objects while Trellis/Owl adopts a variant of 'conditional critical regions' known as *lock blocks*. Since there are no constraints on the activation of methods (normal sequential semantics apply), the programmer is responsible for controlling access to critical regions by encoding the appropriate checks in the body of methods. This approach, therefore, suffers from the same drawbacks of complexity and lack of safety as the original low-level synchronization approaches.

In the 'integration' approach, communication is by means of method calls (or simpler message passing primitives in the asynchronous case), so the most natural strategy for achieving exclusion synchronization is to adopt a monitor-like approach in which method calls (messages) are queued outside the encapsulation boundary of a server object until such time as they may be safely executed. Regarding objects as 'monitors' in this way conceptually extends their resource encapsulation properties, originally designed for abstraction and modularity purposes, to handle access control in concurrent environments. This approach, therefore, represents a further unification of the concept of an object with the generalized notion of a monitor. The main characteristic of this approach is that method activation does not take place as soon as an invocation request (message) is received, as in the other approach, but only when the receiver deems that it is safe.

Kafura and Lee (1989) identify two main ways of realizing this monitor-based approach. The majority of languages adopt a 'centralized' technique in which the synchronization conditions determining the permitted method interleavings are specified in a single, 'centralized' execution thread, which is usually unified with the process part responsible for making objects active. In POOL, for example, the process part of an active object (called the 'body') specifies the conditions under which particular methods may be activated using guarded select statements and special 'receive' primitives. In this respect the concurrency model of these languages is very similar to that of Ada – communication taking place between active processes (tasks in Ada) only when both parties are ready and willing to rendezvous. Other languages adopting this centralized approach include ABCL/1 (Yonezawa *et al*, 1986), Orient84/K (Ishikawa and Tokoro, 1987), ACT++ (Kafura, 1988) and ALPS (Vishnubhotta, 1988).

In the other more *decentralized* approach, which is adopted by the Actor languages and Hybrid (Nierstrasz, 1987), the synchronization constraints determining when queued calls may be accepted and serviced are dispersed among the methods rather than concentrated in a single construct. In Hybrid, for example, pending method calls are stored in *delay queues* until the execution of another method opens the queue and allows the call at the head to be executed.

The main differences between these two approaches is that the centralized version requires the monitor objects to be active, since is relies on guard-like constructs, while the decentralized version does not.

6.2.1   Exclusion synchronization and inheritance

Since DRAGOON was designed to conform as closely as possible to Ada, it might have been thought that the language would have attempted to integrate Ada's tasking constructs with the object-oriented programming model. For example, tasks might have been used for the active part of objects, entry calls as the means of inter-object communication, and (as in POOL and ALPS) the rendezvous, coupled with guarded select statements, to provide exclusion synchronization. As pointed out by Wegner (1987) and Kafura and Lee (1989), however, this approach, like all the others mentioned so far, cannot be satisfactorily combined with the inheritance mechanism.

The conflict between exclusion synchronization and inheritance in these languages arises because they require the synchronization conditions to be explicitly encoded in the source code of classes. Whether they are specified centrally within the process part of a class or dispersed among its methods, exclusion constraints, by their very nature, must involve *all* the methods in the interface of an object. When a class is generated by inheritance, however, the inherited code is unaware of the existence of any new methods which may have been introduced. The inherited synchronization conditions, in particular, do not automatically extend to any methods introduced by the heir. Appropriate constraints covering all the methods in the heir's interface can only be produced either by rewriting the centralized control thread (e.g. the body in POOL) or all the inherited methods (e.g. Hybrid). In either case, the quantity of redefinition involved largely defeats the reuse benefits of inheritance.

The 'orthogonal' approach of Smalltalk, which uses semaphores to protect critical regions, is actually more compatible with inheritance than the monitor-based approaches, because each method is directly responsible for handling the access constraints that apply to it. It is possible, therefore, to include the appropriate operations (e.g. signal and wait) in the new methods introduced by an heir class without having to redefine the inherited methods. However, the already well-known difficulty of programming with semaphores is compounded when methods are added in a subclass since the programmer must ensure that semaphore manipulation by the new methods is compatible with that of all the inherited methods.

Because of these difficulties, few languages to date have managed to combine concurrency concerns with a fully general inheritance mechanism. The only languages that do incorporate facilities for both are those such as Smalltalk which have adopted the 'orthogonal' approach, and which therefore do not attempt to integrate them. Languages such as Emerald, POOL and ALPS, which have concentrated on supporting concurrency entirely within the object-oriented framework, have no implementation-inheritance mechanisms.

6.2.2 Separating synchronization and functionality

One of the fundamental goals of DRAGOON is to improve the opportunities for reuse in the domain of embedded and large-scale software systems. Therefore, since the adoption of Ada-like concurrency features would have severely weakened the usefulness of inheritance, which is the most important reuse mechanism of object-oriented languages, DRAGOON instead employs a completely different strategy for achieving exclusion synchronization in an object-oriented style.

The basic problem with the approaches described so far is that the synchronization conditions have to be explicitly embedded in the source code of classes by the applications programmer, whether they are concentrated in a single process or dispersed among the methods. There is no fundamental reason why this should be so, however. The synchronization conditions applying to a particular method – determining *when* it may be executed – are essentially independent of its functionality – defining *what* it does.

Consider a class, for example, which models simple unibuffer objects with a storage capacity of only one item, and which provides the conventional PUT and GET methods. There are at least three meaningful access protocols which can be used with instances of such a class (Atkinson *et al*, 1990). If PUT and GET were constrained to execute in strict alternation, the buffer object would behave like a mailbox, with the consumer having to 'GET' any produced item before the producer can 'PUT' a new one. If, on the other hand, a simple mutual exclusion protocol was used, the consumer would be guaranteed only to receive the latest version of the produced items, since the producer would be able to overwrite unconsumed ones. Finally, another classic alternative is the readers/writers access protocol in which the buffer behaves more like a 'notice board' with concurrent GET operations but exclusive PUTs. Even this basic protocol has a number of variants depending on the degree of fairness offered to writers wishing to perform a PUT in the face of an incessant stream of readers, and vice versa.

Since the approaches described require the embedding of the access protocol within the class implementation, a different class would have to be defined for each of these protocols, despite the fact that the functionality of the methods remains unchanged. This replication of code runs directly counter to the aims of reuse and incremental development which makes the object-oriented programming approach so popular. To overcome this problem, and the general conflict between inheritance and reuse, it is necessary to decouple the specification of the synchronization constraints applying to the methods of a class from the definition of their functionality.

Kafura and Lee (1989) have gone some way towards achieving this separation of concerns in the context of the Actor model with their notion of 'behaviour abstraction'. Although their language ACT++ has the notion of a centralized 'object manager' to handle access to the internal state of an object, the rules determining which of the methods are 'open' (i.e. may be activated) are specified in separate, explicitly named 'behaviours'. This makes it possible to define subclasses that can extend the interface of the class and add the necessary additional 'behaviours' by renaming those inherited. This approach is enhanced in Rosette (Tomlinson and Singh, 1989) by making the 'behaviours' first-class citizens.

Before describing the DRAGOON solution to this problem, the precise meaning of the term 'behaviour' needs some clarification. In some contexts, such as the pure Actor model, a 'behaviour' refers to the 'functionality' of possible responses to a message, while in others it is used to refer to the set of permissible operations in a given state. In DRAGOON, the *behaviour* of a class is defined as the synchronization constraints defining the permitted interleaving of method executions, and is therefore conceptually independent of the *functionality* of the class's methods.

6.3   Behavioural inheritance

The basic philosophy of DRAGOON's approach to exclusion synchronization is to permit the desired synchronization constraints – the behaviour – to be added to any concrete functional class in a style analogous to the usual inheritance of implementations (Genolini *et al*, 1989). DRAGOON therefore introduces the concept of *behavioural inheritance*, which is a form of multiple inheritance in which one of the parents is a normal (but concrete)

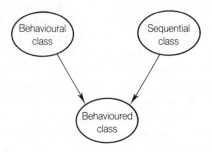

Figure 6.1 Behavioural inheritance.

sequential class, and the other is an abstract description of a *behaviour*. The resulting class, termed a *behavioured* (or monitor) class, thus inherits the functional properties of one class in the normal way and the behaviour of the other.

The abstract behaviour is modelled as a special kind of class, termed a *behavioural class*, which specifies synchronization conditions using logic predicates over abstract method sets. These are not really classes in the true sense of the word, since such a class cannot be directly instantiated like others, but they are referred to as classes to signify that they may act as a parent in a form of inheritance relationship. Figure 6.1 illustrates the way a behavioured class is generated from a sequential and behavioural class using multiple inheritance. A behavioured class is a proper subclass of its unbehavioured parent.

6.3.1   History functions

There are several possible ways of expressing abstract interleaving constraints on a set of operations, the most well-known being path expressions (Campbell and Habermann, 1974). DRAGOON, however, has adopted an approach based on the use of logic assertions over method invocation histories, since these offer more expressive power than path expressions and are in fact the basis of one technique for defining their semantics. These assertions are expressed using an operator 'borrowed' from *deontic* logic – an extension to first-order predicate logic incorporating operators for expressing the deontic[2] concepts of 'may' or 'must'.

The roots of deontic logics go back to Mally (von Wright, 1980), who introduced the term in connection with work on capturing the concept of *willing*, but owe their modern form largely to the work of von Wright

---

[2] From the *Oxford English Dictionary* 'deontic: Pertaining to duty or obligation'.

(1951). One particular variant called M(A)L (Khosla, 1988), developed in the FOREST project on requirements specification, employs two deontic operators: 'obl', indicating that an agent is obliged to perform an operation before it does anything else, and 'per', indicating that an agent has permission to perform a particular operation. In DRAGOON a similar 'per' operator is used in the specification of abstract behaviours to define the conditions under which a given method may be executed. Whereas the FOREST 'per' is interpreted globally, however, so that it is both necessary and sufficient for the execution of an operation, in DRAGOON it is interpreted locally so that it is necessary but not sufficient. An external object must also invoke the method for its execution to begin. In DRAGOON, therefore:

per (op) $\Leftrightarrow$ <boolean expression>

indicates that there is *permission* to activate a method 'op' (from the point of view of the object owning 'op') if, and only if, <boolean expression> holds. 'op' will only be activated, however, if per (op) is true *and* another object invokes the method. Rather than specify the conditions applying to individual operations, however, the generality of behavioural classes in DRAGOON is increased by defining the constraints in terms of *sets* of abstract methods. This then permits the conditions specified by a single boolean expression to be applied to a number of methods that are equivalent as far as the behaviour is concerned. In practice, therefore, the deontic expressions have the form:

per (OPS) $\Leftrightarrow$ <boolean condition>

where 'OPS' represents an abstract set of methods and leads to the following informal interpretation – 'there is permission to activate a method in the set 'OPS' if, and only if, <boolean expression> holds'. 'per (OPS)' is thus effectively defined as:

per (OPS) $\equiv$ $\forall$ op $\in$ OPS, per (op).

Three unbounded and monotonically increasing history functions are used to represent the number of times the methods of a particular set have been requested, activated or completed since system start-up:

req (OPS)   =   number of requests for execution of methods in the set OPS,

act (OPS)   =   number of activations of methods in the set OPS,

fin (OPS)   =   number of completions of methods in the set OPS.

Typically, however, permission to execute a method depends on the number of *currently* unserviced invocation requests (messages) or the number of *currently* active methods, so it is convenient to introduce special auxiliary functions representing these concepts and defined in terms of the primitive history functions:

$$\text{active (OPS)} \quad = \text{act (OPS)} - \text{fin (OPS)}$$
$$= \text{number of currently active methods in the set OPS,}$$
$$\text{requested (OPS)} \quad = \text{req (OPS)} - \text{act (OPS)}$$
$$= \text{number of outstanding calls for methods in the set OPS.}$$

Like the primitive history functions they are defined in terms of, these auxiliary functions should return non-negative integer values.

The use of 'history functions' to handle synchronization is being investigated in other object-oriented languages. Guide (Decouchant *et al*, 1990) (Krakowiak *et al*, 1990) employs an approach based on the use of 'synchronization counters' which provide the same basic information about the history of method invocations, activations and completions as DRAG-OON history functions, but are regarded as variables internal to protected objects rather than as abstract functions. The main difference between the DRAGOON approach and that of Guide is that the latter embeds the boolean expressions specifying when a method may execute within the bodies of classes. Although this provides greater expressive power, since it enables the expressions to be written directly in terms of the class's state variables, it faces the same basic incompatibility with inheritance as the approaches described previously. McHale *et al* (1990) describe an approach in which 'synchronization counters' of the form used in Guide are enhanced by the notion of 'scheduling functions' and 'pre and post ambles'. The synchronization conditions are still embedded within the class bodies, however.

6.3.2   Behavioural and behavioured classes

Using these five functions it is possible to define a large proportion of the behaviours that are likely to be needed in the development of concurrent systems. To illustrate how they are used, consider the possible behaviours that may be required in connection with the simple unibuffer class mentioned earlier, which has a specification of the form:

```
with ELEMENT;                                          (6.1)
class UNI_BUFFER is
    introduces
        procedure PUT (ITEM : in ELEMENT);
        procedure GET (ITEM : out ELEMENT);
end UNI_BUFFER;
```

The simplest behaviour that could be used with such a class would be straightforward mutual exclusion on the methods PUT and GET. In DRAG-

OON this behaviour is represented by the behavioural class MUTEX:

```
behavioural class MUTEX is                                          (6.2)
ruled OPS;
where
      per (OPS) ⇔ active (OPS) = 0;
end MUTEX;
```

The 'ruled' clause defines the names of the method sets that appear in the abstract behaviour. In this case, there need only be one set, called OPS, because as far as the behaviour is concerned there is no logical difference between the operations (i.e. methods) 'ruled' by the behaviour. Informally, the deontic assertion states that 'there is permission to activate a method in the set OPS if, and only if, there are no members of this set which are currently active (i.e. executing)'.

A unibuffer class with a mutual exclusion access protocol can be defined simply by superimposing this behaviour on the methods of UNI_BUFFER using the behavioural inheritance mechanism:

```
class MUTEX_UNI_BUFFER is                                          (6.3)
    inherits UNI_BUFFER;
    ruled by MUTEX;          -- this class is a proper subclass of UNI_BUFFER
where
    OPS => PUT, GET;             -- matches the set OPS with {PUT, GET}
end MUTEX_UNI_BUFFER;
```

This class specifies that MUTEX_UNI_BUFFER is a subclass of UNI_BUFFER which is 'ruled by' (or controlled by) the abstract behaviour specified in the behavioural class MUTEX. The 'where' clause is the crucial part in which the concrete methods of the sequential class are mapped into the abstract method sets of the behavioural class. In this sense, behavioural inheritance can be viewed as the instantiation of the abstract (or generic) behaviour defined in terms of 'formal' method parameters, on a particular set of 'actual' methods provided by the sequential class. However, since in isolation a concrete (i.e. instantiated) behaviour is not a useful component of a DRAGOON system, it is the subclass relationship of the behavioured, or monitor, class to the sequential class that is emphasized.

In this particular case, the concrete methods PUT and GET are symmetric with respect to the behaviour, and therefore are mapped to the same set. This is not the case, however, with the 'alternation' behaviour defined by the behavioural class:

```
behavioural class ALTERNATION is                                   (6.4)
ruled FOP, SOP;
where                                    -- F(irst)_OP and S(econd)_OP
      per (FOP) ⇔ act (FOP) = fin (SOP);
      per (SOP) ⇔ fin (FOP) > act (SOP);
end ALTERNATION;
```

Informally, the deontic part of this class specifies that 'a method in the set FOP may be activated if, and only if, for every activation of a FOP there has been a completion of a SOP, while SOP methods may be activated if, and only if, the number of completions of FOP methods exceeds activations of SOP methods'. A version of UNI_BUFFER with an 'alternation' access protocol is generated in precisely the same way as a 'mutual exclusion' UNI_BUFFER except that on this occasion the methods PUT and GET are not symmetric with respect to the behaviour; the programmer must decide which of the concrete methods is to be assigned to the FOP set (i.e. which must be activated first) and which is to be mapped on to the SOP set. Clearly, in this case, it is activations of the PUT method which must exceed activations of the GET, because an item must be placed into the buffer before it can be removed. The 'where' clause of a behavioured subclass of UNI_BUFFER with this behaviour, therefore, would be of the form:

```
where FOP => PUT, SOP => GET;
```

It is the programmer's responsibility to ensure that the assignments of concrete methods to abstract sets are consistent. Clearly, there must be at least one concrete method assigned to each abstract set, otherwise the conditions necessary to satisfy the deontic assertions would break down.

Finally, the classic 'readers/writers' protocol mentioned earlier, in which it is acceptable to permit concurrent reading of a data structure but writing must be performed in strict exclusion, is defined by the following behavioural class:

```
behavioural class READERS_WRITERS is                            (6.5)
ruled ROP, WOP;
where                                    -- R(eader)_OP and W(riter)_OP
    per (WOP) ⇔ active (WOP) = active (ROP) = 0;
    per (ROP) ⇔ active (WOP) = 0;
end READERS_WRITERS;
```

The informal interpretation of the deontic assertions in this behavioural class is that 'there is permission to execute a method in the set WOP if, and only if, there are no other active methods, while there is permission to activate a ROP method if, and only if, there are no currently active WOP methods'. There may be multiple ROP methods active concurrently, therefore, so the basic requirement of the 'readers/writers' protocol is satisfied.

A behavioured subclass using the READERS_WRITERS behaviour would have a 'where' clause of the form:

```
where WOP => PUT, ROP => GET;
```

There can be many simultaneous activations of the GET buffer, therefore, but only one exclusive activation of PUT.

6.3.3   The exclusion symbol

In many behaviour specifications, it is common for methods to be permitted to execute only in complete exclusion with all other methods covered by the behavioural class. This is the case, for example, with the WOP method in the 'readers/writers' behavioural class READERS_WRITERS just introduced. There is permission to activate a method in this set only if there are no other currently active methods of any kind. Using the notation described Section 6.3.1, however, the only way to express this requirement in the deontic expression is to state explicitly that the number of currently active instances of each formal method set mentioned in the 'ruled' clause is zero. This causes no real problem in behavioural classes dealing with a maximum of two or three abstract method sets, but for behaviours involving more, it becomes extremely verbose and unnecessarily obscures the meaning of the deontic expressions.

To counteract this problem a special composite symbol is introduced, called the *exclusion symbol*, which has precisely this meaning – that the current number of activations of all the method sets appearing in the behavioural class is zero (i.e. no methods are currently active). The symbol is represented by adjacent 'greater than' and 'less than' characters resembling an 'X' shape – '(><)'. Using this symbol, the conditions for execution of the WOP methods in the READERS_WRITERS (6.5) behavioural class would simply have the form:

per (WOP) ⇔ (><);

This means that there is permission to activate a method in the set WOP only when there are zero activations of all methods mentioned in the behaviour.

6.3.4   Alternative readers/writers behaviours

The readers/writers behaviour is one of the most important and ubiquitous behaviours found in concurrent systems. However, the behaviour defined by the READERS_WRITERS (6.5) behavioural class has the drawback that writers may be blocked from writing indefinitely if there is an incessant stream of readers so that 'active (ROP)' never drops to zero. In most scenarios it is preferable to give writers priority, since this ensures that readers will obtain the most up-to-date information. In other words, it is preferable to block any further readers from accessing the shared resource once a writer has signaled its intention to write. Such a behaviour is described by the following class:

behavioural class WRITERS_PRIORITY is   (6.6)
ruled ROP, WOP;
where

```
    per (WOP) ⇔ (><);
    per (ROP) ⇔ active (WOP) = requested (WOP) = 0;
end WRITERS_PRIORITY;
```

The deontic assertion for the WOP formal method set, to which writers are mapped, remains the same as in the simple readers/writers behaviour (6.5). However, the assertion for the ROP formal set, to which readers are mapped, is appended with the condition that 'requested WOP = 0'. Informally, this means that there is permission to execute a method in the set ROP if, and only if, there are no currently executing WOP methods *and* there are no currently outstanding (i.e. queued) calls for WOP methods.

The behavioural class giving priority to readers has a similar form:

```
behavioural class READERS_PRIORITY is                              (6.7)
ruled ROP, WOP;
where
    per (WOP) ⇔ (><) and (requested (ROP) = 0);
    per (ROP) ⇔ active (WOP) = 0;
end READERS_PRIORITY;
```

The provision of a readers/writers behaviour that ensures neither readers nor writers are starved, without favouring either of the categories, is not so simple. There are two scenarios which would satisfy this requirement. They are both similar when only writers or only readers are queued. If the executing method is a writer, then all queued calls must wait, but if the executing method is a reader, queued readers may be activated. The difference between the two scenarios occurs when there are both read requests and write requests outstanding.

The 'fairest' scenario is probably that in which no method call is accepted before a call which arrived earlier, whether a reader or a writer. In essence, this means that calls are held in a single FIFO queue. With an approach based on history functions (or synchronization counters) such a behaviour can only be achieved by providing additional 'registration' methods that readers and writers call before the actual reading and writing methods (Decouchant *et al*, 1990).

The alternative strategy is to make readers and writers execute in strict alternation when there are outstanding calls to both readers and writers. It is not possible to reuse the deontic assertions in the class ALTERNATION (6.4) to describe this alternation behaviour, however, since there is no bound on the difference between the number of times readers and writers are activated or completed. Between the times when the 'alternation' behaviour is active (i.e. when both read and write requests are queued) any number of readers or writers could be executed. The expression of both these behaviours in DRAGOON relies on an enhancement of the simple behavioural inheritance mechanism described in Section 6.8.

6.4   Behavioural class libraries

The behavioural inheritance mechanism outlined in the previous section overcomes the conflict between inheritance and exclusion synchronization because it completely decouples the expression of synchronization constraints (behaviour) from the normal use of inheritance as a specialization mechanism. A DRAGOON programmer designing a concurrent system requiring a particular 'behavioured' class must first develop an 'unbehavioured' class with the required functional properties. Only when this class is complete are the necessary synchronization conditions added by means of the behavioural inheritance mechanism.

In a sense DRAGOON side-steps the essence of the conflict, therefore, which is the *direct* specialization of a behavioured class by inheritance. If a specialized version of such a class is required, the programmer must first specialize the original sequential version using the normal inheritance mechanism and then reimpose the necessary behaviour subsequently. DRAGOON behavioured classes cannot be used as the parent of any other (apart from another special form of inheritance described in Chapter 7) and so a class of this form represents the end of a branch of the (normal) inheritance hierarchy. It is not possible, for example, to generate a specialized version of the MUTEX_UNI_BUFFER class by using it as a parent. If such a class is required it is first necessary to define a specialized version of UNI_BUFFER and then reapply the synchronization constraints using behavioural inheritance.

6.4.1   Booch temporal forms

Because the synchronization conditions specified in behavioural classes are completely abstract, a small number of them are sufficient to handle most of the commonly required behaviours. The behavioural classes already introduced, for example, can be used to produce all of the important *temporal* forms defined by Booch to describe the properties of components in a concurrent environment. Booch identifies four different temporal forms:

- **sequential** – the component is not protected in a concurrent environment.
- **guarded** – the component provides semaphore operations (e.g. signal and wait) which the clients must use to gain mutually exclusive access.
- **concurrent** – the component behaves like a simple monitor enforcing strict mutual exclusion on the exported operations. Operation requests are queued until they can be serviced safely.
- **multiple** – the component behaves like a monitor, but provides a more flexible readers/writers access protocol, which permits multiple simultaneous 'reading' operations, but mutually exclusive (i.e. sequentialized) 'writing' operations.

In the same way that the normal inheritance mechanism aids the definition of different spatial forms of an abstract component, as described in Chapter 4, the behavioural inheritance mechanism of DRAGOON greatly simplifies the definition of these different temporal forms.

A sequential component corresponds directly to a sequential (i.e. unbehavioured) class in DRAGOON, which defines only the functionality of the methods exported. The guarded form employs an approach to exclusion synchronization which is not normally recommended in DRAGOON designs because it relies on the programmer calling methods in the appropriate order, and thus embodies all the risks associated with the 'orthogonal' approach identified earlier. Nevertheless, this form of component can be easily generated in DRAGOON. First a subclass of the required sequential form is introduced which exports two extra methods to act as the 'signal' and 'wait' semaphore operations, and then the required behaviour is superimposed on this class using behavioural inheritance. An appropriate behaviour is the 'alternation' behaviour defined by the class ALTERNATION (6.4). The 'signal' method would be mapped on to the method with permission to execute first, while the 'wait' method would be mapped on to the method which executes second.

The most important component forms are the 'concurrent' and 'multiple' forms, which can be generated quite simply from the sequential form by using the 'mutual exclusion' and 'readers/writers' behaviours introduced in the previous section. The concurrent form, for example, would inherit the behaviour defined by MUTEX, with all the concrete methods of its sequential parent mapped on to the set OPS, while the multiple form would inherit one of the 'readers/writers' behaviours. In this case the designer must decide which of the exported methods are 'readers' and which are 'writers' and bind them to the appropriate method set names.

When Ada is used as the implementation language, each different component form has to be completely reimplemented as a different package. The situation is little better in the majority of concurrent object-oriented languages described earlier, since the different access protocols would have to be explicitly encoded in the body of each different form. In DRAGOON, however, using only three behavioural classes, it is possible to generate all the different 'temporal' forms recognized by Booch without any replication of code.

Of course, the access protocols identified by Booch in his component taxonomy are not the only ones which may be needed in the development of DRAGOON systems. Nevertheless, the majority of behaviours likely to be required can be handled by a fairly small number of commonly recurring schemes. The DRAGOON component library, therefore, contains a standard set of predefined behavioural classes which are intended to cover a wide range of the commonly required behaviours.

The prototype implementation of DRAGOON developed in the DRAGON project does not at present support user-defined behaviours. In other words, it is not possible for the user to define his/her own behavioural class and ask the translation tool to translate it automatically into Ada. While it is hoped that this facility will be available in the long term, it is certainly a non-trivial problem, and for the foreseeable future programmers will be required to provide Ada implementations for any new behavioural classes they may require.

6.5   Active objects

Having introduced the basic strategy for supporting concurrency in DRAG-OON, it is now possible to examine the approach in more detail by considering the introduction of concurrency into the supermarket control system.

In the overall architecture of the system, the interaction of the database with the two other principal object types in the system (i.e. checkout points and the central controller) essentially conforms to the 'readers/writers' scenario. The central controller object 'produces' new product descriptors and 'writes' them to the database object, while the numerous checkout point objects continuously 'read' these descriptors in the database to determine product prices. Since such readers and writers are conveniently handled as autonomous processes, with their own independent execution threads, the central controller and checkout points are most naturally modelled in DRAGOON as active objects, and the database as a behavioured object, protecting its internal data from corruption.

The central control point provides the main interface to the system for human operators, and is therefore likely to be a fairly complex object aiming to make this interface as 'friendly' as possible. So far as its interaction with the database is concerned, however, details of how product descriptors are actually produced, and the handling of the interface, are unimportant. In order to focus on how active objects are defined in DRAGOON, therefore, the central controller object, for the moment, will be regarded as a simple producer, employing the library function NEW_DESCRIPTOR to create new descriptors and then arranging for them to be added to the database.

6.5.1   Threads

As in Modula 3 (Cardelli *et al*, 1988) the independent execution thread which characterizes an object as active is called the *thread* in DRAGOON, and may either be defined explicitly in the class body or inherited from an ancestor. Classes that define a thread directly must indicate this fact to potential clients by means of the keyword 'thread' in the 'introduces' clause of the specification. If the central controller is regarded as a simplified producer of product descriptors, therefore, it would be modelled by a class with a specification of the form:

```
with DATA_BASE;                                        (6.8)
class CENTRAL_CONTROLLER is
    introduces
        procedure SHARE (SHARED_DB : in DATA_BASE);
        thread;
end CENTRAL_CONTROLLER;
```

The method SHARE is introduced as a means of providing instances of
CENTRAL_CONTROLLER with a reference to a shared instance of DATA_BASE
(5.15). Its body, therefore, merely assigns the actual parameter to one of
the class's private instance variables:

```
with PRODUCT_DESCRIPTOR, NEW_DESCRIPTOR;                (6.9)
class body CENTRAL_CONTROLLER is

    DB : DATA_BASE;                     -- stores reference to the shared database
                    -- DB will be changed to a different class type in Section 6.7
    P : PRODUCT_DESCRIPTOR;

    procedure SHARE (SHARED_DB : in DATA_BASE) is
    begin
        DB := SHARED_DB;
    end;

    thread;
        loop
            P := NEW_DESCRIPTOR;
            DB.ADD(P);
        end loop;
end CENTRAL_CONTROLLER;
```

As this body indicates, the thread of a class has a similar appearance
to the initialization part of an Ada package, except that it follows the
keyword 'thread' rather than 'begin'. Furthermore, like the initialization
part of a package, there can be a maximum of one thread per class. Unlike
the initialization code of a package, however, which is executed when a
package is elaborated, the thread of an object is activated only after explicit
invocation of the special method START, which is an implicit part of the
interface of every active object. This approach also distinguishes DRAG-
OON from most other object-oriented languages adopting the active object
approach, since in these the process part of an object is activated as soon as
it is created. The reason for providing an alternative mechanism to this in
DRAGOON is to enable the communication pattern of concurrent systems
to be set up before the processes themselves are activated (Section 6.10).

When the START method is called by an external object, a new thread
of control is generated to execute the sequence of statements in the thread
part of the object. This will only have an extended lifetime (i.e. behave
like a persistent, active process) if it contains a loop, otherwise it will
terminate on completion of the sequence of statements. In this respect, the
DRAGOON approach is similar to the 'asynchronous method execution'
approach described earlier, since the thread is activated by a call to the

method START and proceeds asynchronously until complete. An important difference from this model, however, is that the special START method in DRAGOON can never have any parameters and can only be called once for each instance of an active class. Subsequent invocations of the method result in the exception START_ERROR being raised.

So far as their interaction with the database is concerned, the checkout point objects will have a similar form to the central controller class – the difference being that they are *consumers* of product descriptors, rather than *producers*. Like CENTRAL_CONTROLLER, therefore, the class describing checkout points must export a method similar to SHARE by which the reference of the shared database object can be made visible to the instances.

6.6   Agents

It is possible to define active objects that export no methods whatsoever and whose only function is thus to call other objects in the system. However, such objects, which following the terminology of Booch (1987) are called *actors*[3], are not used frequently because to perform a useful role in a concurrent system a 'calling' object must export at least one method like SHARE to receive reference to shared objects.

Conversely, of course, there are objects which possess no active thread, and which therefore are unable to issue calls spontaneously. Booch terms objects of this nature *servers*, since they can only execute in response to method calls. This term is confusing in the context of object-oriented languages, however, where it refers to any object (including active ones) that provides 'services' to client objects by exporting a set of callable methods. A better term for describing objects that possess no thread is *passive*, therefore. Clearly, normal sequential objects in a non-concurrent system fit the criteria for being passive, but when used in a concurrent system such objects need to be protected by a suitable access protocol using the behavioural inheritance mechanism.

The final category of objects used in building concurrent systems are what Booch refers to as *agents*. These are objects that both export methods for invocation by others and possess their own thread to initiate calls. Since their methods may be called concurrently by other objects, they are likely to require an appropriate behaviour to control *external* access to the internal data. This does not, however, guarantee that the internal state of the object is protected from concurrent access, because the thread of the object, like the methods, has unrestricted access to its state variables. Although the behaviour is able to protect against the erroneous concurrent execution of *methods*, because it does not affect the thread, it is unable to ensure this will not access an internal state variable simultaneously with a

---

[3] Not to be confused with 'actors' in the model of Agha and Hewit (Agha, 1986).

method. In the case of instances of the CENTRAL_CONTROLLER (6.9) class, for example, invocation of the method SHARE while the thread is active could lead to interference and unpredicted results. The problem is avoided in this particular case because the thread should not be activated until the SHARE method has been called to initialize the external reference. In general it remains true, however, that the thread of an object is able to access its state variables concurrently with its methods.

The solution to this problem is to provide 'internal' objects in danger of being concurrently accessed with their own behaviour. In other words, the burden of protection does not reside entirely with the encapsulating object, but also with its private objects. DRAGOON, in fact, places no restriction on the nature of private objects – they may be actors, passive servers and agents in any combination. Concurrency, therefore, may exist at all levels in the DRAGOON dependency hierarchy. Although an object can possess only one sequential thread, it may contain an unlimited number of private active objects, which essentially provide it with further internal threads. Even a passive object, which possesses no thread itself, may possess private objects which are active. DRAGOON also permits the temporary (instance) variables of methods to be active objects.

This contrasts sharply with other concurrent object-oriented languages such as POOL, which enforce strict sequentiality within the encapsulation boundary of an object. In POOL the single execution thread (or body) that an object may possess is used both to make it 'active' and to control external access in the style of Ada 'select' statements. All its private (or internal) objects, therefore, reside in a completely sequential environment in which there is never more than one active thread of control. This approach has the advantage of simplifying the language's semantics, but the disadvantage of imposing an unnaturally flat concurrency structure on POOL systems. The DRAGOON approach, on the other hand, makes the formal definition of semantics more difficult (Breu and Zucca, 1989), but provides the full benefits of concurrency at all levels of the dependency hierarchy of a system. Although this may leave programmers with more leeway to produce erroneous programs which deadlock, it also provides scope for the definition of much more powerful programs.

6.6.1   Condition synchronization

Enabling agents to contain (private) behavioured objects is important because it provides the way of achieving condition synchronization in DRAGOON. This is the form of synchronization in which one process waits for a signal from another before proceeding. Since the behaviour of an object does not affect the execution of its thread, in order to arrange for the thread to be suspended upon a signal it is necessary to make the object a client of another behavioured object. The behaviour of this object must be such that the execution of the method called by the thread is blocked until the

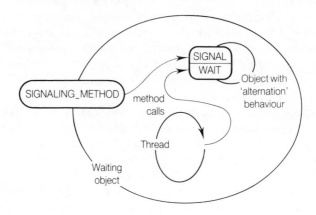

Figure 6.2   Condition synchronization.

appropriate signal is received. The simplest behaviour with this property is the 'alternation' behaviour defined by the class ALTERNATION (6.4).

The object with the 'alternation' behaviour could be *shared* between (i.e. be the peer of) the 'signaling' object and the 'waiting' object with the blocked thread. However, a much more elegant and robust approach is to make the 'alternation' object private to the 'waiting' object in the manner illustrated in Figure 6.2. This ensures that the responsibility for correct synchronization lies solely with the component builder. In this scenario, the thread of the 'waiting' object is blocked by arranging for it to call the method of the internal 'alternation' object which is constrained to execute second. To transmit a signal, the signaling object simply calls a method in the waiting object's interface (usually having no constraints on its execution) which calls the first operation. This then enables the second permitted operation to be executed and the thread to proceed.

At first sight, the reliance on clientship of internal behavioured objects to synchronize the methods and thread of an object might seem clumsy, and vulnerable to the same likelihood of errors as the traditional semaphore-based approaches. However, it is important to realize that active objects, as well as behavioured objects, can be encapsulated within other objects so that there is a great deal of freedom in nesting threads as well as behaviours. If a programmer finds that an overly complicated set of method calls is required to synchronize the thread of an object with the methods of one of its servers, it is probable that the functionality (i.e. sequence of statements) defined in the thread should really be defined as an additional method of the server, and the required execution thread provided by an additional active object. The role of this active object's thread would simply be to loop around calling the appropriate method of the behavioured object. In this way, the sequence of statements originally defined in the thread would still be executed in a separate thread of control.

By the appropriate nesting of behavioured and active classes, therefore, it is possible to use inherited behaviours to handle most synchronization scenarios. However, this facility must be used with great caution because nested behaviours can easily interfere in ways not expected by the programmer. Generally speaking the behaviour of a class is determined not only through the behaviour it inherits directly by the behavioural inheritance mechanism – the *inherited* behaviour – but also by the behaviour conferred upon its methods indirectly by their interaction with the behavioured classes of which it is a client – the *conferred* behaviour. If the programmer does not control the interaction of these two sources of behaviour carefully, they could easily interfere destructively. Suppose, for example, that an active object was required which waits for a particular signal and does not permit any of its own methods, other than that intended for receiving the signal, to be executed before the signal arrives. An appropriate behaviour for such an agent might be:

per (SIGNAL_OP) ⇔ act (OTHER_OP) = act (SIGNAL_OP) = 0;

per (OTHER_OP) ⇔ act (SIGNAL_OP) > 0 and active (OTHER_OP) = 0;

By mapping the signal-receiving method of the agent to SIGNAL_OP and all the others to OTHER_OP in the behavioured class, this behaviour would ensure that no other method of the class could execute before the signal-receiving method, but after the signal was received they would execute in mutual exclusion. If the body of the class is programmed correctly this is a perfectly acceptable behaviour to use in conjunction with the condition synchronization technique. However, if a mistake is made in programming access to the semaphore object, for example, by the signal-receiving method calling the WAIT method of the semaphore, or alternatively the thread of the agent calling the SIGNAL method, the thread of the agent would be blocked indefinitely. Far from conforming to the inherited behaviour described above, therefore, the behaviour of the resulting class could best be described as 'deadlock'.

This is an extreme case of the kinds of interactions that occur between the inherited and conferred behaviour of an object. This can be used constructively to provide subtle behaviours that cannot be satisfactorily expressed by behavioural inheritance alone, but sometimes, of course, if wrongly used the resulting behaviour may not be that desired by the programmer.

Another potential source of problems in the use of behavioural inheritance arises if classes are permitted to invoke their own methods. Most of the behaviours superimposed on classes enforce total exclusion constraints (i.e. (><)) on at least some of the methods in their interface. If one method, therefore, called another of the class's methods with which it was constrained to be mutually exclusive, then deadlock would obviously occur. To avoid this, it is necessary to ensure that mutually exclusive behaviour is never applied to a method making introspective method calls (i.e. calls to SELF). As mentioned in Chapter 3, partly for this reason, and partly because the facilities they offer can be easily achieved by other means, DRAGOON does not permit introspective method calls.

Even with this restriction on introspective method calls, there is still a great deal of leeway for programmer errors in the combination of inherited and conferred inheritance. This could be seen as a weakness of a language intended to reduce the scope for programmer error by such techniques as strong typing. However, it is important to realize that most of the applications of behavioural inheritance involve simple passive classes in which their is no risk of interaction between behaviours. Moreover, concurrency is an application area in which it is notoriously difficult to reduce the chance of errors without significantly reducing the flexibility and expressibility of the language. It is felt, therefore, that the DRAGOON approach provides a reasonable balance between flexibility and safety, providing a concise and easily understood mechanism for handling common synchronization problems while providing features for handling more complex and unusual requirements in an elegant fashion.

6.7   Forwarder objects

The database in the supermarket control system is a good example of an object which needs to be protected by some form of readers/writers behaviour. In general there will be several readers (checkout points) and a writer (central control point) trying to access the database at the same time. One approach would be to use a behaviour which gives priority to writers, since this would ensure that the database always contains the most up-to-date information. However, this approach has the drawback that all the checkout points would be blocked while the single writer updated the database. Furthermore, it could be argued that prompt service of the customers waiting at the checkout points is more important that prompt service of the central controller. This would suggest that a better choice would be a behaviour giving priority to readers. In a real supermarket the database access priorities would be decided by factors far more involved than it is appropriate to discuss here. For the purposes of discussing the concurrency features of DRAGOON it is convenient to adopt the second approach, and it is assumed that a subclass of DATA_BASE has been defined called PROTECTED_DATA_BASE which has inherited the behaviour defined by READERS_PRIORITY (6.7).

To relieve the central control object from having to wait for long periods of time to write to the database during moments of high activity by the checkout points, it is desirable to introduce some form of buffering medium. This could be achieved using a passive instance of the class QUEUE (4.4), for example, into which the central control object 'PUTs' product descriptors and from which the database object 'GETs' them. However, since this would require the database to 'fetch' product descriptors this approach would involve a major redesign of the database to turn it into an active object. Instead an *active* 'forwarding' object will be designed which is able to buffer product descriptors produced by the central controller until it can forward them to the database. Such an object is defined by the class:

```
with DATA_BASE, PRODUCT_DESCRIPTOR;                              (6.10)
class FORWARDER is
    introduces
        procedure SHARE (SHARED_DB : in DATA_BASE);
        procedure ADD (P : in PRODUCT_DESCRIPTOR);
        thread;
end FORWARDER;


with QUEUE;
class body FORWARDER is

    D_BASE : DATA_BASE;
    DESCRIPTOR : PRODUCT_DESCRIPTOR;
    BUFFER : QUEUE;                      -- stores reference to the shared database

    procedure SHARE (SHARED_DB : in DATA_BASE) is
    begin
        D_BASE := SHARED_DB;
    end;

    procedure ADD (DESCRIPTOR : in PRODUCT_DESCRIPTOR) is
    begin
        BUFFER.ADD(DESCRIPTOR);
    end;
thread
    BUFFER.CREATE;
    loop
        DESCRIPTOR := BUFFER.POP;
        D_BASE.ADD(DESCRIPTOR);
    end loop;
end FORWARDER;
```

As illustrated in Figure 6.3, each forwarder has a private QUEUE object to store product descriptors waiting to be added to the database. The method ADD is called by the central controller object to pass new product descriptors to the forwarder. As FORWARDER is not type compatible with DATA_BASE (5.15), therefore, the class CENTRAL_CONTROLLER (6.9) needs to be changed from a client of DATA_BASE, as shown in Section 6.5.1, to a client of FORWARDER (i.e. the variable DB and formal method parameter SHARED should be of class type FORWARDER rather than DATA_BASE).

Unless the buffer is full, the ADD method immediately adds the product descriptor to the buffer. The 'forwarding' is performed by the thread of the forwarder object, which removes product descriptors from the buffer and PUTs them into the database. As with CENTRAL_CONTROLLER objects,

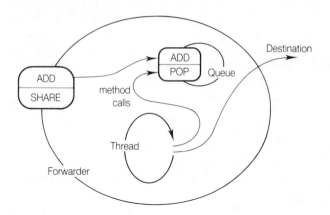

Figure 6.3   Structure of a forwarder object.

the reference to the database is passed to forwarder objects by means of the method SHARE.

This design for forwarder objects is fairly straightforward and can make use of the generic 'queue' component developed in the previous chapter. The main difficulty is in generating a version of the queue with the right kind of behaviour. All the previous behaviours superimposed on sequential classes have been describable in fairly concise and natural terms using the five basic functions, but the behaviour required for the buffer used in FORWARDER objects is more complicated because in addition to exclusion constraints it must handle access conditions related to the size of the buffer. It is only acceptable to execute the buffer's PUT method, for example, provided the buffer is not full, while it is only acceptable to execute its GET method provided it is not empty.

It is quite easy to express the required re-entrancy conditions using the history functions defined earlier. For example, if the buffer had a capacity of 20 items, the appropriate synchronization conditions could be specified by the behaviour:

per (PUT_OP) $\Leftrightarrow$ ($><$) and act (PUT_OP) − fin (GET_OP) < 20;

per (GET_OP) $\Leftrightarrow$ ($><$) and fin (PUT_OP) − act (GET_OP) > 0;

In addition to the basic mutual exclusion requirement, this behaviour expresses the fact that 'there is permission to execute a PUT_OP only if the number of completions of PUT_OPs does not exceed the number of activations of GET_OPs by 20 (i.e. the buffer is not full), while there is permission to execute a GET_OP only if the number of completions of PUT_OPs exceeds the number of activations of GET_OPs (i.e. it is not empty)'. The problem with using this behaviour, however, is that because the size of the buffer it controls has had to be explicitly stated, it is only applicable to buffers of size 20. This, in turn, means that a different behavioural class would have to be defined for each possible buffer size, which is clearly incompatible with the general goal of providing a small number of behavioural classes capable of satisfying most applications.

6.8   Guarded permissions

This is just one example of a more general limitation of the simple behavioural class approach described in Section 6.3. The history functions 'act', 'req' and 'fin', and their auxiliaries 'active' and 'requested', provide a simple record of part of the state of an object. The 'act' and 'fin' information, for example, can easily be recorded by integer variables that are updated each time a method starts and completes, while the information provided by 'req' is available to processes in many other languages[4]. This information alone, however, is very often not enough to define the complete state of an object, and hence further conditions must be satisfied to define the access protocol. The 'fullness' of a bounded buffer, for example, cannot be determined by the method invocation histories alone, but depends crucially on the implementation of the class body – specifically, the size of the data structure storing the buffered items.

There is a wide range of classes of this nature in which the access conditions are determined by aspects of their implementation, as well as the method invocation history. To avoid having to define a specialized behavioural class for each class with particular implementation idiosyncrasies (e.g. the queue size in this example), it is necessary to extend the behavioural mechanism described earlier so that the synchronization conditions can also be made to depend on aspects of the state of the behavioured class.

This is achieved in DRAGOON by permitting the value returned by function methods to be used as one of the logical conditions determining when a particular method may be executed. Instead of an explicit specification of the size of a queue in a 'bounded buffer' behavioural class, therefore, the boolean expression defining the execution permission for the PUT_OP methods has a *guard* controlled by the state of the queue:

```
behavioural class BOUNDED_BUFFER is                          (6.11)
where
ruled PUT_OPS, GET_OPS, FULL_GUARD, OTHER_OPS;
    per (PUT_OPS) ⇔ (><)  and (not FULL_GUARD);
    per (GET_OPS) ⇔ (><)  and (act (PUT_OPS) − act (GET_OPS) > 0);
```

---

[4]In Ada, for example, the COUNT attribute can be used to establish the number of calls queued on a particular entry.

```
        per (FULL_GUARD) ⇔ (><);
        per (OTHER_OPS) ⇔ (><);
    end BOUNDED_BUFFER;
```

When this behavioural class is used as a parent of a behavioured class, each abstract method appearing as a guard in the deontic expressions is instantiated with a method from the sequential parent. Methods used as guards are normal methods in the interface of a class and hence must also have the conditions under which they may execute specified in the behaviour. Any abstract method name used as a guard, therefore, must also appear in the 'ruled' clause of the behavioural class and must have a corresponding deontic expression specifying its execution conditions.

For a method to serve as a guard which returns information about the current state of an object, the only behaviour that can usually sensibly be applied to it is strict mutual exclusion with all other methods in the interface (i.e. $(><)$), otherwise a concurrently executing method could change the state while it is being evaluated. Moreover, unlike other abstract method names in the behavioural class, which can be instantiated with a *set* of methods in a derived behavioured class, abstract methods used as guards may only have *one* method assigned to them, otherwise the execution permissions in which they appear would not be uniquely determined.

Using the behavioural class GUARDED_BUFFER, a behavioured version of the class SIMPLE_QUEUE could be defined by the following class:

```
    class GUARDED_QUEUE is                                      (6.12)
        inherits SIMPLE_QUEUE;
        ruled by BOUNDED_BUFFER;
    where
        PUT => PUT_OPS, GET => GET_OPS, IS_FULL => FULL_GUARD,
                                        IS_EMPTY => OTHER_OPS;
    end GUARDED_QUEUE;
```

With these mappings of concrete methods to abstract set names, the intuitive meaning of this behaviour is clear – 'there is permission to execute a PUT method if, and only if, there are no currently active methods and evaluation of the boolean method IS_FULL returns false (i.e. the queue is not full)'. What is not so clear, however, is how this conceptual interpretation of 'guarded permissions' relates to actual execution of the guard method. In other words, how and when are the guard methods evaluated?

6.8.1   Guard evaluation semantics

At first sight an obvious interpretation might appear to be that the guard method is evaluated whenever a new call is issued. For example, the method IS_FULL guarding invocation of the PUT method would be evaluated when a client object invokes the PUT method. This interpretation is acceptable on the occasions when the conditions for PUT are satisfied and an instance of the method may begin execution immediately, but it is not acceptable when the method does not have immediate execution permission. In this case, the call to PUT needs to be placed on a queue of pending calls until the conditions for activation of the method are satisfied. *Logically* this occurs as soon as another object in the system invokes a GET method to remove an object and create spare space in the queue. The problem is, however, by what mechanism and in which 'thread of control' are the conditions for activation of the PUT method (i.e. the guard method) re-evaluated? Clearly, the originators of queued calls to PUT are unable to do so, because by definition they are blocked. Adopting the interpretation that guards are evaluated only when the guarded method is *called*, therefore, is not a valid approach, because there is no mechanism for 'waking up' a queued call when the logical conditions tested by the guard become true.

As pointed out earlier in this chapter, conventional languages using guards as the basis for synchronization regard monitor objects as possessing internal execution threads responsible for evaluating the guards at the appropriate moment. In Ada, for example, the guards controlling the acceptance of entry calls are evaluated when the task's thread of control enters a 'select' statement encapsulating one or more 'accept' statements. The evaluation of the guards, therefore, takes place in the thread of control of the 'called' rather than the 'calling' task, and completely independently of calls joining the entry queues of the task. In fact, when a '**select**' statement is evaluated, guards are evaluated for *all* the accept alternatives, regardless of whether there are any calls currently queued on the entries concerned. For a rendezvous with a guarded entry to begin, therefore, not only must the 'called' task have executed a '**select**' statement and the corresponding guard evaluated to true, but there must also be a currently queued call.

The required interpretation of guarded permissions must simulate the effect of evaluating the guards independently of method calls, but without relying explicitly on the concept of an active thread of control within the monitor, because it is the avoidance of this concept in defining synchronization constraints which pays such dividends as far as reuse is concerned. To meet these requirements, the following interpretation is adopted for the evaluation of guard methods used to determine the execution permissions of others. *All* the guard methods[5] in the behavioured class are evaluated indivisibly in some undefined order:

- once at object creation time,
- every time a non-guard method is completed (whether or not successfully).

---

[5] Those mapped on to abstract methods appearing on the right-hand side of deontic expressions.

The guard methods are *not*, therefore, evaluated whenever one of the corresponding guarded methods is *called*. On the contrary, except at object initialization time, they are evaluated after the *completion* of every non-guard method, since the execution of such a method may have changed the state upon which the guard conditions depend. If, after the re-evaluation of all the guards, a call that was previously queued now has permission to execute, it is activated by the behaviour implementation and serviced by execution of the appropriate method body.

Strictly speaking, therefore, it is a misnomer to call methods used to determine the execution permission of others as 'guards', because they are not actually 'called' at the moment when the guard is checked to see if an external call may be accepted. More accurately stated, the purpose of the guard functions is to return the *value* to which the real 'guards' are set. This value is then, in a sense, 'remembered' by the behaviour implementation until needed to establish execution permissions or until the completion of a non-guard method causes its re-evaluation.

Because the guard values are only re-evaluated after the completion of non-guard methods, it is important that the guard functions do not have any side-effect on the state of the object, otherwise this could invalidate the value returned by previously evaluated guard functions. This is a general requirement of functions and expressions used to provide guard values, whatever the language or execution model. It follows, also, that the execution conditions associated with guard functions when invoked directly by client objects will usually be total exclusion (i.e. (><)), or at least exclusion with respect to non-guard functions, but it is possible for a guard function to execute concurrently with a non-guard function if the latter manipulates a completely unrelated part of the object's state.

6.9   Future development

The behavioural inheritance mechanism described in the preceding sections is that which is implemented in the current version of the DRAGOON-to-Ada preprocessor, and represents the state of development that existed at the end of the DRAGON project. Although this proves the basic concept of behavioural inheritance and provides a practical vehicle for improving the reusability of software components, it is deficient in one or two areas. This section describes some ideas currently under investigation by the DRAGOON partners for enhancing the behavioural inheritance mechanism described in the previous sections.

The power of behavioural inheritance results from the fact that synchronization policies are defined independently of the methods to which they are ultimately applied. This means that a single behavioural class, such as READERS_WRITERS (6.5), is sufficient to define the behaviour of all classes requiring a readers/writers behaviour, because the formal methods named in the behavioural class are bound to the actual methods of a class only when a behavioured subclass is defined. Thus behaviour descriptions are essentially 'parameterized' with respect to the methods they control.

The conditions determining when a formal method may execute are almost invariably related to the histories of the other formal methods in the behavioural class. In most scenarios where the number of different formal methods (i.e. synchronization points) is fixed, it is perfectly satisfactory to specify independently how the execution conditions for each formal method depend on the execution histories of the others. However, the logic of some behaviours is essentially independent of the number of formal methods. The classic example is that in which the methods of a class need to be executed according to a simple priority ordering – a method may not be executed if there is an outstanding call to a higher priority method. Clearly, this basic rule is independent of the number of formal methods in a behavioural class, but in the version of behavioural inheritance described in Section 6.3 a different behavioural class would have to be defined for each possible number of priority levels. It is not possible to avoid this problem by suitable mapping of actual to formal methods in a behavioured class, because each priority level corresponds to a different synchronization point in which calls of a given priority must be queued. Another example is the generalization of the ALTERNATION (6.4) behaviour to cycle through more than two methods. Clearly, the logic for this is independent of the number of formal methods.

The main shortcoming of the behavioural inheritance mechanism described earlier, therefore, is that behavioural classes cannot be parameterized with respect to the number of formal methods. A useful enhancement to the basic mechanism would be the introduction of 'indexed behaviours'. In their simplest form these are parameterized simply by a number that specifies the size of a family of formal methods. An indexed behavioural class defining a simple priority-based behaviour, for example, might be of the form:

behavioural class PRIORITIES (N : POSITIVE) is   (6.13)

    type PRIORITY is range 1 .. N;
    I, J : PRIORITY;

ruled P_OP (PRIORITY);
where
    per (P_OP(I)) $\Leftrightarrow$ ($><$) and (($I < J$) $\rightarrow$ req (P_OP(J) = 0);
end PRIORITIES;

Informally, the deontic expression in this class states that a method in the set corresponding to the Ith formal method of PRIORITIES may execute if, and only if, there are no other currently active methods and there are no requests to methods in a set with a higher index value (i.e. a higher priority). Suppose a class, CONTROL, say, had methods HIGH_A and HIGH_B requiring a high priority, a method MED requiring medium priority and a method LOW requiring low priority. The required subclass would be as follows:

```
class PRIORITY_CONTROL is                                        (6.14)
    inherits CONTROL;
    ruled by PRIORITIES (3);
where
    HIGH_A, HIGH_B => P_OP (1);
    MED => P_OP (2);
    LOW => P_OP (3);
end PRIORITY_CONTROL;
```

The behavioural class PRIORITIES can therefore be used with classes requiring different numbers of priority levels. In this approach the behavioured class must provide a positive integer specifying the number of different priorities required – the type of the indices being declared in the behavioural class. An alternative approach would be to parameterize a behavioured class with respect to a discrete type and use this as the type of the indices. The deontic expressions would then have to be expressed in terms of the attributes associated with discrete types such as 'FIRST and 'LAST. This provides a more natural correspondence between the types used to define the class of the sequential parent and the type defining the index of the formal method family.

6.9.1   Method families

The idea of indexed behavioural classes described above completes the generality of behavioural classes by enabling them to be parameterized with respect to the number of formal methods, as well as the actual methods that are to be controlled. Indexed behavioural classes in some ways provide a similar facility to families of entries in the Ada tasking model. They both facilitate the description of a family (or array) of synchronization (or queuing) points distinguished by the value of a discrete index. Whereas the formal methods of an indexed behavioural class are quite deliberately separated from the functionality of the methods that will be controlled by the corresponding execution constraints, a task also defines the 'bodies' (i.e. 'accept' statements) that must be executed when one of a family of entries is called.

The purpose of the concept of a family of entries is to provide a certain degree of dynamic control over the queue to which a call is added. A normal entry has only one associated synchronization queue so that all calls to that entry are placed in the same queue no matter what their priority. One of the main uses for the family of entries in Ada is to enable callers of different priorities to enter different queues for essentially the same service.

Another direction in which the DRAGOON behavioural inheritance mechanism could be enhanced, therefore, is in its support for dynamic queue selection depending on the actual parameters of a method call. The most general solution would permit each combination of actual parameter values in a call to be mapped to a different queue. In practise, however, it may be sufficient to let one privileged parameter (such as the family index in Ada) dictate which queue is joined.

It is stressed that the ideas discussed in this section are not implemented in the current version of DRAGOON. They are presented to illustrate the various ways in which the basic behavioural inheritance mechanism described in the previous sections may be enhanced in the future.

6.10   Building concurrent systems

Having discussed the facilities provided by DRAGOON for constructing components of concurrent systems, it is now possible to illustrate how these are assembled into a complete concurrent system. In view of the measures taken to integrate the concurrency features with the object-oriented aspects of the language, it is perhaps not surprising that this is achieved in a very similar way to the construction of a purely sequential system.

In non-concurrent object-oriented languages, a system (or program) is represented as a single class, called the *root* class in Eiffel, which generates all the other entities in the system as its private objects. Although DRAGOON has a different model for compiling and executing such classes, as described in Chapter 8, a non-distributed concurrent system in DRAGOON is similarly defined as a single class which generates and encapsulates all the other objects. Such 'system-defining' objects are usually actors, therefore, which export no methods (other than the special CREATE and START operations).

Suppose, for the sake of argument, that a non-distributed version of the supermarket control system was required in which, initially at least, there were ten checkout points. Using the components developed so far, a class generating such a system would be of the form:

```
class SUPERMARKET is                                          (6.15)
    introduces
        thread;
end SUPERMARKET;


with CENTRAL_CONTROLLER, CHECKOUT_POINT, DATA_BASE;
class body SUPERMARKET is

    CC : CENTRAL_CONTROLLER;
    DB : PROTECTED_DATA_BASE;              -- introduced in Section 6.7
    F : FORWARDER;
    CP : array (1 .. 10) of CHECKOUT_POINTS;

thread

    CC.CREATE;                                  -- create objects
    DB.CREATE;
    F.CREATE;
    for I in 1 .. 10 loop
```

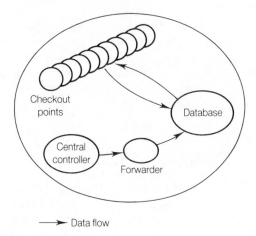

→ Data flow

Figure 6.4   Non-distributed supermarket control system.

```
        CP(I).CREATE;
    end loop;

    CC.SHARE(F);                                        -- see page 115
    F.SHARE(DB);                          -- set up required system configuration
    for I in 1 .. 10 loop
        CP(I).SHARE(DB);
    end loop;

    CC.START;                                           -- start objects
    F.START;
    for I in 1 .. 10 loop
        CP(I).START;
    end loop;

end SUPERMARKET;
```

This demonstrates one of the reasons why the thread of active objects
is activated by a special START method rather than at object creation
time. It permits the required system start-up configuration to be established without concern for synchronization problems while there is only one
execution thread. As pointed out earlier, if the SHARE method of a CEN-
TRAL_CONTROLLER (6.9), FORWARDER (6.10) or CHECKOUT_POINT was called
while the thread was active, untold errors could result. By enabling the
required communication pattern to be established before the threads are
activated, these problems are avoided.

The generation of an instance of the class SUPERMARKET, and subsequent activation of its thread by invocation of its START method, will result
in the generation of a supermarket control system of the form illustrated
in Figure 6.4.

6.10.1   Reconfiguration

As defined above, the thread of the class SUPERMARKET behaves as a piece of initialization code, serving only to generate the required objects in the system, set up the desired communication pattern and then activate the required execution threads. Once the thread of a SUPERMARKET object has performed these actions it terminates and plays no further role in the execution of the system. This does not have to be the case, however. The thread of such an object could contain a non-terminating loop which provides it with an extended lifetime, and permits it to continue regulating the configuration of the system.

Suppose, for example, that a version of the system was required in which a new FORWARDER (6.10) object is generated if the original instance becomes full, and hence the CENTRAL_CONTROLLER (6.9) is blocked. This could be achieved by appending the thread definition with code of the following form:

$$\vdots \hspace{7cm} (6.16)$$

```
declare
    WAITING, WORKING, TEMP : FORWARDER;
    FIRST_RECONF : BOOLEAN := TRUE;
begin
    loop
        <Wait until forwarder is full>
        if FIRST_RECONF then
            WAITING.CREATE;
            WAITING.SHARE(DB);
            WAITING.START;
            FIRST_RECONF := FALSE;
        end if;
        CC.SHARE(WAITING);
        TEMP := WAITING;
        WAITING := WORKING;
        WORKING := TEMP;
    end loop;
    end;
end SUPERMARKET;
```

This 'reconfiguration' code appended to the thread waits for a signal indicating that a new FORWARDER (6.10) is needed. It then checks to see if a backup forwarder object has already been created (i.e. if there has been any previous reconfiguration request). If not, it first arranges for a new forwarder to be generated through the instance variable WAITING, and then proceeds to change the configuration of the system so that the CENTRAL_CONTROLLER object now sends PRODUCT_DESCRIPTOR objects to the new backup forwarder object.

Once the reconfiguration has been performed, the instance variables WAITING and WORKING, which respectively refer to the backup FORWARDER object and the 'working' object being sent new product descriptors by the central controller, are 'swapped' so that they can be exchanged on the next occasion this reconfiguration is required.

There are two outstanding problems with this approach, however. The first, which is considered further in Section 8.6.1, is how to communicate to the thread that a reconfiguration is actually required. The second relates to the fact that this 'reconfiguring code' breaks an important rule mentioned earlier – the calling of the SHARE method of an object (in this case the object referenced through CC) after its thread has been activated. The SHARE method of the central controller referenced through CC is called without any concern for the state of the object. If it happens to be communicating with the forwarder object when the reconfiguration is performed, untold damage could result.

To overcome this problem it is necessary to define extra methods in the interface of CENTRAL_CONTROLLER which SUPERMARKET must call first to gain permission to perform the reconfiguration, and then to inform the CENTRAL_CONTROLLER (6.9) when it has been completed. This could be achieved by defining the appropriate subclass of CENTRAL_CONTROLLER, RECONF_CENTRAL_CONTROLLER:

```
class RECONF_CENTRAL_CONTROLLER is                    (6.17)
    inherits CENTRAL_CONTROLLER;
        procedure REQUEST_RECONF;
        procedure COMPLETED_RECONF;
    redefines
        thread;
end;
```

These methods ensure that the SHARE method, which changes the reference to the FORWARDER object, behaves as an atomic operation as far as the reconfiguration is concerned. The code responsible for performing the reconfiguration (6.16) must call REQUEST_RECONF and COMPLETED_RECONF immediately before and after calling the SHARE method. The REQUEST_RECONF method indicates to the central controller that it should move to a 'quiescent' state in which a new reference may be assigned to the instance variable through which it accesses one of the FORWARDER objects. Since it is the thread of the CENTRAL_CONTROLLER object which calls the methods of the forwarder, this needs to be blocked in order for the reconfiguration to take place. This is achieved by introducing an object with a form of alternation behaviour into the body of the task and arranging for the REQUEST_RECONF method, the thread of the class and the COMPLETED_RECONF to call its methods in the appropriate order. This is why the thread has to be redefined in the subclass. It is not possible to use behavioural inheritance to achieve this effect, since a behaviour cannot directly influence the thread of a class.

In this example, the COMPLETED_RECONF method is actually redundant since only one method, SHARE, has to be invoked to perform a reconfiguration. This method could instead be modified to call the internal behavioured object and arrange for the thread to be unblocked once the appropriate assignments have been made. In general, however, when more than one method is called to implement a reconfiguration, such a COM-PLETED_RECONF method is needed.

Key points

Languages for building current systems must facilitate the description of concurrent execution threads, inter-thread communication and inter-thread synchronization.

Features for supporting concurrency can be added as an extra layer on top of the object-oriented features, or can be fully integrated with them.

Concurrent execution threads may be integrated into the object-oriented model either through the notion of 'active objects' which possess an internal concurrent execution thread, or through the notion of asynchronous methods when the body of a method is executed concurrently with the caller.

Synchronization is the most difficult of the three concurrency requirements to integrate satisfactorily with the object-oriented paradigm. It not only conflicts with inheritance, since methods added in a subclass are not controlled by the synchronization constraints inherited from the parent, but also leads to the unnecessary duplication of code in classes with the same synchronization requirements but different methods.

In DRAGOON, the behaviour of a class is the set of synchronization constraints defining the permitted interleaving of method executions.

DRAGOON overcomes the conflict between inheritance and synchronization by separating the behaviour of a class from the description of its methods using the mechanism of *behavioural inheritance*.

Special *behavioural classes* are used to define abstract behaviours independently of any particular set of methods.

The synchronization conditions in a behavioural class are specified in terms of logic expressions over method invocation histories. These expressions employ the deontic operator 'per'.

A behaviour is applied to a given class by defining a subclass which inherits the appropriate behavioural class. This subclass is known as a *behavioured class* and its instances are protected from concurrent method execution in the style of a 'monitor'.

The exclusion symbol is used to indicate that methods mapped to a given formal method in a behavioural class may execute only if there are no other concurrently executing methods. In other words, the methods must execute in mutual exclusion with any other method of the class.

A small set of 'classic' behaviours, such as 'mutual exclusion', 'alternation' and various forms of 'readers/writers', is sufficient for the majority of behavioured classes required in typical applications. In particular, these three behaviours are sufficient to accommodate all the different concurrent forms in Booch's component taxonomy.

Objects are made active in DRAGOON by providing them with a *thread* which executes concurrently with the method of the objects and the threads of other objects. A thread may be defined explicitly in a class or may be inherited from a parent.

The thread of an object is started by means of the predefined START method.

Condition synchronization, in which one object waits until it receives a signal from another, is programmed by nesting an object with 'alternation' behaviour within the object waiting for the signal.

The three history functions — act, req and fin — are not always sufficient to define the conditions under which a method may be executed. In order to allow the execution conditions to depend on the state of the behavioured object, the deontic expressions may contain a guard method.

The guard values are re-evaluated each time a non-guard method is completed.

Further development of the behavioural inheritance mechanism is desirable to enable behavioural classes to be parameterized with respect to the number of synchronization points, and also to allow calls to be added to synchronization queues dynamically.

Concurrent systems may be generated within objects using the normal object-oriented mechanism.

The thread of an object encapsulating a concurrent system may simply terminate once it has configured the system, or may continue to monitor the system and make suitable configuration changes when required.

Chapter 7
Distribution

The idea of superimposing special qualities on classes by an enhancement of the inheritance mechanism is used again to great advantage in DRAGOON for the construction of distributed systems. This chapter outlines the special difficulties encountered in developing software for such systems and the various ways in which the object-oriented paradigm has been applied to this problem. It then goes on to describe the particular approach followed in DRAGOON.

7.1   Loosely coupled distributed systems

The term 'distributed system' is used to describe a large number of different types of system, ranging from massive international networks of mainframes to small clusters of microprocessors communicating via shared memory. Those employed in the domain of embedded systems are *loosely coupled* distributed processing systems, typically composed of a number of 'embedded' microprocessors, and one or two larger *host* computers. The processors, or *nodes*, are 'loosely coupled' in the sense that they each possess a separate memory unit. As a consequence, software segments executing on different nodes reside in disjoint address spaces and so must communicate by the exchange of messages over the relatively narrow bandwidth communication links.

More complex architectures are of course possible in which several processors in an otherwise loosely coupled network are 'tightly coupled' by shared memory. However, the arrangement of software among such machines is more a problem for the compiler and run-time system than the applications programmer. For the present discussion it is convenient to regard such a 'processor cluster' as simply another independent machine in the network.

Despite their extra complexity, distributed systems are becoming increasingly popular for the implementation of embedded systems because they offer a number of advantages over their uniprocessor counterparts

(Sloman and Kramer, 1987):

Performance. Being composed of multiple processors they are able to support the true parallel execution of concurrent processes, and therefore offer significant potential performance improvements for highly processor-intensive applications.

Processor locality. Processing power may be situated physically close to distributed devices rather than concentrated in a large, centralized computer. 'Long distance' communication can therefore be limited to the essential interaction between the devices, with all independent processing carried out locally.

Configuration flexibility. Both the hardware and software architectures of the system may be modified periodically to reflect changes in the environment or the availability of new devices or processors. These changes may be performed dynamically without disrupting those parts of the system not immediately affected by the reconfiguration.

Fault tolerance. In contrast with a uniprocessor system, the failure of hardware in a distributed system does not necessarily lead to the failure of the system as a whole. Damage can be limited to the node concerned and the remaining software either reconfigured to manage without it, or substitute nodes brought in to compensate for the failure.

The extent to which these potential advantages can actually be realized in a distributed system, however, depends crucially on the nature of the language and design approach used to construct the application software. Languages poorly designed from the perspective of distribution can result in highly inflexible software structures that severely restrict the scope for dynamic reconfiguration and fault tolerance. Despite allusions to the contrary in the Ada Language Reference Manual (DoD, 1983), it is now widely recognized that Ada is one such language whose modularity and concurrency mechanisms are poorly combined for the purposes of flexible software distribution.

Before describing the desirable features of languages intended for developing distributed, embedded systems, and how DRAGOON aims to improve the usability of Ada for this purpose, it is useful to relate the goals of DRAGOON to that of other projects exploiting the object-oriented programming paradigm for the purposes of distribution.

7.1.1   Object-orientation and distributed systems

Many of the concepts of object-oriented programming are currently finding widespread application in loosely coupled distributed systems. Object-orientation is probably most popular in the field of operating systems (Dasgupta, 1986) (Snodgrass, 1983), but projects such as Comandos (1987) are using this approach in the development of office automation systems, and Oscar (Shepherd *et al*, 1988), for distributed robotics applications.

Although they address widely differing application domains, these projects have the common characteristic that they are essentially concerned with the development of object-oriented *environments* in which software is not only *developed* in an object-oriented style, but *executes* within the framework of an object-oriented run-time system. Consequently, they all adopt the philosophy of a 'uniform' or 'virtual' object space which hides the disjoint address spaces in the loosely coupled network and permits all entities in the system, from the highest level application layers to the lowest level systems layers, to be modelled as objects.

Implementing a fully general object-oriented environment on a distributed system is a notoriously difficult problem, however, because of the code sharing mechanisms that have to be supported (Wegner, 1987) (Bennet, 1987). With a dynamic (or reactive (Bennet, 1987)) inheritance mechanism, such as that of Smalltalk, the functionality of a method may not only be inherited from objects situated on remote machines, but may be dynamically updated at any time. Unless large quantities of code are replicated on the separate sites, therefore, the execution of a method developed using dynamic inheritance may involve the execution of code dispersed throughout the network.

While construction of the run-time support and network communication mechanisms in an object-oriented style may well prove to be a suitable choice for DRAGOON systems, the 'object-orientedness' of the final system is not a prime concern in DRAGOON. What is important is that the approach used should reinforce the benefits of distribution outlined previously, should encourage the reuse of software and should be sufficiently efficient to cope with the real-time demands of embedded systems. The motivation for adopting an object-oriented approach in DRAGOON, therefore, is not to apply the concepts uniformly in the construction of a distributed environment, but to bring the reuse advantages of object-oriented programming to the development of distributed software. Consequently, DRAGOON is not concerned with supporting a uniform object model for its own ends nor with supporting dynamic inheritance across the network. As will be explained later, however, the language does enable programmers to take full advantage of inheritance in the development of distributable software components.

7.2   Programming distributed systems

As far as the development of embedded applications software is concerned, the main factor distinguishing loosely coupled distributed systems from uniprocessor systems is the additional overhead of remote communication across the network. Unless steps are taken to identify and minimize the overhead of remote (inter-processor) communication, the potential performance advantage of having multiple processors can easily be outweighed by the communication delays. Given the strict real-time constraints under which embedded systems must typically execute, it is extremely important that applications software is distributed judiciously among the processors in the network.

Traditional approaches for developing distributed software have fallen into two main camps (Atkinson, 1988). In one approach, no special linguistic support is provided for distribution and the programmer must design a separate program for each machine in the network, expressing inter-program communication using the low-level communication facilities provided by the host operating system. A prerequisite for this approach, therefore, which may be conveniently termed the 'operating system' approach, is a knowledge of the distributed nature of the target network and of the desired distribution of software components among the processors. While it permits the most efficient implementation of inter-machine communication, since it provides access to the low-level communication primitives, this approach ties the application software to one particular system architecture and limits its amenability to configuration change. Moreover, it reduces the reliability of the system because inter-node communication is not controlled by the typing rules of the language.

The second approach represents the other extreme in which the programmer has no knowledge of the target configuration and designs the applications software as if it were to execute on a single machine. It is the responsibility of the compiler and/or associated partitioning tools to split the software into components for distribution, and of the run-time system to support any required facilities across the network. This approach, therefore, which may be termed the 'language-oriented' approach, provides the opposite tradeoffs between efficiency and flexibility. Any program is clearly suitable for any configuration, since it contains no specific systems calls tying it to a particular architecture or communication system. However, since the software is designed without regard for potential distribution, its architecture may not lend itself well to efficient distributed execution.

7.2.1 Separation of concerns

In applications where either efficiency or generality/reliability take precedence over all other considerations, one of these approaches may provide a reasonable solution, but in the majority of situations a more equitable balance is required. Recent approaches, therefore, have attempted to combine the advantages of the 'operating system' and 'language-oriented' approaches by providing a compromise between the total visibility and total transparency of the target configuration which they respectively assume.

This is achieved by conceptually splitting the development of distributed applications into two distinct phases.

The functional modules for dispersal over the network, commonly called *virtual nodes*, are designed in the first *programming* (or *partitioning*) phase, while the determination of the exact configuration of the target network and the distribution of the virtual nodes upon it, are handled in the second *configuration* phase. By deferring configuration concerns until the second phase, the virtual nodes in a system can be designed without regard for the exact configuration of a particular target network, or arrangement of software upon it. The resulting configuration independence of the components provides a high degree of flexibility, not only with regard to the initial software architecture of a system but also the scope for dynamic configuration changes. Nevertheless, interactions between virtual nodes are still expressed in terms of the high-level communication constructs of the language, and are thus type checkable by the compiler. This approach, therefore, permits much of the safety of the 'language-oriented' approach to be gained in the first phase, and the efficiency of the 'operating system' approach in the second.

Virtual nodes constitute the atomic units of distribution, whose contents cannot be separated across loosely coupled machines. Consequently, they can be regarded as abstractions of autonomous processing units which define the granularity of distribution and enable application software to be structured in a way that mirrors the loose coupling of the underlying hardware. Programmers must therefore design the virtual nodes in a system in the knowledge that communication between them may ultimately be implemented by message passing over the network, and thus potentially carries a high overhead. The interior of a virtual node can be designed with complete freedom, however, since all its components are guaranteed to be colocated.

Many recent languages/environments designed specifically to support the development of distributed software explicitly embrace this approach. CONIC (Dulay *et al*, 1987), for example, developed at Imperial College, London, provides a special linguistic construct, called a *task module*, to model virtual nodes, and a distinct configuration language to describe the configuration of particular systems. Other linguistic constructs capturing the idea of virtual nodes include the guardian in Argus (Liskov, 1982), the Resource in SR (Andrews and Olson, 1986) and the sequence in MML (Boari *et al*, 1984).

This approach is also proving to be one of the most popular techniques for overcoming the problems of distributing Ada (Tedd *et al*, 1984). Both the DIADEM (Atkinson *et al*, 1988) and Aspect (Hutcheon and Wellings, 1987) projects have developed strategies for modelling virtual nodes in Ada and for supporting Ada-based remote communication mechanisms.

7.2.2   Characteristics of virtual nodes

In view of the advantages of this approach for controlling communication overheads while allowing compile time checking of remote transactions, it would clearly be desirable if DRAGOON could pursue a similar strategy for software distribution. However, supporting the virtual node concept within the object-oriented framework is not as straightforward as might at first be thought. To see why this is so, it is first necessary to identify the main properties required of virtual nodes and the supporting communication system (Goldsack *et al*, 1987) (Hutcheon and Wellings, 1988).

- To perform their role as loosely coupled node abstractions, virtual nodes must not communicate by direct access to shared data structures, but rather by operations that support a message-based protocol and appear in well-defined interfaces.

- To model strongly cohesive modules, virtual nodes must tightly encapsulate their internal state, ensuring that no other virtual node can *ever* access this state directly. In particular, they should never export references to parts of their internal state since this undermines the encapsulation boundary provided by the interface. All 'state' in the system must be encapsulated within virtual nodes, therefore.

- To provide maximum flexibility in system configuration and minimize the dependency between the programming and configuration phases, virtual nodes should be separately compilable library units and should represent module *types* acting as blueprints from which multiple instances can be instantiated.

- To permit dynamic changes in the communication pattern of the system, and incremental upgrades, instances of virtual nodes should not name each other directly in transactions but should identify each other by means of an indirect naming scheme.

- To facilitate the generation of concurrent execution threads and take advantage of the presence of multiple processes, virtual nodes should be able to model active processes with independent execution threads. This does not mean that all virtual nodes have to represent active processes, but merely that the capability for modelling such entities exists.

- To provide maximum flexibility in the allocation of virtual node instances to physical machines in the network, the distributed run-time system should support the same communication mechanisms for local (i.e. intra-processor) and remote (i.e. inter-processor) communication – a property known as *communication transparency* (Kramer and Magee, 1985).

7.2.3   Suitability of objects

At first sight, classes/objects from the object-oriented programming world would seem ideal constructs for acting as virtual nodes in the partitioning of software for distribution. Classes are separately compilable 'types' from which multiple instances (i.e. objects) can be instantiated, and objects not only communicate through well-defined interfaces by means of method calls but name each other indirectly. Moreover, the concurrency extensions of languages like DRAGOON enable objects to have threads and thus model autonomous activities. There is, however, one fundamental aspect of objects that is detrimental to their suitability for acting as virtual nodes – their failure to strongly encapsulate their internal state.

This might seem a surprising statement to make given the frequency with which the modularity and encapsulation properties of objects are emphasized. However, in all object-oriented languages that employ reference semantics for identifying objects, which is the majority (e.g. Smalltalk, Eiffel, Objective C, C++[1] and POOL), objects do *not* guarantee encapsulation of their state (Goldsack and Atkinson, 1989). Despite the fact that all communication between them is expressed in terms of method calls, the use of indirect references breaks down the encapsulation barriers and means that objects can directly access and manipulate the 'internal' state of others.

This problem exists wherever indirect references are used to identify data structures. In Ada, for example, using access types to refer to tasks makes it possible for tasks instantiated within a package body to be directly visible to any other part of the program to which the access value is communicated, regardless of the scoping rules that otherwise apply. The problem is exacerbated in 'pure' object-oriented languages which only provide objects, indirectly referenced through instance variables, as the means of representing data. Unless all communication is performed in terms of special 'immutable objects', which would obviously be extremely tedious, objects are bound to concede visibility of their internal states to others.

Consider the DATA_BASE object in the supermarket control system, for example. This contains a large number of PRODUCT_DESCRIPTOR objects which can be regarded as representing part of its state and which no other object should be allowed to modify directly. The main role of this DATA_BASE object is to provide CHECKOUT_POINT objects with information about particular products stored in the corresponding descriptor. Moreover, since the checkout points require access to several pieces of information on each product (in order to print the receipt, for example), it is clearly undesirable to have to communicate the information in a product descriptor as a sequence of 'immutable objects' (in Smalltalk this would require the exchange of individual characters).

---

[1]Although C++ also supports the direct naming of static objects.

It is true that, initially, the checkout points can only gain access to the information stored in the product descriptors by calling the appropriate method in the database's interface. However, in a pure object-oriented language the only way in which the database can communicate all the information about a given product in one transaction is by supplying the reference to the appropriate PRODUCT_DESCRIPTOR object. From this point onwards, the checkout point which receives the reference has direct and unrestricted access to the PRODUCT_DESCRIPTOR object concerned, without having to call methods of the database. There is nothing the database can do to stop the checkout point altering the state of the PRODUCT_DESCRIPTOR object at will (though it must do so, of course, via the product descriptor's methods).

7.2.4   Reference-free communication

In 'pure' object-oriented languages there is no way around this conflict between reference semantics and encapsulation, except to program all inter-object communication in terms of the primitive 'immutable objects'. Objects in a system must communicate in order to do useful work, but the only sensible way in which they can do so is by exchanging references and end up giving the receiving object unlimited access to the 'state' of the sender. This is not a serious problem in uniprocessor environments since all references, in any case, reside in the same address space and there is no extra overhead in allowing any object to reference any other. The only drawback is from the modularity and reuse point of view in that a reusable component cannot protect itself from misuse when it exports a reference.

In a distributed environment, however, this lack of strong encapsulation is a serious drawback to the realization of the 'virtual node-based' approach to distribution and the control over remote communication overheads which this provides. All conventional languages/environments that adopt this approach strictly forbid the exchange of references between virtual nodes (Liskov, 1982) (Sloman and Kramer, 1987) because this not only defeats the loose coupling of the virtual nodes by permitting remote data structures to be accessed as if they were local but also can easily lead to data corruption if care is not taken to distinguish remote references from local ones.

In order to provide a 'virtual node-based' approach to distribution in an object-oriented language it is necessary to relax the 'pure' philosophy and support a mechanism other than reference passing for object communication. One possible strategy is to define an alternative form of parameter passing semantics in which it is not *references* to objects which are passed in method calls but *deep copies* of the objects themselves. A 'deep copy' of an object in Smalltalk or Eiffel provides a complete (recursive) copy of the object and thus includes all other objects that it references. Indeed, some languages, such as Matroshka (Crowl, 1988) avoid reference semantics altogether and use copy semantics for all communication. C++, on the other hand, supports both approaches. This strategy would certainly avoid the passing of internal references over the network and is feasible for simple objects with few references to others. However, objects do not have to become very large or complex before the overheads of implementing a copy over the network soon outweigh the advantages of avoiding remote references. It is not clear, either, what the semantics of copying active and behavioured objects should be in a concurrent environment.

The most practical way of avoiding communication by references in an object-oriented language is provided by 'hybrid' languages, such as DRAGOON and Simula, which support the use of conventional data types as well as class types. Objects in such languages are not forced to communicate by exchanging references but may also exchange static data values of *non-primitive* types. DRAGOON is particularly powerful in this respect since it permits the full use of Ada's typing mechanism.

It is not desirable, however, to restrict communication between all objects to being by means of data values since this would rule out the use of many of the most powerful features of object-oriented programming. Reference semantics is not only invaluable for exploiting the properties of polymorphism and dynamic binding, which are so important for reuse, but also for permitting the *sharing* of objects. This facility is required in the construction of the supermarket control system, for example. It is essential to permit all these powerful features to be used in *building* distributable objects, since these are often fairly large modules composed of many other objects. All that is required to support the virtual node approach to distribution is to prohibit the exchange of state references between objects that are intended to have the potential for execution on a separate machine – that is, *virtual node* objects.

7.3 Virtual node objects

It is easy to state the general principle that potentially distributable virtual node objects should only communicate by exchanging data values, but without imposing a blanket ban on all reference passing between objects it is not so easy to see how this should be achieved. In traditional implementations of virtual nodes their modularity is guaranteed by requiring that they do not pass references to 'internal', or 'local', data structures to other virtual nodes. In the normal object-oriented model, however, the notion of one object being 'internal' or 'local' to another is not generally applicable since all objects exist in a completely uniform object space and, subject to the typing constraints, any instance variable may be made to refer to any object.

To specify more precisely what structures are permissible for virtual node objects and how they should be designed, therefore, it is first necessary to provide a basis for deciding the 'locality' of objects (i.e. whether they are 'internal' or 'external' to others) by identifying the different purposes for which references are used in a normal, non-distributed object-oriented program.

During the execution of an object-oriented program, an object may bring another into existence by invoking a CREATE method through one of its instance variables. A reference so created will be termed an *ingenerate* (i.e. self-generated) reference of the *creator* object – that is, the object which owns the instance variable and invokes the CREATE 'method'. Not all references used by an object are ingenerate, however. Others may be *imported* from an anonymous client object as an argument of a method call or from a server object identified by a previously imported reference.

During the execution of a program, therefore, the references stored by the instance variables of an object may be divided into two distinct categories:

Ingenerate references – created explicitly by the object through invocation of CREATE operations,

Imported references – not created explicitly by the object but received as parameters of method calls during interaction with other objects.

References of the first kind are used in two distinct scenarios. Either the ingenerate reference:

- is *never* passed to an object identified by an imported reference. In this situation the referenced object may legitimately be regarded as a completely *private* object 'owned' by its creator and used as a *component* in its construction (Goldsack and Atkinson, 1989). An example of such an object is the QUEUE component of a FORWARDER (6.10) object. This is an object used merely in the construction of FORWARDER objects, and need never be referenced by any other object in the system. Used in this way, a reference defines the analogue of the 'include' relationship in HOOD (1987).

- *is* deliberately passed to objects identified by imported references. This scenario is used commonly in producer/consumer situations in which a producer builds objects for use by another. An example is the PRODUCT_DESCRIPTOR (3.4) objects created by the CENTRAL_CONTROLLER (6.9). Immediately after generating such an object and filling its fields through interaction with the user, the CENTRAL_CONTROLLER object passes its reference to a FORWARDER (6.10) object before proceeding to generate another product descriptor. The PRODUCT_DESCRIPTOR objects of the CENTRAL_CONTROLLER cannot, therefore, be regarded as private components because they are designed specifically to have their reference exported. Conceptually, it is probably better to think of the whole PRODUCT_DESCRIPTOR ob-

ject, rather than merely the reference, as being passed in the FOR-
WARD transaction since the CENTRAL_CONTROLLER immediately creates a new PRODUCT_DESCRIPTOR object and relinquishes visibility of
the old one.

Imported references of the second kind enable objects to share access to
other objects in the system and are thus essential for configuring useful
concurrent systems such as that described by SUPERMARKET (6.15) in the
last chapter. FORWARDER (6.10) and CHECKOUT_POINT objects, for example, possess instance variables which store imported references facilitating
the sharing of the DATA_BASE (5.15) object. Such instance variables are
analogous to the *ports* of languages like CONIC, since they act as an indirect name for an external service. Imported references of this form define
the analogue of the 'use' relationship in HOOD (1987).

Having identified these three different ways of using references in normal object-oriented programming, it is possible to state more precisely what
criteria an object must satisfy in order to qualify as a virtual node:

- A virtual node object should never pass an ingenerate reference to an
  object identified by an imported reference.

Essentially, this means that scenarios of the second kind, exemplified by
the exchange of PRODUCT_DESCRIPTOR objects in the supermarket control
system, are not permissible for virtual node objects. Such objects may possess and manipulate private objects in a completely unconstrained fashion
and may possess and exchange references to other virtual node objects, but
they are *not* permitted to exchange ingenerate references.

7.3.1   Instance variable categories

Although 'typed' object-oriented languages, such as DRAGOON and Eiffel,
permit instance variables to refer only to subclasses of their static type, no
restrictions are placed on the 'locality' of the objects to which they refer. In
other words, during the execution of a program any instance variable of an
object can alternatively refer to ingenerate or imported references because,
apart from the typing rules, there are no constraints on assignments to
instance variables. Ensuring that the criteria laid down above are satisfied,
therefore, is a difficult 'bookingkeeping' task analogous to the problems of
programming in untyped languages.

To overcome this problem it is helpful when building virtual node
objects to differentiate instance variables referring to the different kinds of
object identified above and ensure that no assignments take place between
them. Since imported references are analogous to ports in traditional distributed programming languages, as mentioned earlier, it seems sensible to
call instance variables designed to contain such references 'port' variables.

Private objects, on the other hand, constitute part of the state of the creator object, and so it seems reasonable to term instance variables intended to refer to such objects 'state' variables. In the same way that 'port' variables may contain only imported references, 'state' variables contain only ingenerate references.

7.3.2 Method categories

Prohibiting assignments between 'port' variables and 'state' variables is not actually sufficient to ensure that they will always contain the intended kind of reference, however. References may be assigned to instance variables not only by direct assignment statements but also via method call parameters. For complete security, therefore, it is also necessary to identify two different categories of methods.

Since it is only methods that have parameters of a reference type (i.e. a class or access type) that may cause the illegal passing of references, such methods will be termed *unsafe*. Methods with no parameters, or merely parameters of static data types, will correspondingly be termed *safe*.

The final constraints placed on the structure of virtual node objects to ensure a strict separation of the different kinds of references are that the unsafe methods of a class must never manipulate its *state* variables and, conversely, *state* variables must never be supplied as actual parameters of methods called through *port* variables. In effect, the only action an unsafe method of a virtual node object may perform with arguments of reference types is to assign them to the object's port variables. This is illustrated by the ASSIGN_DATA_BASE method of the class FORWARDER (6.10). Such methods, therefore, serve as the mechanism for controlling the 'configuration' of a system of interacting distributed objects.

7.3.3 Virtual node construction rules

Using the terminology introduced above, the guidelines for the construction of virtual node objects can be summarized as follows:

Definitions

- Instance variables should be divided into two categories – 'state' variables and 'port' variables.

- Methods should be divided into two categories – 'safe' methods which possess no parameters of a class or access type, and 'unsafe' methods which do possess parameters of such a (reference) type.

Rule on assignment

- There should be no assignment between state variables and port variables – these should remain completely independent.

Rule on method calls

- A state variable may not be supplied as an actual parameter of a method invoked through a port variable, and a port variable may not be supplied as an actual parameter of a method invoked through a state variable.

Rule on unsafe method bodies

- The body of an unsafe method may not name the state variables of the object.

These rules apply to assignments and method calls appearing directly in the thread or methods of the object concerned and do not extend to subprograms which they may invoke, whether they are defined internally or imported from a template package. It is possible that such a subprogram may surreptitiously assign a reference to the wrong kind of variable. To make the rules completely watertight, therefore, it is necessary to extend the idea of port and state variables to the formal (class) parameters of subprograms called by a virtual node object. The guidelines are therefore completed by the following rules:

Definition

- Like the instance variables in the body of a virtual node class, formal subprogram parameters of a class type should also be divided into the categories – 'state' and 'port' parameters – and should adhere to the same rules.

Rule on parameter matching

- All 'state' formal parameters can only be matched to a 'state' actual parameter, and vice versa.

Rule on functions

- The value returned by a function which has 'mixed' formal parameters (i.e. both 'state' and 'port' parameters) cannot be assigned to an instance variable or used as an actual parameter in a subprogram call, but may be used to call a method.

The basic goal of these rules is to ensure that *virtual node* objects do not communicate by means of reference passing. What they essentially provide, therefore, is a concrete notion of 'locality' in an object-oriented system. Private objects, identified by state variables, can reasonably be regarded as 'internal' to, or encapsulated within, a virtual node object, since the rules guarantee that no other virtual node will be able to reference them. Similarly, objects referenced by port variables are generated elsewhere and can reasonably be regarded as 'external' objects. These construction rules, therefore, serve to enforce the tight encapsulation boundaries which the reference semantics of object-oriented languages undermine.

It is stressed, however, that the only objects which need such strong encapsulation boundaries, and thus need to be designed according to these rules, are those intended to be potentially distributable (i.e. virtual nodes). Objects intended to serve only as components in the construction of others may be designed in the usual way with no restrictions. Moreover, although virtual node objects are potentially distributable, this does prohibit them from also being used as normal components in the construction of other objects.

The purpose of the last rule is to allow the result of a function to be either an imported or ingenerate reference, so that a method call may be bound dynamically to either a remote or local object. This is an important facility for programming mode changes in which a virtual node object may switch to using the (possibly degraded) services of an internal object should an external server break down, or some other circumstance arise.

At present there are no syntactic constructs in DRAGOON to enforce these rules – they are merely guidelines which programmers should follow to be confident before run-time that no attempt is made to export an ingenerate reference. The DRAGOON run-time system has no problem in detecting when such an attempt is made and raises the exception REMOTE_ERROR to indicate that the virtual node construction rules have been broken.

These constraints on the structure of virtual nodes do sacrifice some of the power of the object-oriented programming paradigm across virtual node boundaries. In particular, it is not possible to take advantage of polymorphism over a network. However, this cannot be avoided if the overheads of network communication are to be contained. The important point is that inheritance can be used without restriction in the construction of virtual nodes, since in DRAGOON it is a static mechanism in which all code sharing is resolved at compile time.

7.4   Virtual nodes in the supermarket control system

Although it is certainly possible to control the devices of the supermarket control system from a single centralized program, such as an instance of

SUPERMARKET (6.15), this system clearly lends itself well to implementation as a distributed system with the central controller, database, checkout points and possibly forwarders residing on separate machines. However, as currently defined, none of these classes satisfies the criteria outlined in the previous section as necessary to serve as virtual nodes for distribution because they exchange references to product descriptor objects. To qualify as virtual nodes, objects are not permitted to communicate by passing references or to contain references to other objects that are not virtual nodes. It is not possible, therefore, to build a distributed version of the supermarket system from the current versions of the classes. For this to be possible, the potentially distributed classes should have been designed from the beginning to conform to the virtual node construction rules.

Two main changes must be made to the current implementation of the classes in the supermarket system to make them conform to these rules. The first is to arrange for the information stored in product descriptor objects to be transferred around the system as static data values rather than as object references. The second is to change the way in which the 'fuse rating' associated with electrical descriptors is represented. At present the required rating is specified by means of a reference to the descriptor of the actual fuse product that is needed. However, this is not acceptable when the product descriptor concerned may reside on a separate machine. This property of electrical products, therefore, needs to be represented as an attribute of a simple enumeration type like all the others.

Consider the problem of adding new PRODUCT_DESCRIPTOR (3.4) objects to the database. If the database is to be a virtual node, it is not possible to do this by passing a PRODUCT_DESCRIPTOR reference as a parameter of a single ADD method. Instead the attributes of the objects must be transferred to the database as data values, either individually or collected together into a record.

7.4.1   Transferring object state

If a record is used to transfer the entire state of an object as one (composite) value, the record type must be defined in a template package which is 'withed' by the database and central controller (the producer of the data). Since the data corresponding to different kinds of product descriptor varies, variant records are the most appropriate kind of record to use:

```
package DESCRIPTOR is                                         (7.1)

    type FUSE_RATING is (THREE_AMP, FIVE_AMP, THIRTEEN_AMP);

    type STATE (FORM : PRODUCT_TYPE) is record
                                -- PRODUCT_TYPE defined in (3.1)
        INTERNAL_BAR_CODE : PRODUCT.CODE_NUMBER;
        INTERNAL_PRICE : PRODUCT.VALUE;
        INTERNAL_STOCK_LEVEL : PRODUCT.STOCK_NUMBER;
```

```
        INTERNAL_LABEL : PRODUCT.LABEL;
        case FORM is
           when BASIC =>
              null;
           when ELECTRICAL =>
              INTERNAL_FUSE : FUSE_RATING;
           when PERISHABLE =>
              INTERNAL_DATE : SIMPLE_CALENDAR.DATE;
        end case;
     end record;
  end DESCRIPTOR;
```

The advantage of this approach is that the product descriptor classes can be provided with methods which return 'state' records of type DESCRIPTOR.STATE, and with CREATE methods which take records of this type and use them to initialize new objects. The impact on the communicating virtual node clients is therefore minimal.

Defining a record of this kind is only one step away from defining a full Ada abstract data type to represent the various product descriptors in the system, and the question arises as to whether it is necessary to introduce classes to model them at all. This depends on whether or not the programmer wishes to take advantage of polymorphism and dynamic binding within the bodies of virtual node classes. If not, then the abstract data type view is appropriate. Since it is a trivial task to build a class representation from the abstract data type view, one approach to designing distributed systems in DRAGOON is to provide both representations for abstractions which are likely to be transferred between virtual nodes.

7.4.2   Transferring attribute values

Instead of defining a record type to store the entire state of a product descriptor in a single data structure, the state can be transferred in terms of the individual attribute values. There are two ways in which this can be achieved; either by providing a separate method for each attribute, or by a single method with an argument for each attribute. Although the overloading facility of DRAGOON permits all the different methods needed in the first approach to be given the same name, the second is clearly preferable because it is simpler and carries fewer invocation overheads.

The main problem in the second approach is to retain some of the flexibility that was possible when the full object-oriented features of the language could be used. In the original version of the class DATA_BASE (5.15), a single ADD method was sufficient to insert all the different kinds of product descriptor into the database because the ELECTRICAL_DESCRIPTOR (3.8) and PERISHABLE_DESCRIPTOR (3.6) are subclasses of PRODUCT_DESCRIPTOR. Although it is not possible to support polymorphism directly, it is possible to simulate this using DRAGOON's facility for providing method arguments with default values.

Since the bar-code, stock-level, price and label attributes are common to all the different types of descriptor, these are treated as normal parameters of the method without default values. The arguments corresponding to attributes that are not common, on the other hand, such as the sell-by-date and fuse rating, are provided with default values. This default value indicates to the body of the method that the attribute corresponding to the argument is 'undefined' – that is, not present in the descriptor type denoted by the current call.

Because the method argument must have the same type as the corresponding attribute, this type must contain a value capable of representing this 'undefined' state. It is possible in some cases for a normal value of the type, such as a past date, to satisfy this requirement. In general, however, it is preferable to make explicit provision for this value in the definition of attribute types. The package SIMPLE_CALENDAR (3.3), for example, which defines the type of the date attribute of perishable products (as a private data type) could provide an additional function, UNDEFINED say, which would return this special value. Similarly, the enumeration type which is now needed to represent the fuse-rating attribute of electrical products could contain a special literal for this value:

```
package FUSE is                                                      (7.2)
      type RATING is (THREE_AMP, FIVE_AMP, THIRTEEN_AMP, UNDEFINED);
   end FUSE;
```

Uisng this approach a version of the database conforming to the virtual node construction rules would have an ADD method of the form:

```
procedure ADD (PRICE : in PRODUCT.VALUE;
      BAR_CODE : in PRODUCT.CODE_NUMBER;
      STOCK_LEVEL : in PRODUCT.STOCK_NUMBER;
      LABEL : in PRODUCT.LABEL;
      SELL_BY_DATE : in SIMPLE_CALENDAR.DATE :=
                                    SIMPLE_CALENDAR.UNDEFINED;
      REQUIRED_FUSE : in FUSE.RATING := UNDEFINED);
```

Using these default values it is possible for the body of the ADD method to 'rebuild' a PRODUCT_DESCRIPTOR object of the same form as that whose reference would have been supplied directly in the original version:

$$\vdots$$

```
PROD : PRODUCT_DESCRIPTOR;                                            (7.3)
   PERISH : PERISHABLE_DESCRIPTOR;
   ELEC : ELECTRICAL_DESCRIPTOR;
```

$$\vdots$$

```
begin
    if SELL_BY_DATE = UNDEFINED then
        if REQUIRED_FUSE = UNDEFINED then
            PROD.CREATE;
        else
            ELEC.CREATE;
            ELEC.SET_FUSE_TO(REQUIRED_FUSE);
            PROD := ELEC;
        end if;
    else
        PERISH.CREATE;
        PERISH.SET_SELL_BY_TO(SELL_BY_DATE);
        PROD := PERISH;
    end if;
    PROD.SET_BAR_CODE_TO(BAR_CODE);
    PROD.SET_PRICE_TO(PRICE);
    PROD.SET_STOCK_TO(STOCK_LEVEL);
    PROD.SET_LABEL_TO(LABEL);
```

$$\vdots$$

Clearly, it is possible for the FORWARDER object (6.10) responsible for inserting new product descriptors into the database to 'decompose' a PRODUCT_DESCRIPTOR (3.4) object in a precisely analogous, but reverse fashion, and to supply its individual attributes as actual parameters of this ADD method. Since the methods of virtual node classes can 'decompose' and 'reproduce' objects in this way, the fact that it is not references but data values that are communicated can be hidden from the rest of the implementation. Essentially, the programmer is explicitly coding the 'deep copy' semantics of parameter passing identified earlier as one possible strategy for avoiding the exchange of references.

Although it would certainly be possible for the DRAGOON implementation to generate this code implicitly for simple objects such as product descriptors, the DRAGOON programmer is required to program this explicitly, since this ensures that he/she is aware of the overheads involved and can be sure that only sensibly sized objects are transferred.

Key points

Embedded systems are often implemented as loosely coupled distributed systems composed of networks of independent processors. The term 'loosely coupled' is used to indicate that the processors are connected by relatively low bandwidth communication links rather than by shared memory.

Most projects employing features of the object-oriented paradigm in distributed systems are concerned with organizing software in a *distributed environment*. DRAGOON, in contrast, is interested in adopting an object-oriented approach to the *development* of applications software.

As far as the development of application software is concerned, the main difference between loosely coupled distributed systems and uniprocessor systems is the overhead of inter-processor communication.

In real-time systems it is important that the overhead of remote communication be made visible and minimized.

One approach which is becoming popular for structuring applications software for potential distribution is the so-called *'virtual node'* approach. In this approach, software is designed in terms of atomic units of distribution known as virtual nodes. Virtual nodes must communicate in terms of a message-based protocol rather than through shared memory.

Objects and/or classes of the form supported in object-oriented languages satisfy all of the requirements of virtual nodes except the most important. Because of the reference semantics used to identify objects, they fail to guarantee the tight encapsulation of their internal data structures.

In order to support the virtual node approach to software design in an object-oriented language it is necessary to support *reference-free* communication between objects.

Although an approach based on the 'deep copying' of objects is possible, the most practical solution is to arrange for objects to be able to communicate by exchanging data values rather than references. DRAGOON supports such an approach as a result of its adoption of a mixed paradigm.

To ensure that classes whose instances may potentially be executed independently on separate machines (so-called virtual node classes) communicate only by passing data values, certain constraints are placed on the way in which they may be designed.

In order to define the design rule applying to virtual node classes, it is necessary to identify two categories of references – *ingenerate* and *imported* – two corresponding categories of instances variables – *state* and *port* – and two categories of methods – *safe* and *unsafe.*

The current version of DRAGOON provides no syntactic support for these design rules. If an attempt is made, at run-time, to transmit an internal object reference to a remote site the exception REMOTE_ERROR is raised.

The components of the supermarket control system developed in the previous chapters are not suitable for building a distributed version of the system because they communicate by exchanging object references.

There are two basic approaches for transmitting the state of objects between remote virtual node objects. One is to define a record type that can hold the values of all the attributes of an object. The other is to transmit the values of the attributes independently.

Declaring a record type to store the states of instances of a class is one step away from defining a complete abstract data type for the corresponding data abstraction. Since a class can be easily defined using the facilities of the corresponding abstract data type, a useful design method may be to define both a class and an abstract data type representation of data abstractions which may need to be communicated between virtual node objects.

Chapter 8
System Configuration

The previous chapter described the structure of potentially distributable virtual nodes in DRAGOON, and discussed how the classes in the supermarket system should be designed to satisfy the necessary conditions. Adherence to these rules, however, does not automatically mean that instances of the classes can be distributed among the nodes of a network for execution. Objects that are able to execute independently on network machines possess important properties that are not captured in the virtual node class definition alone. This chapter describes the way in which the appropriate kind of objects are created in DRAGOON.

8.1   Executing programs

There are two basic models by which code written in a high-level language may be executed. The code can either be *interpreted*, in which case small segments, usually individual lines, are executed directly by the processing system and put into immediate effect; or the code can be *compiled*, in which case it must first be translated into a different form before execution is possible. Traditionally, these approaches have tended to be regarded as alternatives, since the 'compilation' process usually translates the 'source' code directly into the machine code of the target computer. However, execution of machine code at this level is essentially just interpretation performed directly by the hardware. It can be argued, therefore, that there is an interpretation phase in all execution strategies. The main factor distinguishing the various approaches is how much of the required processing is performed *before* execution (i.e. interpretation) time in one or more 'compilation' steps. Languages that are primarily interested in run-time efficiency, such as those intended for embedded systems, are implemented in a way which maximizes the work performed in the 'compilation' phase, and are therefore sometimes termed 'compiled' languages.

The precise meaning attached to the term 'compilation', however, differs somewhat depending on the exact nature of the language and development system used. In languages such as Ada and Modula, which permit applications software to be developed as a set of separate modules, 'compilation' describes the act of submitting a new module to the 'compilation system' so that, if error free, it may be added to the library of accepted modules. Compilation in this sense, therefore, is largely concerned with type checking and library management. A certain amount of translation may take place at this stage, but the production of an executable software module requires at least one additional step, typically termed 'linking', which collects together the relevant components and combines them into an executable form. For the present discussion, the exact mechanics of translating source modules into executable form are not important. What is important is that in so-called 'compiled' languages, such as DRAGOON, at least one non-trivial (i.e. time-consuming) translation step is required before code execution is possible.

8.1.1   The 'main program' concept

Although a language may permit many different types of module to be 'compiled', in the above sense, most languages only recognize one construct, usually termed the 'main program', as being translatable by the compilation system into an *executable* module. Pascal, for example, has an explicit 'program' construct which conceptually encapsulates all other declarations, while in Ada any parameterless library *subprogram* may be used as a main program. Compiled object-oriented languages, on the other hand, usually use library classes to serve as main programs.

In languages such as these which were not designed specifically for the purpose of distribution, the constructs representing main programs were designed under the assumption that a *single* program would provide the entire functionality of a given system – in other words, that every program executes completely independently of others. In the case of Ada, which had support for concurrency as one of its main design aims, this assumption required the designers to provide elaborate concurrency mechanisms that are orthogonal to the 'main program' concept. A single Ada program, therefore, may contain multiple concurrent tasks executing under the control of a single program's multi-tasking kernel.

This 'single-program' assumption is not valid in distributed systems, however, where the software modules allocated to individual nodes must clearly be 'compiled' modules capable of independent execution (Atkinson and Di Maio, 1989). In operating system terminology, such modules are sometimes referred to as 'heavyweight' processes, since they carry with them all the special run-time support required by constructs of the language used to write the source code. In contrast, processes (or objects) that exist within the bounds of such a heavyweight process, such as tasks in an Ada program, are termed 'lightweight' processes since they carry no dedicated run-time support but execute under the control of the encapsulating heavyweight process.

Because a distributed system is necessarily composed of multiple, interacting *heavyweight* processes (or objects), the 'single main program' assumption lies at the heart of Ada's incompatibility with distribution. The language does not recognize tasks, the in-built units of concurrency, as being executable outside the context of a main program (in fact, it does not even permit them to be library units), and consequently they cannot easily be used as units of distribution. The only way of doing so depends on viewing the entire distributed applications software as a single 'distributed' Ada program (Burns *et al*, 1985), but as well as being difficult to support, this conflicts with the principle of separating the programming and configuration phases outlined in the previous chapter.

In contrast, main programs, which are the Ada abstractions designed to execute independently, are not able to communicate using mechanisms of the language. Communication between Ada programs can only be achieved using the facilities of the host operating system, in the style of the 'operating system' approach introduced earlier. A programmer adopting this approach must consequently handle two levels of concurrency; one at the level of 'lightweight' tasks 'internal' to an Ada program and one at the level of 'heavyweight' processes communicating using facilities 'external' to a program (Atkinson *et al*, 1990). This situation runs directly against the goals of reuse, since a component designed according to one concurrency model cannot later be reused in the other.

Consider the supermarket control system, for example. To build a version of the system in Ada to execute within the bounds of a single program, the main components (i.e. database, central controller and checkout points) would have to be implemented as (lightweight) tasks. To build a distributable version, however, they would have to be implemented as Ada programs communicating using the message passing facilities of the target system. Not only is the programmer therefore forced to handle two different levels of concurrency, but must decide from the earliest stage of system design which model to pursue. This is much worse than having to decide whether a component should be modelled as a virtual node or not, since in this case the programmer must only decide whether a class is to be a *potentially* distributable object. Deciding whether to structure a component according to the 'internal' or 'external' concurrency model, however, completely rules out its use in the other way.

Ada is by no means the only language that provides a different model for heavyweight and lightweight processes. Most conventional languages designed without regard for distribution but with support for concurrency, such as Modula 2, Simula and CLU (Liskov *et al*, 1981), fall into the same category. Even languages designed to support distribution, such as Argus (Liskov, 1982) and EPL (Almes *et al*, 1985), provide different models of concurrency for lightweight and heavyweight processes (respectively 'CLU clusters' and 'Euclid data structures' versus 'Guardians' and 'Eden objects') (Black *et al*, 1987).

8.1.2 'Heavyweight' and 'lightweight' objects

To enable software components to be reused as either 'lightweight' or 'heavyweight' objects irrespective of their locations or encapsulation within other components, it is necessary to support a uniform concurrency model.   This is demonstrated by many of the recently defined language/environments for developing distributed software such as CONIC (Kramer and Magee, 1985) and Emerald (Black *et al*, 1986). In CONIC, for example, the task module is not only the unit of encapsulation for modelling distributable virtual nodes but can also be used to describe concurrency within virtual nodes. Projects such as DIADEM (Atkinson, 1989) have attempted to overcome Ada's lack of symmetry in this respect by using the notion of virtual nodes to provide a uniform approach to concurrency. One of the main aspects of the DIADEM work was the implementation of a 'remote rendezvous mechanism' enabling distributed virtual nodes to communicate using the same rendezvous mechanism as virtual nodes grouped together on a single machine.

Providing a uniform concurrency model in this way, however, creates the new problem of distinguishing between heavyweight and lightweight versions of a component in environments where they coexist. Emerald essentially avoids the problem because all the objects in a system are essentially 'heavyweight' in the sense outlined above, any object in the system being transferable to any machine. As pointed out above, however, this 'uniform object space' model carries with it too many overheads to be generally acceptable in embedded systems. The CONIC and DIADEM systems in a sense avoid the problem as well because they do not handle the generation of 'heavyweight' components within the language used to design their lightweight counterparts. As in most development environments, the task of compiling and linking components to translate them into an executable form is handled by the host operating system in response to command line instructions.

In these systems, therefore, it is necessary to leave the language environment to produce an executable version of a particular component and return again to configure a system. Not only does this lower their 'user friendliness', but also makes it more difficult to distinguish between the many different versions of a component that may be produced.

8.2   Execution support classes

In DRAGOON all the different kinds of components used in a system, whether executable forms for distribution over a network or non-executable

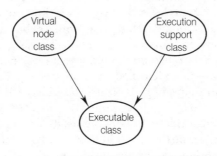

Figure 8.1   Generating executable classes.

forms for use in the construction of others, are represented in the same inheritance hierarchy. This is achieved by using a special form of multiple inheritance to distinguish heavyweight components from their lightweight counterparts (Bayan *et al*, 1989) (Atkinson *et al*, 1990). An executable, or 'heavyweight', version of a normal virtual node class is generated by defining a subclass that also inherits the properties of an appropriate *execution support class*, as illustrated in Figure 8.1. Such a subclass, termed an *executable class*, inherits all the sequential and behavioural properties of the virtual node class in the normal way, but is also empowered to execute on the particular type of machine associated with the execution support class.

Suppose, for example, that a version of the class PROTECTED_DATA-_BASE mentioned in Section 6.7 was required to execute on a VAX under VMS. Such a component would be generated by defining a class that was an heir both of PROTECTED_DATA_BASE and a suitable execution support class:

<pre>
class VAX_EXECUTABLE_DATA_BASE is   (8.1)
      inherits PROTECTED_DATA_BASE, VAX_VMS_EXECUTION_SUPPORT;
end;
</pre>

where VAX_VMS_EXECUTION_SUPPORT is an execution support class with the general form:

<pre>
class VAX_VMS_EXECUTION_SUPPORT is   (8.2)
      introduces LOAD_ONTO (PN : in VAX_VMS_PHYSICAL_NODE);

      :   -- services provided by processes in the VAX/VMS environment
end;
</pre>

Like the behavioural classes of Chapter 6, execution support classes are not classes in the normal sense since they cannot be instantiated independently. Their only function is to serve as parents of executable classes so as to endow them with the quality of executability. Another property they share with behavioural classes is that they have no body. In fact, they cannot even be defined by applications programmers, but are supplied with a DRAGOON development environment as an interface to its (cross) compilation facilities. Executable classes differ from behavioural classes, however, in that they are not identified by a special keyword. Conceptually, executable classes are part of a separate class hierarchy distinct from the application class hierarchy originating at the class APPLICATION_OBJECT.

Execution support classes are distinguishable from normal application classes by the inclusion of the method LOAD_ONTO in their interface. The role of this special method, which appears in the interface of every execution support class, will be described more fully in the next section. Since it is the main distinguishing feature of such classes this name is not available for use in normal application classes.

As well as this special LOAD_ONTO method, execution support classes may export methods representing services provided by processes in the environment they describe. Suppose, for example, that the VMS operating system provided with VAX computers permitted processes under its control to be assigned an execution priority, denoted by an integer value. In the DRAGOON model this priority is an attribute of 'heavyweight' executable objects which may be accessed and updated by external agents. To model this feature, an execution support class for processes in the VAX/VMS environment, such as VAX_VMS_EXECUTION_SUPPORT, would probably export the following additional methods:

$$\vdots$$

```
procedure SET_PRIORITY (P : in POSITIVE);
function CURRENT_PRIORITY return POSITIVE;
```

$$\vdots$$

Submission of the class VAX_EXECUTABLE_DATA_BASE to the compilation system will give rise to a new class which extends the interface of the class PROTECTED_DATA_BASE by the three methods of the execution support class. Moreover, the fact that this class inherits from an execution support class signals that it should not just be inserted into the application library like normal classes, but should be completely translated and linked into an executable module for the appropriate machine – in this case a VAX under VMS. The class VAX_VMS_EXECUTABLE_DATA_BASE, therefore, does not just *describe* the interface of objects intended for execution in a VAX/VMS environment, it *is* an executable module (e.g. relocatable binary) which can be directly loaded on to a VAX and executed. In other words, the executable classes denote modules upon which all the translation steps necessary to facilitate direct execution have been performed. This is not the case with normal classes, on the other hand, which are merely textual templates describing the form of objects and do not actually define objects that can be executed *independently*. Such classes represent 'lightweight' objects which can only be instantiated within the thread of control of 'heavyweight' objects.

This is a very important aspect of the DRAGOON approach to developing distributed systems. In the vast majority of development environments for commercial and industrial software, some form of explicit translation must be performed on high-level code to turn it into a form that can be executed; in the case of distributed systems this takes place between the programming and configuration phases of system building. The programming phase deals with the *description*, in terms of high-level code, of the components to be distributed, while the configuration phase is concerned with actually distributing executable versions of the modules over the network. Few existing systems, however, attempt to handle the transition between these two forms in a uniform way. By capturing the conceptual step of translating a textual template into a directly executable module, DRAGOON permits all aspects of the software development process to be handled within the object-oriented framework and by a single language. This, in turn, permits the many different executable versions of a component to be managed and stored in the same way as other components in the system.

8.3   Physical node objects

The previous sections have outlined how classes should be structured in order to model potentially distributable virtual node objects, and how these can be translated into truly distributable (i.e. executable) objects using execution support classes. In order to build a functioning distributed system, however, it is also necessary to have a way of representing the hardware architecture of the system and the different types of processors that it contains.

There are many different types of machines and processors that could be used to form the nodes of a distributed system, ranging from the largest mainframes to the smallest microprocessors. A network node of the former kind encapsulates extensive hardware and 'systems' software resources providing a wide range of facilities to user processes, while nodes of the latter kind have very little native systems software and offer far fewer facilities. From the point of view of the application processes, however, the distinction between which services of the machine they are running on are provided by the hardware and which by the systems software is irrelevant. What is important is the interface to the range of services provided by the machine and the type of processes that it can execute. As far as configuring distributed systems is concerned, therefore, all the various nodes in the system can simply be regarded as *abstract processing machines*, which make a set of services available to application processes and are able to run suitable (i.e. correctly compiled) executable objects.

To remain faithful to the goal of modelling all aspects of system construction within a uniform object-oriented framework, these abstract processing elements are represented in DRAGOON as special *physical node* classes, which present the services offered by the machine as methods. Assuming that the communications system provides full, logical interconnection between the nodes of a network, a particular network architecture is described by a set of instances of such physical node classes.

A physical node class representing the VAX/VMS abstract machine, for example, on which instances of the VAX_EXECUTABLE_DATA_BASE (8.1) class are intended to run, would have a specification of the form:

```
class VAX_VMS_PHYSICAL_NODE is                          (8.3)
    introduces ACTIVATE (P : in VAX_VMS_EXECUTION_SUPPORT);
        ⋮
                            -- services provided by VAX/VMS machines
    end;
```

As this class illustrates, the structure of such classes is, not accidently, very similar to that of execution support classes. Like such classes, physical node classes conceptually reside in another special class hierarchy and are distinguished by inclusion of the special method ACTIVATE in their interface. Moreover, like execution support classes they usually export an additional set of methods, which in the case of physical node classes represent the services provided by the corresponding abstract machine type for use by the executable objects. These services correspond to what are often called 'system calls' in normal programming parlance. A typical example is a call to the 'system clock'. Other examples include the opening of communication ports and interaction with device drivers.

Assuming that VAX/VMS machines permit application processes to ascertain the current time from the system clock, and perhaps determine the total number of currently active processes, methods of the following form would appear in the interface of VAX_VMS_PHYSICAL_NODE in addition to ACTIVATE:

```
        ⋮

    function CLOCK return TIME;
    function ACTIVE_PROCESSES return NATURAL;

        ⋮
```

8.4   Software and hardware system components

Using execution support and physical node classes of the form introduced in the previous sections it is possible to represent all the different kinds of hardware and software components that need to be manipulated in the configuration phase in order to construct complete distributed systems. The processors in the target network are modelled by instances of physical node classes, while the software modules distributed among them for execution are represented by instances of executable classes.

Suppose, for example, that a distributed system was required in which three software modules were distributed over a network of two VAX/VMS machines. The two VAXes would be represented by instances of the class VAX_VMS_PHYSICAL_NODE (8.3), referenced by instance variables VAX_A and VAX_B, say:

```
      ⋮

   VAX_A, VAX_B : VAX_VMS_PHYSICAL_NODE;

      ⋮
```

while the software modules would be represented as instances of subclasses of VAX_VMS_EXECUTION_SUPPORT (8.2), identified by instance variables EXE_1, EXE_2 and EXE_3, say. Except in the extremely unlikely circumstance in which all three of the modules were required to have precisely the same functionality, these will refer to descendants of different application classes.

Having introduced the various software and hardware components and a means of identifying them, the final stage in system construction is to indicate how the software modules are to be distributed over the machines in the network. This is where the special methods LOAD_ONTO and ACTIVATE described earlier come into play. Together they perform all the initialization actions needed to prepare a given executable object for execution on a given physical node object.

Executable objects generated by invocation of the CREATE method are conceptually brought into existence on the machine on which the CREATE method is executed. Unless this is the required location for the object, it must then be moved to the appropriate site in the network by means of the LOAD_ONTO method exported in its interface. Suppose, for example, that the object generated by invocation of CREATE through EXE_1 was generated on VAX_A but was actually required to execute on VAX_B. The object would be moved to this machine by invoking its LOAD_ONTO method with VAX_B as the argument:

```
      ⋮

   EXE_1.LOAD_ONTO(VAX_B);
```

This has the effect of transferring the object referenced by EXE_1 to the machine VAX_B. Simply transferring the relocatable binary code[1] represented by the object into the memory of the target machine, however, does not make it a functioning component of the distributed system. To turn the *executable* object into an *executing* object capable of responding to method calls, the machine on which it is intended to run must be made aware of its existence so that it can perform the steps necessary to begin its execution. This is achieved by means of the ACTIVATE method exported by physical node objects.

To activate the executable object EXE_1 just transferred to VAX_B, for example, the ACTIVATE method of VAX_B has to be invoked with parameter EXE_1:

```
                    ⋮

    VAX_B.ACTIVATE(EXE_1);

                    ⋮
```

In the same way that the START method starts the *thread* of an active object, invocation of the ACTIVATE method starts the execution, or *elaboration* in Ada terminology, of the entire *object* supplied as its argument. The ACTIVATE method is, in a sense, therefore, the analogue of the START method for 'heavyweight' processes. An important difference, however, is that the ACTIVATE method belongs to the machine responsible for running the object while the START method belongs to the active object itself.

Naturally, if an executable object is derived from an active object (i.e. its 'application' parent is an active class), then after activation of the object by the ACTIVATE method it is also necessary to start the thread by the START method in the normal way.

Together with the CREATE and START methods of normal classes, the LOAD_ONTO and ACTIVATE methods of executable and physical node classes provide all the facilities required to generate and execute DRAGOON systems – both distributed and non-distributed. In general, to bring about the execution of an executable object referenced by the variable EXE on a physical node referenced by the variable P_N, the following method calls must be issued:

```
                    ⋮

    EXE.CREATE;                       -- brings the object into existence
    EXE.LOAD_ONTO(P_N);        -- moves it to the appropriate execution site
    P_N.ACTIVATE(EXE);                -- begins execution of the object
    EXE.START;                                 -- starts the thread
```

---

[1] And possibly initialization data supplied as parameters to the CREATE operation.

Moreover, invocation of these methods must occur in this order. An attempt to execute any of the methods before the preceding operation has been performed will generally result in the raising of an exception. It is not possible, for example, to 'load' an object that has not been 'created', to 'activate' an object on a machine on to which it has not been 'loaded' or to 'start' the thread of an object that has not yet been 'activated' (because it is not actually executing). There are two cases in which certain operations in this sequence need not be performed, however. If the object is passive it is clearly not necessary to invoke the START method, and if an object is to be executed on the machine on which it was created it is not necessary to invoke the LOAD_ONTO method.

From the point of view of the execution model, a non-distributed system is simply viewed as a trivial uninode network composed of one executable object running on one physical node object. In principle, all the operations outlined above still have to be performed, but clearly some of them are redundant in this case and so may not have to be issued in practice. This depends on the user interface offered by the execution environment.

The question of *who*, or *what*, actually performs these variable declarations and method invocations will be considered in Section 8.6. First it is necessary to examine in more detail the relationship of the ACTIVATE and LOAD_ONTO methods.

8.4.1   Corresponding system classes

The ACTIVATE and LOAD_ONTO methods of physical node and executable objects perform complementary roles. Their main role is to perform the initialization actions needed to prepare an executable object for execution. However, they also play an important role in providing the visibility necessary for the interaction between the hardware and software to be viewed as a form of clientship. The ACTIVATE method of a physical node object is used to provide it with 'references' to the executable objects allocated to it for execution while the LOAD_ONTO method of an executable object is used to supply it with a reference to the physical node object on which it has been allocated for execution. When combined with the normal typing rules of the language, this 'clientship' view of software and hardware dependency provides an elegant means of capturing the different kinds of processors that may exist in heterogeneous networks and the different kinds of software modules that may execute on them.

One of the most basic principles of software development using compiler technology is that an executable module produced by a compilation system is targeted to one particular type of machine and cannot be executed on another type with a different architecture or systems software. Conversely, a given computer can only execute software modules specifically targeted to that type of machine.

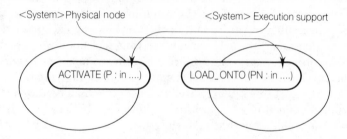

Figure 8.2   Canonical class pairs.

This fundamental principle is neatly captured in DRAGOON using executable and physical node classes by ensuring that every physical node class has a corresponding execution support class, and vice versa. This is the case with VAX_VMS_EXECUTION_SUPPORT (8.2) and VAX_VMS_PHYSICAL_NODE (8.3) classes introduced earlier. The former captures the qualities that an application class must inherit in order to be able to execute on a VAX/VMS machine while the latter defines the properties of the machines acting as processors for such objects.

For each different kind of processor architecture supported by the DRAGOON (cross) compilation system there is at least one pair of associated execution support and physical node classes. Moreover, as illustrated in Figure 8.2, the parameter type of the physical node class's ACTIVATE method is the corresponding execution support class, while the parameter type of the execution support class's LOAD_ONTO method is the corresponding physical node object. The normal typing rules of DRAGOON, therefore, ensure the correct match of executable objects to physical node classes. In the case of a VAX/VMS system, for example, it is only possible to load descendants of VAX_VMS_EXECUTION_SUPPORT on to VAX_VMS_PHYSICAL_NODE objects, and vice versa. In a heterogeneous network, in which there is a number of different types of processor, and hence executable objects, this prohibits inappropriate allocation of software modules to physical nodes.

The careful reader will notice that it is not actually possible to generate classes with this relationship in normal user-defined DRAGOON programs because of the mutual dependence of their interfaces. Not only are the classes clients of each other but also this dependency is expressed in their interfaces since each uses the other as a method parameter type. Both classes, therefore, rely on the prior compilation of the other!

Such mutual dependencies are not supported for normal DRAGOON classes. It is important to remember, however, that physical node and execution support classes are not normal application classes that may be defined by the user, but predefined classes supplied with a DRAGOON

environment. Although they are known to the DRAGOON compilation
system, therefore, and exist in the library of classes reachable by the applications programmer, they do not have to be 'compiled' as such in the
normal way. The role of these classes is in fact to provide an interface
to the various possible system architectures supported by the DRAGOON
environment and compilation system.

8.5   System calls and interrupts

The correspondence of physical node classes to execution support classes
need not necessarily be a one-to-one relationship. In general, there may be
many specialized versions of execution support and physical node classes
for a basic machine architecture. In the case of execution support classes
these would correspond to different kinds of processes supported in a given
system or of processes in a specialized version of the system, while in the
case of physical node classes these correspond to different versions of the
basic processor type that extend or modify the set of operations made
available to the executable objects.

In DRAGOON these different specialized versions are defined as descendants of the most simple, or *canonical*, versions of the physical node
and execution support classes. For every type of machine architecture supported by the DRAGOON compilation system there must be at least a
canonical pair which defines the LOAD_ONTO and ACTIVATE methods. The
classes illustrated in Figure 8.2 represent a canonical pair, therefore. The
specialized descendants of these classes inherit the LOAD_ONTO and ACTI-
VATE methods and so do not need to redefine them explicitly.

8.5.1   Device drivers

Machines connected to particular types of devices are commonly modelled
as subclasses of a canonical physical node class. Suppose, for example, that
one of the VAXes in the network was connected to a laser printer. Although
this VAX provides the same basic facilities as other VAXes in the network
and can only execute objects that have inherited the appropriate execution
support, it also provides the additional set of operations associated with a
laser printer. This particular machine in the network, therefore, is modelled
by an instance of a subclass of VAX_VMS_EXECUTION_SUPPORT (the canonical
physical node class) whose interface has been extended by the appropriate
operations.

Another good example of where this facility would be needed is in
the construction of the checkout points used in a distributed version of the
central control system. It is unlikely that the machines used to provide
local processing power at the many checkout points in the store will be

VAXes, but rather small dedicated microprocessors. Moreover, these microprocessors are not only 'attached' to the cash register device which they are responsible for controlling but are completely 'embedded' within them. The normal set of facilities provided by the embedded microprocessor type will therefore be extended by operations used to control the cash register hardware.

A typical example of such an operation is the opening of the till which stores the money. A common feature of many cash registers is that the till cannot be opened until the total bill of a customer has been calculated, at which point it is opened automatically. To handle this interaction between software and hardware in DRAGOON it is necessary to define the OPEN_TILL operation as a method of the physical node class for cash registers.

Suppose for the sake of argument that the cash registers chosen for a particular version of the supermarket system were based on Motorola 68000 microprocessors with a canonical physical node class of the form:

```
class MC_68000_PHYSICAL_NODE is                                    (8.4)
    introduces
        procedure ACTIVATE (P : in MC_68000_ EXECUTION_SUPPORT);
        ⋮
                            -- facilities provided by MC68000 processors
        ⋮
    end MC_68000_PHYSICAL_NODE;
```

where MC_68000_EXECUTION_SUPPORT is the corresponding canonical execution support class. The physical node class describing cash registers whose facilities are extended by those of the encapsulating devices would thus be modelled as a subclass of MC_68000_PHYSICAL_NODE. This extends its interface with the additional methods necessary for controlling the register hardware, such as OPEN_TILL and PRINT_BILL:

```
class CASH_REGISTER_PHYSICAL_NODE is                                (8.5)
    inherits MC_68000_PHYSICAL_NODE;
    introduces
        procedure OPEN_TILL;
        procedure PRINT_BILL;
        ⋮
                    -- other operations provided by the cash register hardware
    end CASH_REGISTER_PHYSICAL_NODE;
```

Objects executing on an instance of this class can control the associated device directly by invoking the additional methods exported in the interface. Consider the checkout point objects, for example. While they are calculating customer bills, such objects interact intensely with the database in order to establish the price of the products selected. Once it has calculated a bill, however, a checkout point object needs to arrange for the till of the cash register it is controlling to be opened ready for payment. To do this it needs to be a *client* of the CASH_REGISTER_PHYSICAL_NODE object on which it is intended to run. The instruction to open the till can thus be issued simply by invoking the corresponding method in the normal way. The body of CHECKOUT_POINT, the class defining the checkout point objects, would thus contain declarations and statements of the following form:

```
class body CHECKOUT_POINT is                                    (8.6)

    ⋮

    CR : CASH_REGISTER_PHYSICAL_NODE;

    ⋮

thread

    ⋮

    CR.OPEN_TILL;              -- activates till-opening action in the hardware

    ⋮

end;
```

The remaining question is how an executable object obtains a reference to the physical node object on which it is to execute. As mentioned earlier, there is no CREATE 'method' associated with instances of physical node classes since such instances do not correspond to software modules that can be generated dynamically. How, then, can instance variables such as CR be made to refer to the physical node on which the encapsulating executable object is to execute?

Recall that the only mechanism for executing software in DRAGOON (even in a non-distributed system) is the inheritance of an appropriate execution support class and the allocation of instances of the resulting subclass to a corresponding physical node object. This involves the invocation of the LOAD_ONTO method inherited from the execution support class with the reference of the machine on which the object is to execute supplied as the actual parameter. This is precisely the reference that needs to be assigned to instance variables like CR above in order to provide executable objects with the capacity to call the system methods of their host machine.

The problem of assigning the appropriate reference to 'physical node' instance variables is not a concern of the application class, therefore, but rather of the executable class generated from it by inheritance of an execution support class. When executable objects such as CHECKOUT_POINT are required which need to invoke methods of the underlying system, the LOAD_ONTO method of the class must be redefined so that its parameter is assigned to the appropriate instance variables inherited from the application class. The executable class MC_68000_EXECUTABLE_CHECKOUT_POINT, for example, which defines the executable classes needed to control the

Motorola 68000 based cash registers, would be of the form:

```
class MC_68000_EXECUTABLE_CHECKOUT_POINT is                        (8.7)
    inherits MC_68000_EXECUTION_SUPPORT, CHECKOUT_POINT;
    redefines LOAD_ONTO;
end;


class body MC_68000_EXECUTABLE_CHECKOUT_POINT is

    procedure LOAD_ONTO (P : in MC_68000_PHYSICAL_NODE) is
    begin
        CR := P;
    end;

end;
```

This conforms to the normal class redefinition rules, except that the method LOAD_ONTO is a special method which has a far greater effect than that described in the new body. As with the 'redefinition' of CREATE, therefore, the redefinition of LOAD_ONTO is best thought of as defining *extra* operations performed when the method is invoked rather than providing an *alternative* redefinition of its entire functionality. The new body is able to assign the reference held in the parameter P to CR, and indeed to any other 'physical node' instance variable in the body of the application class, since by the normal rules of inheritance these are visible in the body of subclasses.

8.5.2   Abstract hardware interfaces

By providing CHECKOUT_POINT with an instance variable of class CASH_REGISTER_PHYSICAL_NODE and redefining the LOAD_ONTO method of executable subclasses, the programmer is able to define interaction with the physical node classes using clientship. This is satisfactory provided the programmer knows beforehand the type of machine on which instances of CHECKOUT_POINT will run, and that this will never be changed. In general, however, it is undesirable to bind application classes to clientship of one particular type of machine at such an early stage. This conflicts with the fundamental DRAGOON philosophy of deferring binding decisions until as late as possible in the development process.

Precisely this problem was encountered in Chapter 4 where clients of a QUEUE component were required to name a particular implementation even though they may have been unconcerned about which form of component eventually provides the service. The solution was the introduction of abstract classes which permitted the implementation of methods to be 'deferred' to subclasses. The same approach can be used here to decouple the class CHECKOUT_POINT from any particular 'implementation' of the cash register methods:

```
class REGISTER_HARDWARE_INTERFACE is                              (8.8)
    introduces
        procedure OPEN_TILL is deferred;
        procedure PRINT_BILL is deferred;

        .
        .                              -- other methods of a cash register device
end;
```

This class is a normal abstract class which exports a set of methods defining the interface to cash register devices. It is possible to define ordinary subclasses that complete the deferred methods in the normal way. However, it is also possible to define a subclass of REGISTER_HARDWARE_INTERFACE which is also a subclass of the physical node class and is therefore itself a physical node class:

```
class ALTERNATIVE_CASH_REGISTER_PHYSICAL_NODE is                  (8.9)
    inherits MC_68000_PHYSICAL_NODE, REGISTER_HARDWARE_INTERFACE
        completes OPEN_TILL, PRINT_BILL ...;
end;
```

This class is a physical node class with precisely the same interface and properties as CASH_REGISTER_PHYSICAL_NODE (8.5). The only difference is that the methods for the cash register device are inherited from an abstract class rather than introduced explicitly. The 'completes' keyword indicates that the class provides an implementation for the abstract methods, as before, but in this case they are implemented by the hardware and/or systems software rather than the DRAGOON application. No bodies need be, or in fact can be, provided for the methods since physical node classes possess no bodies.

The advantage of defining the class representing cash register physical nodes in this way is that its clients, particularly CHECK-OUT_POINT (8.6) can be defined to be clients of its abstract parent REG-ISTER_HARDWARE_INTERFACE. In other words, the instance variable CR in CHECKOUT_POINT would be of class REGISTER_HARDWARE_INTERFACE rather than CASH_REGISTER_PHYSICAL_NODE and could therefore execute on any type of physical node supporting the 'cash register' methods. In fact, the server object may even be a normal software object rather than a physical node object. The important point is that the choice is made at system configuration time because CHECKOUT_POINT is decoupled from any particular implementation.

The only special rule applying to the inheritance of an abstract class by a physical node class is that it must be fully abstract (all methods must be deferred). It is not possible for a physical node class to inherit a partially deferred class.

8.5.3   Interrupt methods

The preceding section has described how independent executable objects in a network can interact with the hardware they execute on by invoking the methods exported by the physical node object. In other words, what are normally termed 'system calls' in normal program development are modelled in DRAGOON as methods of the underlying physical node object. Essentially, this provides a mechanism by which the applications software may communicate with, or initiate actions in, the machines on which they are running. It is equally important, however, to support communication in the reverse direction in which the 'hardware' initiates actions in the 'software'. This type of interaction between hardware and software has traditionally been termed an 'interrupt'.

The interaction between the cash registers and the checkout point objects which they execute again provides a good example of this type of communication. As mentioned earlier, a common property of cash registers is that the till (containing the money) cannot be opened until the calculation of a bill is complete, and while it is open no further calculation can take place. As well as the signal from the software to the hardware to indicate that the till should be opened, therefore, a signal is required in the reverse direction to indicate when it has been shut again. In other words, the hardware must send an 'interrupt' to the appropriate application object to indicate that the till has been closed and the calculation of the next customer's bill may begin.

Traditionally, the code executed in response to an interrupt – the 'interrupt handler' – is defined as a form of subprogram which is invoked directly by the hardware and takes precedence over all other activities being performed by the process (or object) concerned. In Ada, with its in-built concurrency model, an interrupt handler is defined as the body of an entry (i.e. an '**accept**' statement) which is associated with an 'interrupt address' by means of an address clause. Interrupts are conceptually raised by a task with a priority higher than any other so that the corresponding '**accept** statement is executed with the highest priority.

In the object-oriented framework of DRAGOON an interrupt handler naturally corresponds to a method of an executable object whose activation is not restricted by the object's behaviour – that is, a method which always has permission to execute. Moreover, since these methods are characteristic of the type of abstract machine on which an application object is running, the natural place to define the set of callable 'interrupt methods' is in the execution support classes for the system concerned. The execution support classes for a given type of system therefore export a method for each interrupt supported by the system and provide a default implementation which will usually do nothing. User-defined interrupt handlers are provided by redefining the body of the corresponding method when an executable class is created.

Suppose for the sake of argument that the MC68000 processors upon

which the cash register abstract machines are based have the capacity to
raise three different interrupts: INT_1, INT_2 and INT_3. To enable these
interrupts to be 'caught' by executable objects, these interrupts would be
declared as methods in the interface of the execution support class for
MC68000s:

```
class MC_68000_EXECUTION_SUPPORT;                                    (8.10)
    introduces
        procedure LOAD_ONTO (P : in MC_68000_EXECUTION_SUPPORT);
        procedure SET_PRIORITY (P : in POSITIVE);
        procedure INT_1;
        procedure INT_2;
        procedure INT_3;
end;
```

In this particular example the interrupt methods are defined to have no
parameters, but other execution support classes may be defined with 'interrupt methods' that have parameters.

The applications programmer is not actually concerned to which particular addresses these interrupts correspond, or the mechanisms by which
they are raised, but merely that the hardware engineer has arranged for the
closing of the till to raise an interrupt at the address corresponding to INT_2,
for example. In order to ensure the appropriate response to the raising of
the interrupt, which in this example probably means the calling of a method
of a behavioured object blocking the thread, the applications programmer
must 'redefine' the body of the method in an executable class. As with the
'redefinition' of other special methods, such as CREATE and LOAD_ONTO,
redefinition of an interrupt method does not change its special semantics
but merely associates additional functionality with the method name.

In the case of checkout points, the INT_2 method would be redefined
in the executable subclass of MC_68000_PHYSICAL_NODE (8.7) to perform the
required actions:

```
class MC_68000_EXECUTABLE_CHECKOUT_POINT is
    inherits MC_68000_EXECUTION_SUPPORT, CHECKOUT_POINT;
    redefines INT_2;
end;


class body MC_68000_EXECUTABLE_CHECKOUT_POINT is

    procedure INT_2 is
    begin

        :                              -- actions performed when till shuts

    end;

end;
```

The actions that are performed in response to the raising of the INT_2 exception by the underlying system can be programmed in precisely the same way as for any other method of a subclass with multiple parents. In particular, all the instance variables and internal procedures of the 'application' parent are visible in the executable class and can be invoked as required.

This approach completes the symmetry of the clientship which exists between the execution support classes and physical node class. Methods of the former define the 'system calls' that instances of the latter may invoke, while methods of the latter define the 'interrupt handlers' that instances of the former may invoke. The references passed as parameters to the ACTIVATE and LOAD_ONTO methods conceptually provide the visibility necessary for the mutual clientship to exist.

8.5.4   Network specification

The final question to be resolved in connection with the use of physical node objects is the mechanism by which references to physical node objects are introduced into the system. Because applications software cannot 'generate' new hardware in the same way that it can generate new software components, some other mechanism than the CREATE method is required to provide references to physical node objects. In the previous examples of the use of physical node objects it was merely assumed that the instance variables of a physical node class contained reference to the appropriate physical node object.

One approach would be to have some form of special syntax to indicate with which reference physical node instance variables are initialized. However, since the physical configuration of the network is not under the control of the applications software but is determined by external forces beyond its control, all that is needed is for the relevant parts of the applications software to have visibility of a predefined specification of the initial hardware configuration. Any subsequent changes, such as the introduction of new physical nodes, can be communicated to the applications software from the terminal object (Section 8.6) as method parameters.

Following the DRAGOON convention of using template packages to define shareable declarations that may need to be visible to a number of classes, the initial network specification is best contained in a special kind of template package, called a *configuration package*, for example. Such packages would simply contain instance variables storing the references to the physical node objects in the initial configuration of the network. The initial physical configuration of the network used by the distributed version of the supermarket control system would thus be represented by a configuration package of the form:

```
with VAX_VMS_PHYSICAL_NODE;                                    (8.11)
with SUN_PHYSICAL_NODE;
with CASH_REGISTER_PHYSICAL_NODE;
package SUPERMARKET_NETWORK is

    VAX : VAX_VMS_PHYSICAL_NODE;
    SUN : SUN_PHYSICAL_NODE;
    REGISTER : array (1 .. 10) of CASH_REGISTER_PHYSICAL_NODE;

end;
```

Any class which 'withs' this package would have access to the physical node objects in the initial configuration of the network and could copy the references to its own instance variables.

8.6   Execution model

The previous section has described how the different kinds of components making up a distributed system are modelled using physical node and execution support classes, and the various facilities available for configuring them. However, the question as to how these facilities are employed and who or what is actually responsible for configuring systems is yet to be discussed.

At first sight there would appear to be two basic strategies by which the objects needed to produce a functioning system in DRAGOON could be generated and configured – *interactively*, under the control of a human operator, and *automatically*, under the control of some form of configuration program.

Interactively

Pursing the object-oriented model to its limit, the terminal (or shell in UNIX terminology) which the human operator uses to perform the configuration actions can be regarded as an *active* object which permits the normal declarations and operations possible in a DRAGOON class to be performed interactively, as illustrated in Figure 8.3. The operator at this *terminal object* may therefore define instance variables (c.f. UNIX shell variables) and use them to invoke methods (c.f. command line instructions) in order to arrange for the execution of executable objects in the manner described in Section 8.4.

This is true for non-distributed as well as distributed systems. To execute the non-distributed version of the supermarket control system represented by the class SUPERMARKET (6.15), for example, it would first be necessary to define (by instructions at the command line) an instance variable of the appropriate executable subclass of SUPERMARKET and then generate an executable object by invocation of the CREATE method. Since there is only one machine in the network and the executable object was

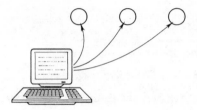

Figure 8.3   Interactive configuration from a terminal object.

generated on the machine on which it is to run, it is not necessary to invoke the LOAD_ONTO method of the object in this case. It is still necessary to invoke the ACTIVATE method of the host machine, however, in order to load the corresponding binary module and begin its execution. A terminal object, therefore, needs some predefined variable, HOST say, which contains a reference to the physical node object to which the terminal is connected. The executable 'supermarket' would therefore be activated by invoking the ACTIVATE method through the pseudo-variable HOST. Finally, since SUPER-MARKET is an active class, the thread of the executable object just activated needs to be started by invoking the START method.

The construction of distributed systems is just a generalization of this scenario, in which physical node objects and executable objects are generated by instructions issued from the *terminal object*, and the LOAD_ONTO, ACTIVATE and START methods are used to define the allocation of software modules to physical nodes and the communication pattern of the executable objects.

This view of system generation and execution is an idealistic model in which the object-oriented framework of DRAGOON is pushed to its limit. To what extent this is actually realized in practice is more a concern for the environment/operating system in which the software is executed than for the language itself. It is certainly possible to provide a fully object-oriented environment for DRAGOON, perhaps similar to that of Smalltalk, where sophisticated mouse-driven browsers are provided to analyze the contents of the library and invoke the methods of executable objects. On the other hand, the system may provide a very primitive user interface that does not support the full object scheme for activating executable objects.

Automatically

Since all the system configuring operations are performed by normal mechanisms of the object-oriented paradigm, another natural approach is to define the required configuration steps in a 'class' rather than to enter them interactively from a terminal object. The 'execution' of an instance of such a 'class' would therefore perform the necessary configuration steps automatically. Such an instance is, therefore, closely analogous to the *con-*

figuration programs of languages such as CONIC which are used to build and configure distributed systems in the second phase of program construction.

Two immediate questions spring to mind with this approach, however – who is responsible for instantiating this class and how is an instance executed once produced? Because such a class manipulates 'heavyweight' executable objects and physical node objects, and therefore essentially encapsulates the whole network, it would at first sight seem to be very different from the normal application classes of DRAGOON. The operations performed by instances of such classes, such as the invocation of LOAD_ONTO and ACTIVATE methods, cannot be compiled directly into machine code as normal but must be implemented by appropriate calls to the services of the underlying operating system. Moreover, the references to objects are not implemented as memory addresses but as network addresses for the machines and processes concerned.

Despite the fact that operations performed by such a class are mapped into operating system commands rather than into machine code, as with normal classes, instances of the class clearly still need to be executed on a machine in the network, typically the host. There is no reason, therefore, why the same execution model cannot also be adopted for such 'configuration' classes – namely that executable subclasses have to be generated by inheritances of the appropriate run-time support. This also means that the generation and activation of such classes can be performed for the terminal object in the same way as for normal application classes. The only difference is that whereas in the interactive case *all* configuration concerns have to be handled explicitly from the command line, in this case the activation of a single object can lead to the generation of a complete distributed system.

Integrated execution model

The two alternative approaches described above represent the two extremes. In the first, all configuration operations are performed interactively from an (active) terminal object by the user, while in the second, all the configuration operations are performed by an instance of a special class which exclusively manipulates physical node and executable ('heavyweight') processes. It is not necessary to have such a sharp dichotomy, however.

The 'automatic' approach described above, in which special 'configuration' classes are used to perform the configuration operations necessary for constructing distributed systems, would on the face of it appear to divide DRAGOON *application* classes into two distinct sets – the normal application classes which are clients of other normal ('lightweight') classes and the special 'configuration' classes which are clients of executable ('heavyweight') and physical node classes. However, because DRAGOON enables all the different types of object in a system to be distinguished by their ancestry and the same execution model is used for both categories, there is no reason why a class cannot be a client of all these different kinds of classes simultaneously. When a class is analyzed by the compilation system it can determine unambiguously whether a server object is 'lightweight', in which case the operations applied to them must be compiled into machine code as usual, or whether they are executable or physical node class, in which case the operations must be mapped into the appropriate calls to the operating system.

The important point is that the compiler is able to determine purely from the class text what kind of objects are being manipulated and how particular operations should be translated. It is not necessary, therefore, to have different categories of class according to the types of objects they manipulate and in which phase of system construction they are used. All classes can manipulate all the three different kinds of object recognized in DRAGOON systems without ambiguity. The only difference between objects which are clients of one or more physical node or executable objects, and those which are not, is that they can not be translated into pure machine code, but rely on calls to the underlying operating system to put some of their actions into effect.

This is the approach adopted in DRAGOON. There is no distinction between 'configuration' and 'normal' objects or between interactive and automatic configuration. Any DRAGOON class can be a client of any other kind of class without restriction and in particular can perform any of the actions required to configure a system. Moreover, any kind of class can only be executed by generating the appropriate executable subclass and instantiating it from the terminal object. It is up to the programmer, therefore, how much of the configuration is performed 'automatically' by objects in the system or 'interactively' from the terminal object.

8.6.1 Centralized reconfiguration

This integrated model for executing objects and configuring systems has a number of important advantages from the point of view of dynamic reconfiguration. If a single object is used to construct a system in the style of the 'automatic' approach it can play a role in monitoring and upgrading the configuration of the network because it is also a normal executing object in the system just like an instance of the class SUPERMARKET (6.15) defining a non-distributed version of the system.

A class defining a distributed version of the supermarket control system would have a similar form:

```
class DISTRIBUTED_SUPERMARKET is                              (8.12)
    introduces
        thread;
end DISTRIBUTED_SUPERMARKET;
```

```
with SUN_EXECUTABLE_CENTRAL_CONTROLLER;
with VAX_EXECUTABLE_DATA_BASE;
with SUN_EXECUTABLE_FORWARDER;
with MC_68000_EXECUTABLE_CHECKOUT_POINTS;
with VAX_VMS_PHYSICAL_NODE, SUN_PHYSICAL_NODE;
with CASH_REGISTER_PHYSICAL_NODE;
class body DISTRIBUTED_SUPERMARKET is

        CC : SUN_EXECUTABLE_CENTRAL_CONTROLLER;      -- declare variables for
        DB : VAX_EXECUTABLE_DATA_BASE;               -- executable objects
        F : SUN_EXECUTABLE_FORWARDER;
        CP : array (1 .. 10) of MC_68000_EXECUTABLE_CHECKOUT_POINTS;

        VAX : VAX_VMS_PHYSICAL_NODE;
        SUN : SUN_PHYSICAL_NODE;
        REGISTER : array (1 .. 10) of CASH_REGISTER;

thread

        CC.CREATE;                                   -- create objects
        DB.CREATE;
        F.CREATE;
        for I in 1 .. 10 loop
            CP(I).CREATE;
        end loop;

        CC.LOAD_ONTO (SUN);          -- load executable objects on to machines
        DB.LOAD_ONTO (VAX);
        F.LOAD_ONTO (SUN);
        for I in 1 .. 10 loop
            CP(I).LOAD_ONTO (REGISTER(I));
        end loop;

        CC.SHARE(F);
        F.SHARE(DB);                 -- set up required system configuration
        for I in 1 .. 10 loop
            CP(I).SHARE(DB);
        end loop;

        SUN.ACTIVATE (CC);                    -- activate executable objects
        VAX.ACTIVATE (DB);
        SUN.ACTIVATE (F);
        for I in 1 .. 10 loop
            REGISTER(I).ACTIVATE (CP(I));
        end loop;

        CC.START;                                    -- start objects
        F.START;
        for I in 1 .. 10 loop
            CP(I).START;
        end loop;

end DISTRIBUTED_SUPERMARKET;
```

An instance of this class activated from the terminal object will issue the
necessary operating system instructions to generate a distributed version
of the supermarket system. The central controller and forwarder objects
will execute on the same Sun workstation, the database on a VAX and the
checkout points on MC68000 based cash registers.

Notice how similar this class is to the class SUPERMARKET (6.15) defining a non-distributed version. Precisely the same method calls are performed to set up the logical configuration of the system (i.e. the population of application objects and their communication pattern) in both cases. The only difference is that the distributed version must also handle the physical configuration of the system (i.e. the number and type of physical node objects) and the allocation of executable objects to physical nodes.

As in the non-distributed version of the system, the thread of the configuring class DISTRIBUTED_SUPERMARKET need not terminate after it has set up the system, but by containing a loop may become a permanent active object which plays a role in the execution of the system. For example, it could provide a similar reconfiguration service with respect to the forwarder objects as the non-distributed version, described in the previous chapter, by generating a new forwarder when the old one becomes full.

Such a reconfiguration is termed a *logical* or *software* reconfiguration since it changes only the logical structure of the applications software. In distributed systems, however, other forms of reconfiguration are possible because the hardware in the network may be changed dynamically. Should extra physical nodes become available during the execution of the program, the configuring class could be programmed to move the existing objects on to the new processing sites or to add new executable objects to the system to execute upon them. Such adjustment is termed *physical* reconfiguration since it affects the structure of the hardware as well as, or instead of, the software. An important feature of the DRAGOON approach is that all these different possibilities are programmed using the normal mechanisms of object-oriented programming. In contrast with systems such as CONIC, therefore, which use a purely declarative form of 'configuration language' to describe the final structure of distributed systems, this means that in DRAGOON the usual imperative 'flow-control' mechanisms (i.e. loops, conditional statements etc.) may be used in the configuration process.

However, the problem faced in the non-distributed version of the system, and left open in connection with the forwarder reconfiguration, also exists here – how does the *reconfiguring* object know when the reconfiguration should be performed?

Environment-driven reconfiguration

One strategy is to include a method in the interface of the configuring object which the human operator may call from the terminal object when a reconfiguration is required. This method could either perform the reconfiguration itself or 'unblock' the thread to do the job. In the case of the 'forwarder reconfiguration' (Section 6.10), for example, the configuring class (SUPERMARKET or DISTRIBUTED_SUPERMARKET in the non-distributed and distributed versions respectively) would export an additional method, GENERATE_NEW_FORWARDER say, which could be called from the terminal object to indicate that a new forwarder should be generated.

This approach is fine for reconfigurations in which the human user is genuinely the agent that detects or decides that the change is needed, such as those generally required as a result of a change in the encapsulating environment. The prime examples are hardware reconfigurations where processors are added or removed from the system. As pointed out earlier, it is impossible for the applications software to issue commands that 'generate' new hardware, so it must ultimately be notified of such changes by the external environment.

Another reconfiguration that might be required is the generation of a new CHECKOUT_POINT (8.6) object to execute on any new CASH_REGISTER_PHYSICAL_NODE (8.5) objects which may be added to the supermarket. In order to provide the DISTRIBUTED_SUPERMARKET configuring class with a reference to the new physical node object and request that a new CHECKOUT_POINT object be generated to execute upon it, another method would be required with a parameter of the appropriate type.

Since such reconfigurations are driven by changes in the environment, one of the major problems is ensuring that the objects affected by the change are in an appropriate state for the change to be made safely. In general, this requires the configuring object to ensure that the objects are in a *quiescent state* (Kramer and Magee, 1988) by calling a number of extra methods specially defined for this purpose in the interface of application objects. Essentially, this requires the configurer to request permission to perform a change, and then subsequently informing the object of its completion, as indicated in Section 6.10.

System-driven reconfiguration

There are many reconfigurations, however, such as the 'forwarder reconfiguration' under consideration that depend on the state of the applications software rather than events in the external environment. Quite apart from the question of how the human operator can actually detect when such a state is reached, it is clearly more desirable for such reconfigurations to be performed automatically than for the user to act as an interface between the application modules and reconfiguring agent.

The basic virtual node approach to distribution, in which the distributable objects developed in the programming phase are made as independent as possible from any configuration concerns, does not readily support automatic reconfiguration of this form. The decoupling of the programming and configuration concerns, which provides much of the flexibility for building different system configurations, makes it much more difficult to arrange for interaction between the application objects and configuring object(s).

Since it is the application objects in the system that detect *when* a reconfiguration is needed (e.g. the central controller becomes aware when the forwarder is full) but the encapsulating object that knows *how* a reconfiguration can be performed, the problem is to facilitate communication between them. In other words, how does the central controller object *notify* the encapsulating system-configuring object that the forwarder is full and a new one required?

The basic cause of this 'notification' problem in the majority of languages is that the reconfiguring object, and the objects it controls, can not both have visibility of the other. In object-oriented languages like DRAGOON, however, it is possible to arrange for the interfaces of classes to depend on each other by arranging for the interface of one of them to be constructed in two steps using inheritance.

To arrange for the interfaces of the classes CENTRAL_CONTROLLER and DISTRIBUTED_SUPERMARKET to depend on one another it is first necessary to define a limited interface to one of them. The interface that a central controller would provide for a DISTRIBUTED_SUPERMARKET object could be defined by a class with the following specification, for example:

```
class PARTIAL_CENTRAL_CONTROLLER is                        (8.13)
    introduces
        procedure SHARE is deferred;
        procedure COMPLETED_RECONF is deferred;
    end;
```

which contains the 'reconfiguring' method SHARE and the method COMPLETED_RECONF which the configuring object calls to indicate that it has completed the required reconfiguration. It is not necessary to provide the method REQUEST_RECONF, as in the class RECONF_CENTRAL_CONTROLLER (6.17) in Section 6.10, because in this scenario the central controller object is responsible for calling the reconfiguring object to request a reconfiguration and so can be assumed to be in an appropriate state when the reconfiguring object responds.

Once this specification has been compiled, it is possible to define an interface for a version of DISTRIBUTED_SUPERMARKET modified to enable the central controller object it contains to call one of its methods:

```
with PARTIAL_CENTRAL_CONTROLLER;                           (8.14)
class CALLABLE_DISTRIBUTED_SUPERMARKET is
    introduces
        procedure NEW_FORWARDER_NEEDED
                        (CC : PARTIAL_CENTRAL_CONTROLLER);
    end;
```

Although not strictly necessary in this particular case, the method NEW_FORWARDER_NEEDED, which a central controller object will call when its forwarder is full, has a parameter of type PARTIAL_CENTRAL_CONTROLLER so that the central controller can send its identity (i.e. its reference) to the configuring object. In this example there is only one central control object, but in general when there are more such objects in a system it is necessary for the one requesting the reconfiguration to identify itself. The method

NEW_FORWARDER_NEEDED is responsible for unblocking the thread so that it may perform the reconfiguration in the manner illustrated in Section 6.10.

Now that the interface of the 'configuring' object has been defined, it is possible to complete the interface of central controller objects in a subclass of PARTIAL_CENTRAL_CONTROLLER:

```
with CALLABLE_DISTRIBUTED_SUPERMARKET;                          (8.15)
class FULL_CENTRAL_CONTROLLER is
    inherits PARTIAL_CENTRAL_CONTROLLER;
    introduces
        procedure CONFIGURING_OBJECT
                    (CO : CALLABLE_DISTRIBUTED_SUPERMARKET);
    completes
        SHARE, COMPLETED_RECONF;
end;
```

This class completes the methods deferred by PARTIAL_CENTRAL_CONTROL-LER and introduces a new method CONFIGURING_OBJECT which has a parameter of the class type of the object which will ultimately build the system. As part of the task of building the system, the 'configuring' object must pass its reference (obtained through the SELF pseudo-variable) to the instance of FULL_CENTRAL_CONTROLLER which it generates. This enables the central controller object to call the configuring object to indicate when it detects that a reconfiguration is required. In order to detect that the forwarder it is using is full, the forwarders used in a reconfigurable system of this nature must export an appropriate boolean IS_FULL method which the central controller can call prior to the ADD method.

8.6.2   Decentralized reconfiguration

The above discussion has demonstrated how 'centralized' configuration schemes, similar to those of CONIC, can be handled in DRAGOON with full support for both user-driven and system-driven reconfiguration. However, because of the fully integrated execution model it is possible to distribute the responsibility for system configuration among executable objects at sites throughout the system.

It is possible, for example, to define an application class FORWARD-_MONITOR, say, whose sole function is to generate a new FORWARDER object when so instructed by the central controller:

```
with FORWARDER, CENTRAL_CONTROLLER, DATA_BASE;                  (8.16)
class FORWARDER_CONTROLLER is
    introduces
        procedure CONTROLLER (CC : in CENTRAL_CONTROLLER);
        procedure DATA_BASE (DB : in DATA_BASE);
        procedure CREATION_SITE (S : in SUN_PHYSICAL_NODE);
        procedure PRIMARY (F : in FORWARDER);
        procedure RECONFIGURE;
end;
```

```
with SUN_EXECUTABLE_FORWARDER;
with SUN_PHYSICAL_NODE;
class body FORWARDER_CONTROLLER is

    C : CENTRAL_CONTROLLER;
    D : DATA_BASE;
    SEF : SUN_EXECUTABLE_FORWARDER;
    WAITING, WORKING, TEMP : FORWARDER ;

    FIRST_RECONF : BOOLEAN := TRUE;
    SITE : SUN_PHYSICAL_NODE;

    procedure CONTROLLER (CC : in CENTRAL_CONTROLLER) is
    begin
        C := CC;
    end;

    procedure DATA_BASE (DB : in DATA_BASE) is
    begin
        D := DB;
    end;

    procedure CREATION_SITE (S : in SUN_PHYSICAL_NODE) is
    begin
        SITE := S;
    end;

    procedure PRIMARY (F : in FORWARDER) is
    begin
        WORKING := F;
    end;

    procedure RECONFIGURE is
    begin
        if FIRST_RECONF then
            SEF.CREATE;
            SEF.LOAD_ONTO (SITE);
            SITE.ACTIVATE (SEF);
            SEF.SHARE (DB);
            SEF.START;
            FIRST_RECONF := FALSE;
            WAITING := SEF;
        end if;
        C.SHARE(WAITING);
        TEMP := WAITING;
        WAITING := WORKING;
        WORKING := TEMP;
    end;
end;
```

As in the non-distributed version of the system created by the class SUPER-MARKET (6.15), the first time a reconfiguration is required to compensate for the primary forwarder being full, a new forwarder object is generated. In this case, however, since the system is distributed an executable subclass has to be instantiated and the appropriate steps taken to arrange for its execution on the required machine. Once a new forwarder has been created, however, instances of FORWARDER_CONTROLLER maintain references to the 'working' and 'waiting' forwarder objects, and after sending the central controller the reference to the currently waiting forwarder, swaps over the references.

Provided it is supplied with all the appropriate references, which is the function of the first four methods in FORWARDER_CONTROLLER, this class can perform the same reconfiguring role as an encapsulating object, such as SUPERMARKET (6.15). The important difference is that instances of FORWARDER_OBJECT may execute on the same physical node as the objects it is responsible for controlling. It may therefore continue performing its function should other machines in the network fail. In general, by defining suitable classes, it is possible to arrange for 'reconfiguring' software to be distributed as required among the machines on which the controlled objects are executing. Ultimately, the distinction between 'controlling' and 'controlled' objects is lost and the system is viewed as a collection of interacting, distributed objects.

Key points

There are two basic models by which code in a high-level language may be executed – *interpretation* in which small segments (usually lines) of the program are executed immediately and *compilation/linking* in which at least one explicit translation step must be performed on a completed software module.

Languages designed primarily with the second 'compiler-oriented' implementation in mind introduce the concept of a 'main program' which represents the module of execution.

Most languages, including object-oriented languages, are designed under the assumption that the functionality of an entire system is captured by a single main program, so that main programs only execute in isolation. This assumption is not valid in distributed processing systems.

In distributed systems it is useful to distinguish the notion of 'heavyweight' processes (or objects) which possess the run-time support necessary to execute independently on a network node, and the notion of 'lightweight' processes (or objects) which execute under the support of heavyweight processes.

In Ada, heavyweight processes correspond to main programs and lightweight processes correspond to tasks. Ada therefore provides different mechanisms for representing lightweight and heavyweight processes and provides no support for describing the interaction of heavyweight processes.

A distributed system is composed of multiple, interacting heavyweight (or executable) processes distributed among the nodes of a network.

To develop a distributed application in Ada, therefore, a programmer must work at two levels of abstraction, and with two models of concurrency.

The reusability of software components is significantly improved by providing a uniform model of concurrency and deferring the decision as to whether a particular object is 'lightweight' or 'heavyweight' to the latest possible moment in the development process.

DRAGOON introduces the notion of *execution support classes* to differentiate classes describing heavyweight objects and classes describing lightweight objects.

A heavyweight, or executable, version of a virtual node class is generated by defining a subclass that also inherits an appropriate execution support class. The resulting execution support class is endowed with the ability to execute on a machine of the appropriate type.

Execution support classes are complemented by the notion of *physical node classes*. Instances of such classes represent the processing sites in a loosely coupled network.

Each execution support class has a corresponding physical node class and each physical node class has a corresponding execution support class. Moreover, the special 'initialization' methods of these classes have a parameter whose type is of the corresponding class. The normal typing rules of DRAGOON therefore ensure that executable objects can only be allocated to physical nodes for which they have been appropriately compiled, and vice versa.

Execution support classes export methods that represent the services provided by processes in the associated environment. These include the 'interrupts' which may be called by the hardware (i.e. by the instance of the physical node class on which an instance of an executable subclass is executing).

Physical node classes export methods that represent the services provided by the associated 'abstract machines'. These services are commonly termed 'system calls'.

Since it enables the various different components of a distributed system to be represented as classes/objects, a distributed system can be *configured* in DRAGOON using the normal 'imperative' mechanisms and relationships of object-oriented programming.

The operations needed to configure a distributed system can either be performed *interactively* from a special 'terminal' object, *automatically* by executing an appropriately designed 'configuring' object, or by a combination of these.

When a distributed system is configured by a single 'configuring' object, the thread of this object may terminate once it has generated the system or may contain a loop which permits it to continue to monitor the system and update the configuration when circumstances demand.

DRAGOON overcomes the 'notification' problem which often arises in a centralized approach to reconfiguration by permitting the interfaces of the configuring and configured objects to depend on one another. This is achieved by building the interface of one of these objects in two steps using inheritance.

By designing suitable objects, the reconfiguration code can also be distributed. This is important for defining fault-tolerant systems whose reconfiguration capabilities are not lost should a crucial processor in the system fail.

Chapter 9
Translation into Ada

One of the main goals of DRAGOON was that it should be readily translatable into Ada for execution. This chapter describes how, despite the *prima facie* incompatibility of the languages, DRAGOON is translated into Ada in a fairly succinct and natural style. The aim of the discussion is to describe the underlying principles of the translation rather than provide an exhaustive specification.

9.1   Implementation strategies

Thanks to its extensive modularity, concurrency and typing mechanisms, Ada provides more support for object-oriented programming than most other conventional imperative languages, such as Pascal and Modula 2. In fact, to a limited extent it is possible to emulate all the fundamental features of the object-oriented paradigm in Ada, including inheritance, polymorphism and dynamic binding (Seidewitz, 1987). For reasons explained later, however, most of these *direct* emulation techniques cannot be used in the implementation of a general object-oriented language like DRAGOON. Not only do they fail to support the object-oriented mechanisms in their full generality, but are disjointed and impossible to use together. Nevertheless, before discussing the particular implementation strategy developed for DRAGOON it is helpful to review these different possibilities.

9.1.1   'Abstract state machine' packages

There are, in fact, three basic techniques for representing objects and classes in Ada. The most direct representation of an object is as a state-encapsulating package (sometimes termed an abstract state machine) exporting a set of subprograms (c.f. methods) which can be used to access and update the encapsulated state. A product descriptor object, for example, of the kind used in the supermarket control system and defined in

183

DRAGOON as an instance of the class PRODUCT_DESCRIPTOR (3.4), could be represented explicitly in Ada as an 'abstract state machine' package of the form:

```
with PRODUCT;                                               (9.1)
package ASM_PRODUCT_DESCRIPTOR is

    function PRICE return PRODUCT.VALUE;
    procedure SET_PRICE_TO (PRICE : in PRODUCT.VALUE);
    function BAR_CODE return PRODUCT.CODE_NUMBER;

        :                -- similarly for other 'methods' of PRODUCT_DESCRIPTOR

end ASM_PRODUCT_DESCRIPTOR;


package body ASM_PRODUCT_DESCRIPTOR is

    INTERNAL_BAR_CODE : PRODUCT.NUMBER;
    INTERNAL_PRICE : PRODUCT.VALUE;

        :                        -- other attributes and subprogram bodies

end ASM_PRODUCT_DESCRIPTOR;
```

Superficially, this package is very similar to the class PRODUCT_DESCRIPTOR (3.4), but represents a product descriptor *object* rather than a *template*.

Using generic packages, this approach can be extended to achieve something of the notion of classes. A generic state-encapsulating package with this interface defines an object template from which multiple structurally identical instances can be generated. However, generic packages are static entities that can only be instantiated at compile time and thus do not support the concept of dynamically instantiable objects identified by references.

This approach is probably the least satisfactory of the three, therefore, because it does not provide a faithful implementation of classes as dynamically instantiable object types, let alone support for the accompanying mechanisms of inheritance, polymorphism and dynamic binding.

9.1.2   Tasks

The second technique is to represent objects as tasks. Since Ada supports the notion of task types as well as instances, this approach has the immediate advantage of supporting dynamically instantiable classes and reference semantics. In this approach the class PRODUCT_DESCRIPTOR (3.4) would be represented by a task type of the form:

```
task type PRODUCT_DESCRIPTOR_TASK is                        (9.2)

    entry PRICE (P : out PRODUCT.VALUE);
    entry SET_PRICE_TO (PRICE : in PRODUCT.VALUE);
```

entry BAR_CODE (B : out PRODUCT.CODE_NUMBER);

⋮   -- similarly for other 'methods' of PRODUCT_DESCRIPTOR

end PRODUCT_DESCRIPTOR_TASK;

Notice that methods such as PRICE and BAR_CODE defined as functions in the DRAGOON representation of such objects have to be defined as value-returning entries in this representation.

One of the main advantages of this approach is that it supports the notion of concurrency and enables objects to be active. It can also be used to realize a form of dynamic binding because Ada permits a task type to define several different 'accept' statements (c.f. method bodies) for each entry (c.f. method) exported in the interface. The body of the task type PRODUCT_DESCRIPTOR_TASK, for example, could contain several different 'accept' statements for the entry PRICE. By parameterizing the task with a flag indicating which of the 'accept' statements is to be executed, it is possible for different instances of a single task type to provide alternative implementations for the entry concerned. Moreover, since such instances are identified by access values of the same type and may all be assigned to a single variable of that type, the particular implementation of the entry executed in response to an entry call is established (bound to the entry name) dynamically.

As with the first approach, the main problem with using task types for implementing classes is that they provide no support for inheritance. There is also the additional problem that tasks, unlike classes, cannot be library units.

9.1.3 Abstract data types

The final strategy for representing objects in Ada is based on the notion of abstract data types. Instead of modelling an object as a package defining an abstract state machine, the abstraction is defined by a package exporting an abstract data type. The package exporting the type and associated subprograms does not itself represent an object but rather variables of the exported data type. The package defining the abstract data type corresponds more to a class, therefore, than to an object.

In this approach the class PRODUCT_DESCRIPTOR (3.4) would be represented as an abstract data type of the form:

```
with PRODUCT;                                              (9.3)
package ADT_PRODUCT_DESCRIPTOR is

    type OBJECT is private;

    function PRICE (OB : in OBJECT) return PRODUCT.VALUE;
    procedure SET_PRICE_TO (OB : in out OBJECT;
                            PRICE : in PRODUCT.VALUE);
```

```
        function BAR_CODE (OB : in OBJECT) return PRODUCT.CODE_NUMBER;
    :                    -- similarly for other 'methods' of PRODUCT_DESCRIPTOR
private

    type OBJECT is record
        INTERNAL_BAR_CODE : PRODUCT.CODE_NUMBER;
        INTERNAL_PRICE : PRODUCT.VALUE;
        INTERNAL_STOCK_LEVEL : PRODUCT.STOCK_NUMBER;
        INTERNAL_LABEL : PRODUCT.LABEL;
    end record;

end;
```

Product descriptor *objects* are generated by elaboration of variables of type
ADT_PRODUCT_DESCRIPTOR.OBJECT, and operations on the objects are performed by supplying the appropriate variable as a parameter of the corresponding subprogram. Each of the methods in the class is, therefore,
mapped into a subprogram with an extra parameter for receiving the 'state'
of the object upon which the operation is to be performed. The type OB-
JECT is defined as 'private' so that clients of the class cannot manipulate the
state of instances directly but only by means of the subprograms defined
in the interface.

One problem with this simple mapping into an abstract data type
is that it fails to provide the reference semantics and the associated facility for dynamically generating objects, which is an important aspect of
object-oriented languages. This is easily overcome, however, by making the
exported type an access type rather than a static type:

```
with PRODUCT;                                                      (9.4)
package ADT_PRODUCT_DESCRIPTOR is

    type STATE is private;
    type OBJECT is access STATE;

    function PRICE (OB : in OBJECT) return PRODUCT.VALUE;

    :                         -- subprogram specifications as above
private
    :

end;
```

This models the references and object creation semantics of DRAG-
OON much more faithfully, since variables of type ADT_PRODUCT_DESC-
RIPTOR.OBJECT are now access variables to which different references may
be assigned dynamically, and product descriptor objects are generated dynamically by means of the allocator 'new'.

Inheritance

The main advantage of this approach is that it provides limited support for two other important mechanisms associated with classes/objects, inheritance and polymorphism. Something of the effect of inheritance is provided by the derived type and subtype mechanisms of Ada. If, for example, a new type PERISHABLE_OBJECT is derived from the type OBJECT defined in (9.4) by a declaration of the form:

$$\vdots$$

```
type PERISHABLE_OBJECT is new ADT_PRODUCT_DESCRIPTOR.OBJECT;
```

$$\vdots$$

a copy of each of the subprograms declared in the specification of ADT_PRODUCT_DESCRIPTOR along with OBJECT is generated for the derived type. Strictly speaking; these are different subprograms which overload the names of the originals and operate on the new type. In effect, however, the subprograms operating on type OBJECT, and defined in the same package specification, are 'inherited' by the PERISHABLE_OBJECT and any other type derived from OBJECT. Moreover, it is possible to extend the set of 'methods' applicable to the derived type PERISHABLE_OBJECT by defining new methods.

The derived type mechanism of Ada, therefore, provides a faithful representation of inheritance with respect to the *operations* associated with a 'class'. In particular, it is possible to specialize a 'class' by expanding the set of 'methods' applicable to it. The subtyping mechanism – involving the specification of dynamic constraints on the set of values that entities of the subtype may assume - provides similar facilities. While derived types are incompatible, however, values of a subtype may be assigned to variables of the parent type.

The main shortcoming of both the subtyping and derived type approaches is that they do not permit the set of state variables associated with an abstraction to be extended. Neither of these mechanisms, therefore, is able to support directly the specialization of a product descriptor template to a perishable descriptor template because it is not possible to add the necessary attribute of type SIMPLE_CALENDAR.DATE.

Perez (1988) describes how this problem can be ameliorated to some extent by embedding 'inherited' state variables in a record containing the additional state variables introduced by a subclass. The resulting type, however, is still not type compatible with the parent type.

Polymorphism

The 'abstract data type' approach also supports a limited form of polymorphism by means of the variant record facility. As in Pascal and Modula 2, variant records permit data structures with different numbers and types of fields to be treated as if they were of the same type. The different kinds of records are actually regarded as different 'variants' of a single variant record type controlled by a *discriminant*. Using the type PRODUCT_TYPE (3.1) defined in Chapter 3 as a discriminant, the different kinds of product descriptors used in the supermarket control system (modelled in DRAG-OON by the classes PRODUCT_DESCRIPTOR (3.4), PERISHABLE_DESCRIPTOR (3.6) and ELECTRICAL_DESCRIPTOR (3.8)) would be represented as variants of a record of the form:

```
with PRODUCT, SIMPLE_CALENDAR, FUSE;                          (9.5)
package VARIANT_ADT_DESCRIPTOR is

    type STATE(FORM : in PRODUCT_TYPE) is private;
    type OBJECT is access STATE;

    function PRICE (OB : in OBJECT) return PRODUCT.VALUE;

      :
      :                                  -- subprogram specifications as in (9.3)
private
    type STATE(FORM : PRODUCT_TYPE) is record
        INTERNAL_BAR_CODE : PRODUCT.CODE_NUMBER;
        INTERNAL_PRICE : PRODUCT.VALUE;              -- common attributes
        INTERNAL_STOCK_LEVEL : PRODUCT.STOCK_NUMBER;
        case FORM is
            when PERISHABLE =>
                INTERNAL_DATA : SIMPLE_CALENDAR.DATE;
            when ELECTRICAL =>
                INTERNAL_RATING : FUSE.RATING;
            when BASIC =>
                null;
        end case;
    end record;
end;
```

Using this package, instances of the classes PRODUCT_DESCRIPTOR, PER-ISHABLE_DESCRIPTOR and ELECTRICAL_DESCRIPTOR would be regarded as BASIC, PERISHABLE and ELECTRICAL variants of the record type VAR-IANT_ADT_DESCRIPTOR.STATE respectively. Since they are thus of the same Ada type, they can be assigned to access variables of type VAR-IANT_ADT_DESCRIPTOR.OBJECT. This approach, therefore, supports the desired polymorphic behaviour with respect to the different kinds of descriptors in the supermarket system.

9.1.4   DRAGOON translation strategy

Using these different techniques, it is possible to achieve something of the effect of all the principal object-oriented mechanisms outlined in the previous chapters. In fact, Ada probably has more in-built features supporting 'object-oriented programming' than most other languages not generally credited with this title. This level of support is quite adequate for implementing object-based *designs* which do not rely on fully fledged inheritance, polymorphism or dynamic binding, and is largely responsible for the current popularity of such design methods in connection with Ada. In implementing designs constructed using such methods, the most appropriate mapping can be used for each particular circumstance. Booch (1987), for example, uses all three techniques outlined in the previous sections for modelling classes and objects depending on the particular context in which they appear.

As they stand, however, none of these strategies is acceptable for implementing a general object-oriented language like DRAGOON because they each support only a certain subset of the required properties. One of the most important aspects of DRAGOON is its use of the 'object' as a *unifying* concept acting as a focus for all the mechanisms supporting reuse, concurrency, distribution and reconfiguration. It is important, therefore, that its translation into Ada permits *all* these to be usable together in the construction and manipulation of classes and objects. The main problem in using Ada as the implementation language for DRAGOON, therefore, is the basic orthogonality of its limited support for inheritance, polymorphism and dynamic binding.

If a class is modelled by a task type, for example, so as to take advantage of the dynamic binding and reference semantics this offers, it is not possible to use inheritance. If derived types are used, on the other hand, to make use of the partial inheritance, it is not possible to use dynamic binding. These two mechanisms, therefore, are mutually exclusive in any of the previous implementations of objects in Ada.

Alternatively, consider the three different versions of product descriptor objects. As demonstrated in the previous sections, it is possible to provide polymorphism exploiting their similarity using variant records. A client of PRODUCT_DESCRIPTOR, such as a queue of such objects, can manipulate all the different versions of the objects since they are all represented by the same Ada type.

The major drawback of this technique, however, is that all these different versions need to be known and included in the record *at the time of definition*. It is not possible to introduce new subclasses of PRODUCT_DESCRIPTOR into the system and make them type compatible with access variables corresponding to existing classes, without redefining the variant record. This has repercussions throughout the system because all the Ada code corresponding to clients of the class has to be redefined and modified. The use of variant records to achieve polymorphism is completely incompatible with inheritance, unless all the ancestors and clients of a class are to be modified and recompiled.

Apart from the limited possibilities provided by variant records, polymorphism is in direct conflict with the strong typing principles of Ada. If variant records are not used to represent objects, the translation needs to break the strong typing rules of Ada using UNCHECKED_CONVERSION.

Because of these problems and the unsuitability of the standard implementation strategies just described, the translation adopted for DRAGOON aims to support inheritance, polymorphism and dynamic binding in a more uniform way.

9.2   Representation of object state

Of the three strategies for implementing classes and objects outlined in the preceding section, the translation of DRAGOON into Ada has most in common with the third 'abstract data type' approach. In particular, it adopts the same basic philosophy of representing classes as 'abstract data types' (i.e. types with associated subprograms), objects as dynamically instantiated data structures and method calls as the application of these subprograms to the appropriate data structure.

The main difference between the approach adopted in the implementation of DRAGOON and the simple 'abstract access type' approach is that the state of objects is not represented by a single record but by a (linked) *list* of records. Each node in the list stores the state variables added by ancestors of the object's class. Thus the state of a PERISHABLE_DESCRIPTOR object would be represented by a list with the 'node' storing the SIMPLE_CALENDAR.DATE attribute specific to PERISHABLE_DESCRIPTOR objects added to a 'node' storing the four attributes belonging to PRODUCT_DESCRIPTOR objects.

Although it is not reflected explicitly in the specification of classes, conceptually the root of the DRAGOON inheritance hierarchy is the class APPLICATION_OBJECT. In other words, all user-defined application classes in DRAGOON are descendants of APPLICATION_OBJECT and may be assigned to instance variables of this class. For logical as well as practical reasons, therefore, the first node of every such *state list* corresponds to an instance of the class APPLICATION_OBJECT. The form of other nodes appended to this list then depends on the position of the object's class in the inheritance hierarchy.

The Ada record type used to generate this special first node in state lists is defined in the following package forming part of the predefined environment of every Ada library used for implementing DRAGOON:

```
package APPLICATION is                                    (9.6)

    type STATE;
    type OBJECT is access STATE;

    type STATE is record
        OFFSPRING_NO : NATURAL := 0;
        SELF : OBJECT;
        MULTIPLE : OBJECT;
        HEIR : OBJECT;
    end record;
```

```
        function CREATE (OFFSPRING_NO : in NATURAL := 0) return OBJECT;
    end;


    package body APPLICATION is
        function CREATE (OFFSPRING_NO : in NATURAL := 0) return OBJECT is
            OB : OBJECT;
        begin
            OB := new STATE;
            OB.OFFSPRING_NO := OFFSPRING_NO;
            OB.SELF := OB;
            OB.MULTIPLE := null;
            OB.HEIR := null;
            return OB;
        end;
    end APPLICATION;
```

All objects in the system are represented by state lists whose first node is a record of type APPLICATION.STATE, referenced by an access variable of type APPLICATION.OBJECT. Instances of class APPLICATION_OBJECT are a special case in that their state is represented by a 'uninode' list containing a single record of this type. The state lists corresponding to descendants of APPLI-CATION_OBJECT are composed of an APPLICATION.STATE record followed by records holding the state variables introduced by each of the classes in the inheritance chain.

This is the basic strategy for overcoming the incompatibility of DRAGOON's polymorphism features and Ada's strong typing mechanism. Since the first node of every state list is of the type APPLICATION.STATE, all objects in the system are referenced by access values of the same Ada type – APPLICATION.OBJECT. All of the DRAGOON typing rules related to classes and objects, therefore, have to be checked and enforced by the DRAGOON translation tool, not by the typing rules of Ada.

The OFFSPRING_NO and MULTIPLE fields of APPLICATION.STATE are used to handle multiple offspring and multiple inheritance situations, respectively, and will be described fully later. The field SELF, on the other hand, simply points back to the record so that objects may access their own state. The last field HEIR is the one that contains the 'links' or references to other nodes to build a linked list for non-trivial objects. In the case of instances of the class APPLICATION_OBJECT, this field is left containing the value 'null' since the 'state' of such objects is represented by an instance of APPLICA-TION.STATE alone. However, for objects of descendent classes this field is used to point to the next node in the list.

In the previous package the HEIR field of the record STATE is defined to be of type OBJECT for convenience, but in fact any access type would have sufficed because it is impossible to predict at the time of its definition what the type of the next node will be. This information is only available when an heir of APPLICATION_OBJECT is transformed. This is the point at which the Ada typing rules need to be broken so that the nodes representing newly

defined heir classes can be 'linked' on to the list corresponding to objects of
the parent class. To make the HEIR field point to a record with a different
type to APPLICATION.OBJECT, the generic function UNCHECKED_CONVERSION
must be used to change its apparent type. The implementation of DRAG-
OON in Ada is therefore based on the assumption that access values to all
record types are of the same size and form.

Consider the class PRODUCT_DESCRIPTOR (3.4), for example. This is
transformed into a package with the following specification:

```
with APPLICATION, PRODUCT;                                    (9.7)
package PRODUCT_DESCRIPTOR is

    type VARIABLES;
    type STATE is access VARIABLES;

    type VARIABLES is record
        INTERNAL_BAR_CODE : PRODUCT.CODE_NUMBER;
        INTERNAL_PRICE : PRODUCT.VALUE;
        INTERNAL_STOCK_LEVEL : PRODUCT.STOCK_NUMBER;
        INTERNAL_LABEL : PRODUCT.LABEL;
        OFFSPRING_NO : NATURAL := 0;
        HEIR : APPLICATION.OBJECT;
    end record;

    function PART_OF (OB : in APPLICATION.OBJECT) return STATE;
    function CREATE (OFFSPRING_NO : in NATURAL := 0)
                                return APPLICATION.OBJECT;
    function PRICE (OB : in APPLICATION.OBJECT)
                                return PRODUCT.VALUE;
    procedure SET_PRICE_TO (OB : in APPLICATION.OBJECT;
                                PRICE : in PRODUCT.VALUE);
    function BAR_CODE (OB : in APPLICATION.OBJECT)
                                return PRODUCT.CODE_NUMBER;

        ⋮              -- similarly for other 'methods' of PRODUCT_DESCRIPTOR
end PRODUCT_DESCRIPTOR;
```

9.2.1   The CREATE function

As illustrated in Figure 9.1, the state of a PRODUCT_DESCRIPTOR object
is represented by a linked list with two nodes, the first of type APPLICA-
TION.STATE and the second of type PRODUCT_DESCRIPTOR.VARIABLES, storing the four attributes specific to product descriptor objects. The job of
linking the two nodes together transparently is performed by the CREATE
function exported in the specification.

To enable the HEIR field of the first node to point to a record of
type PRODUCT_DESCRIPTOR.VARIABLES, the CREATE function has to make
references of type PRODUCT_DESCRIPTOR.STATE appear to be of the expected
type APPLICATION.OBJECT using UNCHECKED_CONVERSION. The body of the
CREATE function declared in PRODUCT_DESCRIPTOR is thus of the form:

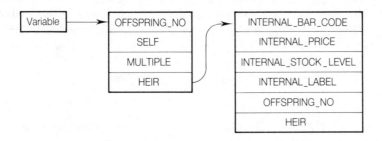

Figure 9.1   List structure holding state of PRODUCT_DESCRIPTOR objects.

$$\vdots \qquad\qquad\qquad\qquad\qquad\qquad\qquad\qquad (9.8)$$

```
function CREATE (OFFSPRING_NO : in NATURAL := 0)
                                   return APPLICATION.OBJECT is
    APP : APPLICATION.OBJECT;
    PROD : PRODUCT_DESCRIPTOR.STATE;
begin
    PROD := new PRODUCT_DESCRIPTOR.VARIABLES;
    PROD.OFFSPRING_NO := OFFSPRING_NO;
    PROD.HEIR := null;
    APP := APPLICATION.CREATE(1);
    APP.HEIR := APPLICATION_VIEW_OF(PROD);
    return APP;
end;
```

where APPLICATION_VIEW_OF is an instantiation of the generic function UNCHECKED_CONVERSION converting access values of type PROD-
UCT_DESCRIPTOR.STATE to the type APPLICATION.OBJECT:

$$\vdots$$

```
function APPLICATION_VIEW_OF is new UNCHECKED_CONVERSION
            (PRODUCT_DESCRIPTOR.STATE, APPLICATION.OBJECT);
```

$$\vdots$$

As far as the Ada typing system is concerned, therefore, PROD-
UCT_DESCRIPTOR objects, and indeed all objects in the system, are of
type APPLICATION.STATE referenced by an access variable of type APPLI-
CATION.OBJECT. Not only does this solve the problem of polymorphism,
but it also means that there are no typing obstacles to the incremental
introduction of new subclasses of PRODUCT_DESCRIPTOR, since instances of
these are also represented by state lists referenced by accessed variables of
type APPLICATION.OBJECT. Nevertheless, it is quite easy to tell at any time
to which type of object such a reference actually points by testing the HEIR
fields of the nodes in the list. For example, if the HEIR field of the first

node is 'null', the list represents an instance of class APPLICATION_OBJECT. If not, then it must correspond to a descendant of APPLICATION_OBJECT and therefore can be supplied as a parameter to a method of a descendent class.

9.2.2   The PART_OF function

The PART_OF function defined in the package specification performs the inverse 'UNCHECKED_CONVERSION' to the CREATE function so that the 'methods' of the class can manipulate the state variables stored in the corresponding state node. Given a reference of type APPLICATION.OBJECT, it returns a reference of the access type defined in the package specification – in this case PRODUCT_DESCRIPTOR.STATE. The PART_OF function declared in PRODUCT_DESCRIPTOR, for example, would have a very simple body of the form:

$$\vdots$$

```
function PART_OF (OB : in APPLICATION.OBJECT) return STATE is     (9.9)
begin
    return PRODUCT_DESCRIPTOR_VIEW_OF (OB.HEIR);
end;
```

$$\vdots$$

where PRODUCT_DESCRIPTOR_VIEW_OF is an instantiation of UNCHECKED-_CONVERSION providing the reverse conversion to APPLICATION_VIEW_OF used by the CREATE method:

$$\vdots$$

```
function PRODUCT_DESCRIPTOR_VIEW_OF is new UNCHECKED_CONVERSION
                (APPLICATION.OBJECT, PRODUCT_DESCRIPTOR.STATE);
```

$$\vdots$$

Apart from the two functions CREATE and PART_OF, no other part of the Ada code makes use of UNCHECKED_CONVERSION. The breaking of the typing rules is therefore performed 'transparently' in a disciplined manner within the bodies of these methods.

9.2.3   Linear inheritance

In a linear inheritance hierarchy (i.e. one in which classes have only one parent), this process of adding nodes on to the list is repeated for each new addition to the hierarchy. Thus, as illustrated in Figure 9.2, the state

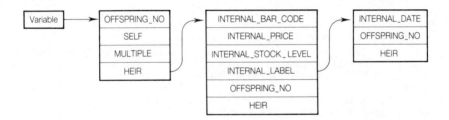

Figure 9.2   List structure holding state of PERISHABLE_DESCRIPTOR objects.

of a PERISHABLE_DESCRIPTOR (3.6) object is stored as a linked list of three nodes – the two nodes corresponding to the PRODUCT_DESCRIPTOR part and an extra node for storing the additional SIMPLE_CALENDAR.DATE attribute of PERISHABLE_DESCRIPTOR objects. The Ada package into which PERISH-ABLE_DESCRIPTOR is translated, however, is completely independent of the record types used to generate the first two nodes in the list. In other words, the transformation of a subclass into Ada does not depend in any way on the nature of the inherited classes but merely on the form of the class itself. PERISHABLE_DESCRIPTOR, for example, would be transformed into a package of the form:

```
with APPLICATION, SIMPLE_CALENDAR;                          (9.10)
package PERISHABLE_DESCRIPTOR is

    type VARIABLES;
    type STATE is access VARIABLES;

    type VARIABLES is record
        INTERNAL_DATE : SIMPLE_CALENDAR.DATE;
        OFFSPRING_NO : NATURAL := 0;
        HEIR : APPLICATION.OBJECT;
    end record;

    function PART_OF (OB : in APPLICATION.OBJECT) return STATE;
    function CREATE (OFFSPRING_NO : in NATURAL := 0)
                                    return APPLICATION.OBJECT;

    function SELL_BY_DATE (OB : in APPLICATION.OBJECT)
                                    return SIMPLE_CALENDAR.DATE;
    procedure SET_SELL_BY_DATE (OB : in APPLICATION.OBJECT;
                                DATE : in SIMPLE_CALENDAR.DATE);

end PERISHABLE_DESCRIPTOR;
```

whose structure is not affected in any way by that of the package PROD-UCT_DESCRIPTOR corresponding to its parent class. The only place in which reference is made to this package is in the implementation of the CREATE and PART_OF functions. The CREATE function of PERISHABLE_DESCRIPTOR uses the CREATE function of PRODUCT_DESCRIPTOR to generate the appropriate state list:

$$\vdots \qquad\qquad\qquad\qquad\qquad\qquad\qquad\qquad (9.11)$$

```
function CREATE (OFFSPRING_NO : in NATURAL := 0)
                                   return APPLICATION.OBJECT is
      APP : APPLICATION.OBJECT;
      PER : PERISHABLE_DESCRIPTOR.STATE;
begin
      PER := new PERISHABLE_DESCRIPTOR.VARIABLES;
      PER.OFFSPRING_NO := OFFSPRING_NO;
      PER.HEIR := null;
      APP := PRODUCT_DESCRIPTOR.CREATE(1);
      PRODUCT_DESCRIPTOR.PART_OF(APP).HEIR :=
                               APPLICATION_VIEW_OF(PER);
      return APP;
end;
```

where APPLICATION_VIEW_OF performs precisely the same kind of conversion as in the earlier version of CREATE (9.8) but from PERISHABLE_DESCRIP-TOR.STATE to APPLICATION.OBJECT.

Notice how this CREATE function, belonging to PERISHABLE_DESCRIP-TOR, uses the CREATE and PART_OF functions corresponding to the parent class PRODUCT_DESCRIPTOR to generate a PRODUCT_DESCRIPTOR list and then to append the record containing the variables specific to PERISH-ABLE_DESCRIPTOR objects on to the end. The function is not in any way concerned with the structure of the list returned by the parent's CREATE function, but is merely interested in 'tagging' a PERISHABLE_DESCRIPTOR node on to the end.

Similarly, the PART_OF function of PERISHABLE_DESCRIPTOR uses the PART_OF function exported by its parent's package:

$$\vdots \qquad\qquad\qquad\qquad\qquad\qquad\qquad\qquad (9.12)$$

```
function PART_OF (OB : in APPLICATION.OBJECT) return STATE is
begin
      return PERISHABLE_DESCRIPTOR_VIEW_OF
                        (PRODUCT_DESCRIPTOR.PART_OF(OB).HEIR);
end;
```

$$\vdots$$

This technique of implementing the CREATE and PART_OF functions for one class using the corresponding functions of its parent classes lies at the heart of the DRAGOON technique for supporting inheritance and incremental development. The key benefit of this mechanism is that the structure of these two functions, and consequently of the whole package, is not at all influenced by the implementation of the parent class. All classes can therefore be translated according to the same rules irrespective of their position in the inheritance hierarchy.

The Ada code corresponding to methods and threads, which are the only things in DRAGOON that can affect the state of an object, knows the type of the Ada record in which it is stored, and can call the appropriate PART_OF function to do the UNCHECKED_CONVERSION necessary to access it. All such conversions are guaranteed to be safe since they are only performed if the HEIR field of the preceding node is not 'null'. At the same time, however, since all objects are referenced by the same Ada type (APPLICATION.OBJECT), no retransformation or recompilation is needed when new classes are added to the system.

9.2.4   Clientship

This method of implementing DRAGOON classes in Ada makes the translation of client code very straightforward. *All* instance variables, of whatever class type, are translated into Ada access variables of type APPLICATION.OBJECT since the first node of all state lists is of type APPLICATION.STATE. The translation of method invocations employs the same principle used in the simple 'abstract data type' mapping outlined in Section 9.1.3. In other words, the Ada access variable corresponding to the called object is supplied as the first parameter of the subprogram implementing the method. Thus a method call of the following kind in a client of PRODUCT_DESCRIPTOR:

```
        ⋮

   PROD.SET_PRICE_TO(PRICE);
        ⋮
```

where PROD is a PRODUCT_DESCRIPTOR instance variable and PRICE an INTEGER value, would be transformed into the following subprogram invocation:

```
        ⋮

   PRODUCT_DESCRIPTOR.SET_PRICE_TO(PROD, PRICE);
        ⋮
```

where PROD is now an access variable of type APPLICATION.OBJECT.

Similarly, the generation of objects by invocation of the CREATE method is simply translated into a call to the CREATE function in the corresponding Ada package:

```
        ⋮

   PROD := PRODUCT_DESCRIPTOR.CREATE;
        ⋮
```

To illustrate these principles in a concrete example consider the class SIM-PLE_QUEUE (4.1) introduced in Chapter 4. This would be translated into an Ada package with the following specification:

```
package SIMPLE_QUEUE is                                        (9.13)
    type QUEUE_POINTER;
    type QUEUE_NODE is record
      ITEM : APPLICATION.OBJECT;
      NEXT : QUEUE_POINTER;
    end record;
    type QUEUE_POINTER is access QUEUE_NODE;

    type VARIABLES;
    type STATE is access VARIABLES;

    type VARIABLES is record
      FRONT, LAST : QUEUE_POINTER;
      OFFSPRING_NO : NATURAL := 0;
      HEIR : APPLICATION.OBJECT;
    end record;

    function PART_OF (OB : in APPLICATION.OBJECT) return STATE;
    function CREATE (OFFSPRING_NO : in NATURAL := 0)
                                    return APPLICATION.OBJECT;
    function POP (OB : in APPLICATION.OBJECT)
                                    return APPLICATION.OBJECT;
    procedure ADD (OB, ITEM : in APPLICATION.OBJECT);
    function IS_EMPTY (OB : in APPLICATION.OBJECT) return BOOLEAN;

    UNDER_FLOW : exception;

  end SIMPLE_QUEUE;
```

The first three types in this package are those used to define the list structure implementing the queue and appear in the body of the class. In general, any type definitions appearing in a class specification or body declarative part are simply copied into the specification of the corresponding Ada package.

Note also how all the method parameters and variables that were originally of a class type (i.e. EXAMPLE in the case of SIMPLE_QUEUE) are translated into the Ada type APPLICATION.OBJECT.

9.3   Dynamic binding

The preceding sections have illustrated how the inheritance and polymorphism features of DRAGOON can be faithfully translated into Ada. The remaining object-oriented feature of DRAGOON most alien to Ada is dynamic binding.

To illustrate the problems involved in implementing this mechanism, consider the class BOUNDED_SIMPLE_QUEUE (4.3) defined in Chapter 4. The most important feature of this class as far as dynamic binding is concerned is that it reimplements some of the methods inherited from SIMPLE_QUEUE.

Consequently, when one of the redefined methods is invoked through an instance variable of class SIMPLE_QUEUE, the particular version of the method which is executed depends on the dynamic type of the instance variable – that is, the type of the object to which it is referring at the time of the call. The problem, therefore, is to decide at run-time which of the Ada subprograms implementing the alternative versions of the method should be executed. Moreover, since the incremental development facilities of DRAGOON mean that the programmer may define further subclasses at any later stage, the range of different versions that may be invoked does not remain fixed.

9.3.1   Method selection shells

Clearly, there must be some Ada code in the system which knows about all the different current versions of a method in the system and is able to select the appropriate version at run-time. If this was embedded in the body of the Ada packages into which classes are translated, however, the code would have to be reproduced and recompiled each time a new version of a method was defined in a subclass. The incremental development principle of DRAGOON, and all the benefits gained by the linked list technique for representing state, would thus be largely undermined.

Ada's facility for defining the bodies of methods in physically separate subunits, however, provides an elegant mechanism for avoiding this problem. It permits the amount of code that has to be updated to cater for the introduction of new method versions to be limited to a single procedure body.

The foregoing discussion has described how the methods of a class are transformed into subprograms exported by the corresponding Ada package. None of the subprograms declared in the package *specification* actually implements the corresponding method *directly*, however. This job is, in fact, performed by an additional set of methods declared in a package SELF contained in the body of the main package. The bodies of the visible subprograms declared in the specification of the main package are contained in 'separate' units and use the subprograms defined in the inner package SELF to implement the original DRAGOON method.

Consider the class SIMPLE_QUEUE, for example. For each of the methods exported by this class there are *two* subprograms in the corresponding Ada code – one declared in the specification of the package SIMPLE_QUEUE and the other declared in the body. The body of the Ada package SIMPLE_QUEUE therefore has the general form:

```
package body SIMPLE_QUEUE is                              (9.14)

    function POP (OB : in APPLICATION.OBJECT) return
                            APPLICATION.OBJECT is separate;
    procedure ADD (OB, ITEM : in APPLICATION.OBJECT) is separate;
```

```
        function IS_EMPTY (OB : in APPLICATION.OBJECT)
                                            return BOOLEAN is separate;

        package SELF is
            function POP (OB : in APPLICATION.OBJECT)
                                    return APPLICATION.OBJECT;
            procedure ADD (OB, ITEM : in APPLICATION.OBJECT);
            function IS_EMPTY (OB : in APPLICATION.OBJECT) return BOOLEAN;
        end SELF;

        package body SELF is

            :                               -- bodies of the 'implementing' methods

        end SELF;


            :

                                  -- bodies of the CREATE and PART_OF methods

    end;
```

Since the subprograms declared in the inner package SELF contain the Ada image of the code in the body of the corresponding methods, these are termed the *'implementing'* subprograms. The implementing subprogram for the POP method, for example, would be of the form:

```
            :                                                       (9.15)
    function POP (OB : in APPLICATION.OBJECT)
                                    return APPLICATION.OBJECT is
        FRONT_NODE : QUEUE_POINTER := SIMPLE_QUEUE.PART_OF(S).FRONT;
    begin
        if SIMPLE_QUEUE.PART_OF(S).FRONT = null then
            raise UNDERFLOW;
        else
            SIMPLE_QUEUE.PART_OF(S).FRONT :=
                            SIMPLE_QUEUE.PART_OF(S).FRONT.NEXT;
            return FRONT_NODE;
        end if;
    end;


            :
```

In addition to the translation of clientship dependencies in the manner described previously, the main change occurring in the translation of a DRAGOON method body into the corresponding 'implementing subprogram' is the extension of instance variable and actual parameter names by the PART_OF function to provide access to the appropriate node of the state list. A similar translation is performed for all the other methods introduced by SIMPLE_QUEUE.

Since SIMPLE_QUEUE is an heir only of APPLICATION_OBJECT and does not inherit any user-defined method, when it is first translated into Ada there is only one version of each of its methods known to the system. Until a subclass of SIMPLE_QUEUE is added to the library, therefore, the subprograms declared in the specification of the corresponding Ada package are essentially redundant. The only action they perform is to call the corresponding method contained in SELF. The body of the exported POP subprogram, for example, has a *separate* body of the form:

```
separate (SIMPLE_QUEUE)                                           (9.16)
function POP (OB : in APPLICATION.OBJECT)
                                    return APPLICATION.OBJECT is
begin
    return SELF.POP(SIMPLE_QUEUE.PART_OF(OB));
end;
```

At this stage, therefore, this subprogram makes no useful contribution to the implementation of the method. It is when the programmer defines new versions of the method in subclasses of SIMPLE_QUEUE that the purpose of these subprograms becomes apparent. One subclass of SIMPLE_QUEUE that does just this is the class BOUNDED_SIMPLE_QUEUE which redefines the CRE-ATE, POP and ADD methods of SIMPLE_QUEUE to provide a bounded version of the component according to the implementation defined in Section 4.3.

When subclasses such as this are translated into Ada, methods *introduced* or *redefined* by the class (i.e. those for which it must provide a body) are translated according to the principles just described. In other words, each such method is translated into two Ada subprograms, one exported in the specification of the corresponding package and the other 'implementing method' defined in the inner package SELF. No methods are produced, however, for methods such as IS_EMPTY which are inherited by the subclass but not redefined.

However, generation of the corresponding Ada package is not the only action performed during the translation of a class which redefines inherited methods such as POP. In addition, the translation tool updates, or replaces, the subunits (i.e. the bodies) of the subprograms exported by the parent class's package in order to take account of the new version of the method introduced into the system. When BOUNDED_SIMPLE_QUEUE is translated into Ada, for example, the separate body of the subprogram SIMPLE_QUEUE.POP illustrated above is replaced by the following:

```
separate (SIMPLE_QUEUE)                                           (9.17)
function POP (OB : in APPLICATION.OBJECT)
                                    return APPLICATION.OBJECT is
begin
    if SIMPLE_QUEUE.PART_OF(OB).HEIR = null then
        return SELF.POP(OB);
    else
        return BOUNDED_SIMPLE_QUEUE.POP(OB);
    end if;
end;
```

When invoked, this function analyzes the form of the state list OB to see whether the node corresponding to BOUNDED_DESCRIPTOR_QUEUE is present (i.e. whether the list represents an instance of DESCRIPTOR_QUEUE or its subclass BOUNDED_DESCRIPTOR_QUEUE); if not (i.e. it represents the former) it invokes the DESCRIPTOR_QUEUE implementation, otherwise it invokes the BOUNDED_DESCRIPTOR_QUEUE version. Essentially, therefore, this function forms a kind of 'shell' around the true method implementations in order to select, at run-time, the appropriate one for execution according to the dynamic binding rules of DRAGOON. Such a subprogram is thus termed a 'selection shell' for the method concerned.

The great advantage of this approach is that because the method body that is replaced is a subunit of the main package, not even the body of the package, let alone the Ada code for clients of the class, need to be recompiled when method-redefining subclasses are added to the system. The client Ada code may therefore exploit the new version of the method without any modification. All the modification and recompilation needed to cater for the new version is limited to the selection shells of the methods concerned.

9.3.2   Multiple offspring

This technique is fine for distinguishing between the different versions of a method that may be introduced in a linear inheritance chain – that is, when each class has only one parent and one heir. In general, however, neither of these two conditions need be satisfied since the multiple inheritance facilities of DRAGOON (whose implementation is discussed in the next section) permit classes to have more than one parent, while it is a normal feature of most object-oriented languages that a class may have more than one heir or *offspring*.

Clearly, merely checking the HEIR field of a state node is not sufficient to indicate which of the numerous offspring of the corresponding class the state list represents. If the HEIR field of a PRODUCT_DESCRIPTOR (3.4) node was not 'null', for example, the next node could either correspond to a PERISHABLE_DESCRIPTOR (3.6) object or to an ELECTRICAL_DESCRIPTOR (3.8) object. Before using a PART_OF function to convert its type, it is essential to determine to which of the subclasses the next node in the list actually corresponds, otherwise serious conversion errors could result. Another field is needed in the nodes of the state lists, therefore, to indicate which of the potential offspring the subsequent node represents – that is, which of the branches of the inheritance tree the class represented by the subsequent node lies in.

There are a number of possible ways of storing this information. One way is simply to store the class name. For example, the record type defining the node corresponding to PRODUCT_DESCRIPTOR could contain a string field holding either 'PERISHABLE_DESCRIPTOR' or 'ELECTRICAL_DESCRIPTOR', depending on the nature of the following node. In the prototype version of the translation tool, however, an alternative strategy is used in which an integer identifier, called the 'offspring number', is assigned to the heirs of a class according to the order in which they are submitted to the translation tool. This is the purpose of the OFFSPRING_NO field introduced earlier.

If PERISHABLE_DESCRIPTOR was the first successfully compiled subclass of PRODUCT_DESCRIPTOR, for example, it would be assigned the offspring number 1 *with respect to* PRODUCT_DESCRIPTOR. In other words, in a state list corresponding to a PERISHABLE_DESCRIPTOR object, the OFFSPRING_NO field of the PRODUCT_DESCRIPTOR (i.e. the second) node would contain the value 1. The next successfully translated classes would be assigned the offspring number 2 with respect to PRODUCT_DESCRIPTOR and so on.

Although this limits the number of offspring of a particular class to the value of MAX_INT (the largest integer in an Ada implementation), this is not felt to be a practical constraint on the development of class libraries. The advantage of this approach is that it reduces the size of the state list nodes and also the time taken to test the equality of different offspring identifiers.

Together, the HEIR and OFFSPRING_NO fields of state nodes provide all the information needed by selection shells to determine which version of a method to execute in response to a call. Suppose, for example, that the programmer defined another subclass of SIMPLE_QUEUE, ANOTHER_SIMPLE_QUEUE say, which also redefined the POP method. Assuming that this was translated *after* the BOUNDED_SIMPLE_QUEUE and that there are no other subclasses, ANOTHER_SIMPLE_QUEUE would be assigned the offspring number 2 and BOUNDED_SIMPLE_QUEUE the offspring number 1. In order to choose the appropriate implementation when the POP method is invoked through an instance variable of class SIMPLE_QUEUE, the body of the POP selection shell would be updated to:

```
separate(SIMPLE_QUEUE)                                            (9.18)
function POP (OB : in APPLICATION.OBJECT)
                                         return APPLICATION.OBJECT is
begin
    if SIMPLE_QUEUE.PART_OF(OB).HEIR = null then
        return SELF.POP(OB);
    else
        case SIMPLE_QUEUE.PART_OF(OB).OFFSPRING_NO is
        when 1 =>
            return BOUNDED_SIMPLE_QUEUE.POP(OB);
        when 2 =>
            return ANOTHER_SIMPLE_QUEUE.POP(OB);
        when others =>
            return SELF.POP(OB);
        end case;
    end if;
end;
```

Notice that if the HEIR field checked by a selection shell is not 'null' and a version of the method defined by a subclass is required, it does not directly call the required implementing subprogram (in fact, it cannot because it is hidden in a package body) but rather the *selection shell* corresponding to the subclass indicated by the OFFSPRING_NO field. A selection shell, therefore, does not in general choose between *all* the available versions of a method, but merely decides whether to call the version defined by the associated class (implemented by the subprogram contained in the inner SELF package) or whether to call a *selection shell* of one of the class's descendants. In the second case, the called selection shell continues the selection process in the same way. The call hierarchy of the selection shells, therefore, directly corresponds to the inheritance hierarchy of the associated classes.

This means that the time taken to select between the various versions of a method is not constant but is proportional to the actual number of different versions. This, in turn, is proportional to the depth of the inheritance hierarchy. Since there is, in principle, no limit to the depth of class inheritance hierarchies, and hence the number of potential versions of a method that could be executed in response to a method call, the time taken to select the version required is potentially unbounded. Experience has demonstrated, however, that inheritance hierarchies developed in practical programming situations tend to remain fairly shallow and the number of times a method is redefined is fairly small. The time taken to search for the appropriate method body to execute, therefore, is unlikely to present significant difficulties in most applications. Nevertheless, it is important that applications programmers are aware of the mechanism used to search for method versions so that they may avoid the overheads involved in time critical situations.

One solution in a future version of DRAGOON might be to include an additional keyword in the language which programmers could use in such situations to indicate that the invocation time for a particular method is more important than the dynamic binding facility. In other words, the keyword - 'fixed' or 'immutable', say – would indicate that the corresponding method cannot be redefined in subclasses and that its access time is therefore fixed. Such methods correspond to the 'non-virtual' member functions of C++.

9.3.3   Abstract classes

Since the nodes in the state lists are not used just for storing the state variables of the corresponding classes but also for representing the position of the corresponding object in the inheritance hierarchy, a state list for an object of a given class must contain nodes for every ancestor of the class, even if they introduce no additional instance variables. In particular, this means that nodes are needed for abstract classes no matter whether they are completely 'abstract' and define no state variables or method implementations.

Abstract classes are, in fact, translated into packages with precisely the same structure as those produced for normal classes. The only difference is that the implementing subprograms corresponding to deferred methods simply contain a statement to raise the exception CONSTRAINT_ERROR should it be invoked erroneously. The packages corresponding to abstract classes even contain a CREATE subprogram, since this is needed by the CRE-ATE subprograms of descendent classes in order to generate the appropriate state list. The 'concreting' of deferred methods in subclasses is handled in precisely the same way as the redefinition of normal methods.

9.4 Multiple inheritance

The discussion so far has been concerned with translating classes possessing a maximum of one parent. In common with a number of other object-oriented languages, however, DRAGOON permits classes to have multiple parents. The extra possibilities that this introduces, particularly the range of different assignments that it makes possible, significantly increases the complexity of the translation into Ada because it means that the straight-forward linked list structure is no longer adequate for storing the state of objects.

To see why this is so, consider the class DATED_DESCRIPTOR (3.13) introduced in Chapter 3 as an heir of both PRODUCT_DESCRIPTOR (3.4) and DATED_ITEM (3.12). Since it is a normal (although perhaps somewhat trivial) class, DATED_ITEM will be transformed, according to the principles outlined previously, into an Ada package with the following specification part:

```
with APPLICATION, SIMPLE_CALENDAR;                          (9.19)
package DATED_DESCRIPTOR is

    type VARIABLES;
    type STATE is access VARIABLES;

    type VARIABLES is record
        INTERNAL_DATE : SIMPLE_CALENDAR.DATE;
        OFFSPRING_NO : NATURAL := 0;
        HEIR : APPLICATION.OBJECT;
    end record;

    function PART_OF (OB : in APPLICATION.OBJECT) return STATE;
    function CREATE (OFFSPRING_NO : in NATURAL := 0)
                                    return APPLICATION.OBJECT;

    function DATE (OB : in APPLICATION.OBJECT)
                                    return SIMPLE_CALENDAR.DATE;
    procedure SET_DATE_TO (OB : in APPLICATION.OBJECT;
                                    DATE : in SIMPLE_CALENDAR.DATE);
end;
```

The main problem presented by multiple inheritance is the fact that a class with multiple parents does not have a unique ancestry chain and cannot therefore be represented by a single list. Consider an instance of the class DATED_DESCRIPTOR, for example. Since this is a subclass of PROD-

UCT_DESCRIPTOR, it can be assigned to PRODUCT_DESCRIPTOR instance variables and can respond to the same set of method invocations as instances of PRODUCT_DESCRIPTOR. In terms of the Ada implementation described above, this means that the state list representing this instance can be supplied to the subprograms defined in the PRODUCT_DESCRIPTOR package, which expect the first part of the list to be the same as that for PRODUCT_DESCRIPTOR objects.

By the same token, however, since DATED_DESCRIPTOR is a subclass of DATED_ITEM also, instances can be supplied to DATED_ITEM instance variables. In terms of the Ada transformation, this means that the state list for such an object can be assigned to subprograms that expect the first part of the list to be that of a DATED_ITEM object. Clearly, it is impossible for a single list to be both a PRODUCT_DESCRIPTOR list and DATED_ITEM list at the same time. In order to support this duality in the translation of DRAGOON, instances of classes with multiple parents are not represented by a single state list but by a composite data structure containing all the necessary state lists. Provided that the appropriate list, or *form*, can be reached from any instance variable, the Ada subprograms implementing the methods of parent classes need only be supplied with the list they are interested in.

Perhaps not surprisingly, it is the role of the one remaining field of the APPLICATION.STATE record to link together the necessary lists into the required composite data structure. When more than one state list is needed to store the state of an object because of multiple inheritance, the MULTIPLE field in the first node in each list is made to point to the first node of the next list (except of course the last, which points to the first list). The result, therefore, is perhaps best described as a 'ring' of linked lists.

The data structure for storing the state of DATED_DESCRIPTOR objects is represented in Figure 9.3. As indicated in this figure, one of the lists in the ring structure is given special status in that all the SELF fields in the first nodes reference the first node of this list. This list, and the corresponding class, is known as the *default* form of the ring structure since it is this list that is referenced when an object is created by the CREATE function for the class. The default form is arbitrarily chosen to be the first class named in the 'inherits' clause of the class being transformed.

Since the class DATED_DESCRIPTOR inherits the methods of both its parents, it is possible to invoke the methods inherited both from PRODUCT_DESCRIPTOR and DATED_ITEM through an instance variable of this class. When translated into Ada, this means that from an access variable corresponding to an instance variable of class DATED_ITEM it must be possible to provide (or reach) references to all the different state lists in the structure. As indicated in Figure 9.3, from an access variable DD referring to the PRODUCT_DESCRIPTOR list, the DATED_ITEM equivalent can be reached by dereferencing the MULTIPLE field of the first node (i.e. by DD.MULTIPLE). For classes that inherit from more than two classes the ring structure of lists is simply extended. In other words, the MULTIPLE field of the second

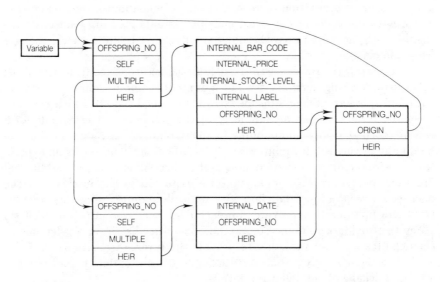

Figure 9.3   Data structure for DATED_DESCRIPTOR objects.

list would not point back to the first but would point to the next list in the ring. Therefore, extra dereferencing on the MULTIPLE fields is sometimes required to reach other lists in the structure (e.g. DD.MULTIPLE.MULTIPLE ...).

By dereferencing the MULTIPLE fields the appropriate number of times, therefore, it is possible to reach any of the other forms of an instance of a class with multiple parents from a reference to the default form. In many object-oriented languages this would be sufficient, because if there is only one remaining reference to an object and this points to one of the forms, the typing rules of the language would imply that the other forms could never be reached anyway. Suppose, for example, that an instance of the class DATED_DESCRIPTOR was 'pushed' on to an instance of SIMPLE_QUEUE. In languages that make no provision for type conversion, the typing rules mean that this object can only be treated as being (i.e. assigned to instance variables) of the class PRODUCT_DESCRIPTOR. As described in Chapter 3, however, DRAGOON permits the type of the object to be explicitly converted back to DATED_DESCRIPTOR where it can also be treated as a DATED_ITEM again.

In general, therefore, it is important not only to be able to reach any list in the structure from the default form but also to reach the default form from a reference to any of the other lists. The first approach which springs to mind for achieving this is simply to continue dereferencing the MULTIPLE fields until the complete ring structure is traversed and the original reference is regained. While this clearly works for this simple example, it is not an acceptable solution in general, because when more complex classes, which have multiple parents with multiple parents etc., are translated the size of the ring, and hence the number of required dereferences, changes from one class to another.

To permit the reference to the default list to be gained from any of the other lists in a ring, as indicated in Figure 9.3, the node defined for classes with multiple parents contains an extra field, called ORIGIN, which contains a reference back to the default form of the structure. The default form can be reached at any point simply by dereferencing the ORIGIN field of the final node in the list. To relieve the client Ada code from having to express this dereferencing explicitly at all points where it is required, additional functions performing this operation are exported in the interface of the package corresponding to a class with multiple parents. More specifically, two extra functions are provided for each additional parent (after the first) – one to provide a reference to the parent's state list from a reference to the default form and the other to provide the reverse transition.

The DRAGOON class DATED_DESCRIPTOR is therefore translated into an Ada package of the following form:

```
with APPLICATION, PRODUCT_DESCRIPTOR, DATED_ITEM;              (9.20)
package DATED_ITEM is

    type VARIABLES;
    type STATE is access VARIABLES;

    type VARIABLES is record
        OFFSPRING_NO : NATURAL := 0;
        ORIGIN : APPLICATION.OBJECT;
        HEIR : APPLICATION.OBJECT;
    end record;

    function PART_OF (OB : in APPLICATION.OBJECT) return STATE;
    function CREATE (OFFSPRING_NO : in NATURAL := 0)
                                return APPLICATION.OBJECT;
    function FROM_DATED_ITEM (OB : in APPLICATION.OBJECT)
                                return APPLICATION.OBJECT;
    function DATED_ITEM_FORM (OB : in APPLICATION.OBJECT)
                                return APPLICATION.OBJECT;
end;
```

The FROM_DATED_ITEM is the function which, given a reference to the DATED_ITEM list in the ring structure, returns a reference to the default form using the ORIGIN field of the final node. Its body is thus of the form:

```
function FROM_DATED_ITEM (OB : in APPLICATION.OBJECT)
                                return APPLICATION.OBJECT is
    begin
        return DATED_DESCRIPTOR_VIEW_OF
                        (DATED_ITEM.PART_OF(OB).HEIR).ORIGIN;
    end;
```

This function is only used in the translation of explicit type conversions. The other function DATED_ITEM_FORM, which provides a reference to the DATED_ITEM list in the structure given a reference of the default form, is much more commonly employed and also simpler to implement:

```
function DATED_ITEM_FORM (OB : in APPLICATION.OBJECT)
                                    return APPLICATION.OBJECT is
begin
    return OB.MULTIPLE;
end;
```

9.5   Generic classes

As described in Chapter 4, in common with Eiffel and POOL, DRAGOON supports the notion of generic classes that can be parameterized with respect to data types or class types. Generic classes are surprisingly easy to implement in Ada because of the language's own advanced generic facilities and also because of the policy that instances of actualizations of generic classes are not type compatible with any other class.

This means that it is not necessary to tackle the problems of polymorphism, dynamic binding and incremental program development encountered in the implementation of normal classes and objects. Consequently, there is no need for the elaborate linked list mechanisms used to permit instances of subclasses to be treated like instances of their parents, or for the selection shell mechanisms needed to handle the dynamic selection of method versions. In fact, the state of instances of generic actualizations can be represented using the basic 'abstract data type' approach outlined in Section 9.1, enhanced to provide the required reference semantics. The main problem encountered in the translation of generic classes is not surprisingly concerned with the generic parameters.

A generic class whose parameters are only of data types can be translated into a generic Ada package with precisely the same generic formal part as the class. Moreover, an actualization of the generic class is translated into an instantiation of the corresponding Ada package with precisely the same allocation of actual to formal parameters. The type and subprograms exported by the resulting generic actualization (instantiation) can be used just as any other enhanced 'abstract data type' to generate dynamically state records and perform operations upon them.

In the case of generic classes with one or more parameters of a class type, the generic class is again translated into a single generic package, but the generic class parameters are mapped into a generic type parameter together with a set of associated formal subprograms corresponding to the methods of the formal class type. In other words, the Ada package generated in the translation is parameterized with respect to the same *data abstraction* as the corresponding class but represented as a type with associated formal subprograms rather than as a formal class parameter.

Consider, for example, the generic class PAR_CHRONO_QUEUE (5.8) introduced in Chapter 5. This has the class DATED_ITEM as a parameter and is therefore translated into a generic package with the following generic formal part:

```
generic                                                          (9.21)
    type T is private;
    with function DATE(OB : in T) return SIMPLE_CALENDAR.DATE;
    with procedure SET_DATE_TO (OB : in T;
                                DATE : in SIMPLE_CALENDAR.DATE);
    with function CREATE (OFFSPRING_NO : in NATURAL) return T;
package PAR_CHRONO_QUEUE is

    type STATE is private;
    type OBJECT is access STATE;

    function POP (OB : in APPLICATION.OBJECT) return OBJECT;

        ⋮
                                        -- similarly for other methods
private

        ⋮

    end;
```

Notice the way in which instances generated from actualizations of this class are represented by single records in the basic 'abstract access type' style rather than as linked lists. Furthermore, the subprograms exported in the interface are not selection shells but 'implementing' methods whose bodies contain the image of the method bodies.

An actualization of this class of the form:

```
class DATED_SIMPLE_QUEUE is new PAR_CHRONO_QUEUE
                        (DATED_ITEM => DATED_DESCRIPTOR);
```

would then be translated into the following instantiation of the generic:

```
package DATED_SIMPLE_QUEUE is new PAR_CHRONO_QUEUE
                    (T => APPLICATION.OBJECT,
                     DATE => DATED_ITEM.DATE,
                     SET_DATE_TO => DATED_ITEM.SET_DATE_TO,
                     CREATE => DATED_ITEM.CREATE);
```

This example illustrates how actualization of PAR_CHRONO_QUEUE, with the actual parameter DATED_DESCRIPTOR (3.13), would be translated into Ada. Since all subclasses of the formal generic parameter DATED_ITEM export at least these methods, the corresponding subprograms can clearly be used to instantiate the generic package.

9.5.1 Inheriting genericity

One of the novel features of DRAGOON is that it permits generic classes to be specialized by inheritance. In other words, new generic classes can be created by enriching existing generic classes in the same way as normal classes. An important difference, however, resulting from the typing rules associated with generics is that the actualizations of a generic *subclass* are not type compatible with actualization of its generic *superclass*.

Again, therefore, there is no need to worry about the problems of dynamic binding and polymorphism associated with the translation of normal classes. The state of actualizations of generic subclasses can therefore also be modelled by the extended 'abstract data type' approach outlined in Section 9.1. The new problem introduced by inheriting genericity is to arrange for the inherited state to be incorporated into the state records of instances of subclass actualizations while at the same time ensuring that the parameters in the inherited generic formal part remain generic.

This is achieved by actualizing the generic package corresponding to the parent class within the package corresponding to the subclass using the generic formal parameters of the latter as the actual parameters of the former. Consider the generic class EXTENDED_CHRONO_QUEUE (5.14), for example, which is a subclass of PAR_CHRONO_QUEUE (5.8) whose translation into Ada has just been illustrated. Assuming that, in addition to the new method NUMBER_WITH_DATE, EXTENDED_CHRONO_QUEUE also introduced a new variable, NUMBER of type NATURAL say, it would be translated into the following package:

```
generic                                                        (9.22)
    type INHERITED_T is private;
    with function INHERITED_DATE (OB : in INHERITED_T)
                            return SIMPLE_CALENDAR.DATE;
    with procedure INHERITED_SET_DATE_TO (OB : in INHERITED_T;
                            DATE : in SIMPLE_CALENDAR.DATE);
    with function INHERITED_CREATE (OFFSPRING_NO : in NATURAL)
                            return INHERITED_T;
package EXTENDED_CHRONO_QUEUE is

    package INHERITED is new PAR_CHRONO_QUEUE (T => INHERITED_T,
                DATE => INHERITED_DATE,
                SET_DATE_TO => INHERITED_SET_DATE_TO,
                CREATE => INHERITED_CREATE);

    type STATE is private;
    type OBJECT is access STATE;

    function POP (OB : in APPLICATION.OBJECT) return OBJECT;

    ⋮                           -- similarly for other inherited methods

    function NUMBER_WITH_DATE (OB : in APPLICATION.OBJECT;
                D : in SIMPLE_CALENDAR.DATE) return NATURAL;
private

    type STATE is record
        INHERITED_STATE : INHERITED.OBJECT;
```

```
        NEW_VARIABLE : NATURAL;
    end record;

  end;
```

In this particular example, the generic subclass EXTENDED_CHRONO_QUEUE does not introduce any more generic parameters. It is only generic with respect to those parameters it has inherited. There is no reason why a generic subclass cannot introduce new parameters, however, in which case they are transformed in the same way as the parameters of directly defined generic classes.

The same is true of any additional instance variables the generic class may introduce. Had EXTENDED_CHRONO_QUEUE introduced any new state variables, these would have simply been included in the private record type STATE.

By using the formal generic parameters of the package EX-TENDED_CHRONO_QUEUE as the actual parameters of the instantiation IN-HERITED of PAR_CHRONO_QUEUE, the genericity of the inherited state is maintained but can also be added to the state record corresponding to the generic subclass.

9.6   Concurrency

Having described how the 'sequential' features of DRAGOON are imple-mented in Ada, it is now time to consider the concurrent aspects. These may be conveniently split into two parts – the handling of 'active' objects and the handling of behavioural inheritance, since these are orthogonal features of DRAGOON.

9.6.1   Active objects

As the task is the unit of concurrency in Ada, the implementation of active objects, with their concurrent execution threads, must clearly be based on the use of tasks. The only problem in using a task to represent the thread of an object is in integrating it with the state list representation of objects used so far. In fact, this turns out to be fairly straightforward because Ada permits tasks generated from task types to be identified by access variables that can be included in the appropriate record structure. In addition to the fields storing the state variables of the object, therefore, the state node of active objects has an additional field holding a reference to a task.

Consider the active class FORWARDER (6.10), for example. This would be translated into a package with a specification of the form:

```
package FORWARDER is                                              (9.23)

    type VARIABLES;
    type STATE is access VARIABLES;
    type THREAD_FORM;
    type THREAD_REF is access THREAD_FORM;

    type VARIABLES is record
        DB, P, BUFFER : APPLICATION.OBJECT;       -- FORWARDER variables
        OFFSPRING_NO : NATURAL := 0;
        HEIR : APPLICATION.OBJECT;
        THREAD : THREAD_REF;
    end record;

    task type THREAD_FORM is
        entry START (S : in APPLICATION.OBJECT);
    end;

    function PART_OF (OB : in APPLICATION.OBJECT) return STATE;
    function CREATE (OFFSPRING_NO : in NATURAL := 0)
                                        return APPLICATION.OBJECT;
    procedure START (OB : in APPLICATION.OBJECT);
    function SHARE (OB, SHARED_DB : in APPLICATION.OBJECT);
    procedure ADD (OB, P : in APPLICATION.OBJECT);
end;
```

The procedure START corresponds to the START method used to activate the thread of active classes. Invocation of the START method by a client of an active object is thus translated into the invocation of the START procedure whose body is of the form:

$$\vdots$$

```
procedure START (OB : in APPLICATION.OBJECT) is              (9.24)
begin
    FORWARDER.PART_OF (OB).THREAD := new THREAD_FORM;
    FORWARDER.PART_OF (OB).THREAD.START(OB);
end;
```

$$\vdots$$

The first action performed by this procedure is to instantiate the task type THREAD_FORM and assign its access value to the THREAD field of the state node associated with FORWARDER. The procedure then calls the START method of the task to give it the reference to the state list so that the thread may manipulate the variables of the object. The calling of this entry also serves to unblock the task so that it may begin execution of the code corresponding to the body of the thread. The THREAD_FORM task type therefore has the following body:

$$\vdots$$

```
task body THREAD_FORM is                                     (9.25)
    SELF : FORWARDER.STATE;
```

```
begin
   accept START (S : in APPLICATION.OBJECT) do
   begin
      SELF := FORWARDER.PART_OF(S);
   end;
   SELF.BUFFER := QUEUE.CREATE;
   loop
      SELF.P := GUARDED_QUEUE.POP(SELF.BUFFER);
      DATA_BASE.ADD(SELF.DB, SELF.P);
   end loop;
end;
```

$$\vdots$$

Once the START procedure has generated an instance of task type THREAD_FORM and provided it with a reference to the object's state list by calling its START entry, the task will execute concurrently with other threads and method invocations, as required. Moreover, as it is included in the state node of the corresponding object, it is intimately associated with the corresponding object state for the duration of the program.

9.6.2   Behavioured classes

The implementation of behavioured classes in Ada has some similarities to that of active classes in that an additional task is added to the state node corresponding to the class. Unless the behaviour contains a guard, however, the task implementing the behaviour does not require visibility of the state list of the object. Its function is to export a set of methods that are called before and after the execution of the 'implementation' subprograms to enforce adherence to the specified access protocol.

The task types used for this purpose are contained in predefined packages corresponding to the behavioural classes. In the long term, tools will be available to generate such packages automatically in the same way as the other parts of the implementing Ada code, but in the short term these packages are predefined along with the library of behavioural classes.

The package corresponding to the behavioural class READERS_WRITERS (6.5), for example, which describes the typical 'multiple readers – single writers' access protocol, is as follows:

```
package READERS_WRITERS is                                    (9.26)

   task type BEHAVIOUR is

      entry ROP_REQUEST;
      entry ROP_COMPLETION;

      entry WOP_REQUEST;
      entry WOP_COMPLETION;

   end BEHAVIOUR;

end READERS_WRITERS;
```

```
package body READERS_WRITERS is

    task body BEHAVIOUR is
        READERS, WRITERS : NATURAL := 0;
    begin
        loop
            select
                when WRITERS = 0 =>
                    accept ROP_REQUEST do
                        READERS := READERS + 1;
                    end;
            or
                when WRITERS = 0 and READERS = 0 =>
                    accept WOP_REQUEST do
                        WRITERS := WRITERS + 1;
                    end;
            or
                accept ROP_COMPLETION do
                        READERS := READERS - 1;
                end;
            or
                accept WOP_COMPLETION do
                        WRITERS := WRITERS - 1;
                end;
            end select;
        end BEHAVIOUR;

end READERS_WRITERS;
```

For every formal method set appearing in the behavioural class, there are two entries in the corresponding task type – one used to request permission to execute the associated method and the other to indicate completion of the method.

Suppose that a behavioured version of the SIMPLE_QUEUE class discussed earlier was required, for example. Such a class would be represented by the following behavioured class:

```
behavioural class SAFE_SIMPLE_QUEUE is                          (9.27)
    inherits SIMPLE_QUEUE;
    ruled by READERS_WRITERS;
where
    ADD => WOP;
    POP => ROP;
end SAFE_SIMPLE_QUEUE;
```

and would be translated into a package with the following specification:

```
with APPLICATION, READERS_WRITERS;                              (9.28)
package SAFE_SIMPLE_QUEUE is

    function PART_OF (OB : in APPLICATION.OBJECT)
                                return READERS_WRITERS.BEHAVIOUR;
    function CREATE return APPLICATION.OBJECT;

end;
```

Since a behavioured class such as this constitutes the end of the normal inheritance chain, there is no need for the OFFSPRING_NO and HEIR fields usually included in the state record for classes. Furthermore, since it is not possible to introduce new instance variables in the behavioural inheritance step, there is no need for fields corresponding to these either. In fact, conceptually the only 'field' needed in the state node for a behavioured class is a reference to an instance of a task defining the appropriate behaviour. Under such circumstances, therefore, the record essentially 'collapses' into a single access variable referenced by the HEIR field of the SIMPLE_QUEUE state list. This access variable is consequently redundant since the HEIR field could easily refer directly to the task rather than to an intermediate access variable.

For this reason no state record is defined in the package generated for a behavioured class. Instead, the CREATE method simply generates an instance of the appropriate 'behaviour' task (in this case READERS_WRITERS.BEHAVIOUR) and appends it to the end of the state list for the application superclass. The PART_OF function accordingly returns a reference to this task.

Updating selection shells

The crucial part of the translation of behavioured classes is the updating of the selection shells of the affected methods. As well as producing the package illustrated above, when the behavioured class SAFE_SIMPLE_QUEUE is translated, the selection shells corresponding to the methods inherited from the application class are updated as if they had been redefined in the behavioured class. The difference is that the 'case' statement alternative corresponding to the behavioured class invokes the 'request' and 'completion' methods of the 'behaviour' task before, and after, the implementing method in the package SELF.

Consider, for example, the POP method of SIMPLE_QUEUE. Assuming this class is assigned the 'offspring number' 3 with respect to SIMPLE_QUEUE, then because POP is allocated to the abstract set ROP in the behavioured class SAFE_SIMPLE_QUEUE, the POP selection shell of this class would be updated as follows:

```
separate(SIMPLE_QUEUE)                                            (9.29)
function POP (OB : in APPLICATION.OBJECT)
                               return APPLICATION.OBJECT is
begin
   if SIMPLE_QUEUE.PART_OF(OB).HEIR = null then
       return SELF.POP(SIMPLE_QUEUE.PART_OF(OB));
   else
       case SIMPLE_QUEUE.PART_OF(OB).OFFSPRING_NO is
       when 1 =>
          return BOUNDED_SIMPLE_QUEUE.POP(OB);
       when 2 =>
          return ANOTHER_SIMPLE_QUEUE.POP(OB);
       when 3 =>
```

```
        SAFE_SIMPLE_QUEUE.PART_OF (OB).ROP_REQUEST;
        SAFE_SIMPLE_QUEUE.PART_OF (OB).ROP_COMPLETION;
        return SIMPLE_QUEUE.POP(OB);
    when others =>
        return SELF.POP(SIMPLE_QUEUE.PART_OF(OB));
    end case;
  end if;
end;
```

If the selection shell is applied to the state list for a behavioured object before the actual implementing subprogram is executed, permission to do so must first be gained from the appropriate 'request' entry of the associated 'behaviour' task. This is referenced by the HEIR field of the last state node. Similarly, once the execution of the implementation method is completed, the appropriate 'completion' entry is called to update the state of the 'behaviour' task. The client Ada code, therefore, is blocked until the required logical conditions for execution of the corresponding method are satisfied.

9.6.3   Guarded permissions

This strategy for implementing the synchronization conditions specified in a behavioural class can easily be extended to cope with situations in which the conditions defining the execution permission of methods are determined not only by the history functions but also by other methods. The main modification to the translation just described is to allow subprograms in the sequential class's Ada package to affect the acceptance of entry calls in the 'behaviour' task and to give this task visibility of the state list of the object it is protecting. The 'behaviour' task type defining the entries that must be called before and after executing the implementing methods is generalized with respect to the guard methods by defining it in a generic package.

Consider the behavioural class BOUNDED_BUFFER (6.11), for example, which includes guarded permissions. The corresponding 'behaviour' task would be defined in a generic package of the following form:

$$(9.30)$$

```
generic
    with FULL_GUARD (OB : in APPLICATION.OBJECT) return BOOLEAN;
package BOUNDED_BUFFER is

    task type BEHAVIOUR is

        entry INITIALIZE (OB : in APPLICATION.OBJECT);

        entry PUT_OPS_REQUEST;
        entry PUT_OPS_COMPLETION;

        entry GET_OPS_REQUEST;
        entry GET_OPS_COMPLETION;

        entry FULL_GUARD_REQUEST;
        entry FULL_GUARD_COMPLETION;
```

```
            entry OTHER_OPS_REQUEST;
            entry OTHER_OPS_COMPLETION;

        end BEHAVIOUR;

    end BOUNDED_BUFFER;


    package body BOUNDED_BUFFER is

        task body BEHAVIOUR is

            SIZE : NATURAL := 0;
            F_GUARD : BOOLEAN := FALSE;
            SELF : APPLICATION.OBJECT;

            procedure EVALUATE_GUARDS is
            begin
                F_GUARD := FULL_GUARD(SELF);
            end;

        begin
            accept INITIALIZE (OB : in APPLICATION.OBJECT) do
                SELF := OB;
            end;
            loop
                select
                    when not F_GUARD =>
                        accept PUT_OPS_REQUEST;
                or
                    when not SIZE = 0 =>
                        accept GET_OPS_REQUEST;
                or
                    accept FULL_GUARD_REQUEST;
                or
                    accept OTHER_OPS_REQUEST;
                or
                    accept PUT_OPS_COMPLETION do
                        SIZE := SIZE + 1;
                        EVALUATE_GUARDS;
                    end;
                or
                    accept GET_OPS_COMPLETION do
                        SIZE := SIZE - 1;
                        EVALUATE_GUARDS;
                    end;
                or
                    accept FULL_GUARD_COMPLETION;
                or
                    accept OTHER_OPS_COMPLETION do
                        EVALUATE_GUARDS;
                    end;
                end select;
            end loop;
        end BEHAVIOUR;

    end BOUNDED_BUFFER;
```

Before the required 'behaviour' task can be appended on to the state list for an instance of a class such as GUARDED_QUEUE (6.12) controlled by BOUN-DED_BUFFER, this package must first be instantiated with the 'implementation' subprogram corresponding to the guard method. GUARDED_QUEUE, for example, would be translated into the following package:

```
with APPLICATION, BOUNDED_BUFFER;                              (9.31)
package GUARDED_QUEUE is

    package QUEUE is new
            BOUNDED_BUFFER (SIMPLE_QUEUE.IS_FULL => FULL_GUARD);

    function PART_OF (OB : in APPLICATION.OBJECT)
                                    return QUEUE.BEHAVIOUR;
    function CREATE return APPLICATION.OBJECT;

end;
```

The task at the end of the state list for a GUARDED_QUEUE object is generated from an instance of the generic package BOUNDED_BUFFER which has the guard method SIMPLE_QUEUE.IS_FULL as its actual parameter. Evaluation of the procedure EVALUATE_GUARDS on completion of each non-guard method will result in the guard variable F_GUARD being assigned the value returned by the subprogram implementing IS_FULL, as required.

9.7 Executable objects

According to the DRAGOON execution model outlined in the previous chapter, in order to execute instances of a user-defined class on a particular type of machine it is first necessary to define the appropriate executable subclass. Submission of an executable class to the DRAGOON compilation system results not only in the generation of new Ada software but also the complete translation of the class into a self-contained executable load module. In typical compiler terminology, executable classes are not only translated into Ada modules and then subsequently 'compiled', but the 'linker' is also invoked to combine the necessary Ada modules into an executable image of the class.

Since Ada recognizes only library subprograms as 'main programs' that can be mapped into an executable image (i.e. linked), when processing an executable class the DRAGOON compilation system must generate some kind of library subprogram that can be used by the Ada compilation system to generate an executable module. Consider, for example, the version of the FORWARDER (6.10) needed in the distributed version of the supermarket system for execution on a Sun workstation. This would be defined as an executable class of the following kind:

```
class SUN_EXECUTABLE_FORWARDER is                             (9.32)
    inherits FORWARDER, SUN_EXECUTION_SUPPORT;
end;
```

where SUN_EXECUTION_SUPPORT is an execution support class for Sun workstations. To make it possible for the Ada compilation system to generate an executable image of such a class, the DRAGOON translation tool would generate a subprogram of the following form:

```
with APPLICATION, FORWARDER;                              (9.33)
with <other 'system' packages>;
procedure FORWARDER_ROOT is
    OB : APPLICATION.OBJECT;
begin
    OB := FORWARDER.CREATE;
end;
```

The only actions this procedure actually performs are to declare an access variable for the associated application object and to instantiate it using the corresponding CREATE subprogram. Its most important role, however, is to act as the 'root' of the dependency graph for all the Ada library units that need to be linked together to provide the desired properties. These are not just the Ada library units generated from the application class (i.e. FORWARDER) and its ancestors, but also the library units needed to support the properties the executable class inherits from the execution support class. Even in the case of the canonical form, which is the most primitive execution support class for the machine concerned, a certain amount of Ada code will be needed to support the LOAD_ONTO method and the other properties associated with processes in the target environment (i.e. Sun workstations in this case). In general, however, execution support classes may export an unlimited number of methods representing the operations performable on such processes – methods whose invocation must be supported across the network.

The potential strategies for supporting distributed execution of DRAGOON objects will be outlined in the following section. For the present it is only necessary to be aware that a certain quantity of Ada software must be included in the 'main program' for an executable class in order to include the functionality provided by the execution support class. The Ada library units concerned, however, are not application specific and form part of the predefined DRAGOON environment.

As illustrated by MC_68000_EXECUTABLE_CHECKOUT_POINT (8.7) in the previous chapter, it is possible for the user to redefine methods in the body of executable objects and even to introduce new variables. In such circumstances, an additional package is produced by the translation tool (according to the principles outlined previously) to implement the methods introduced or redefined by the programmer in the executable object and define a record holding the new variables. The special 'root' procedure, therefore, is a client of this package rather than of the package corresponding to the inherited application class.

9.7.1   Cross compilation

One of the most powerful features of execution support classes in the DRAGOON distribution model is that they permit the compilation of objects for different machine types to be modelled in the language and hence represented in the normal class library. The different machine types that can be supported, however, and the stages to which a class can be translated before specific targeting is necessary, depend largely on the cross-compilation facilities provided by the host Ada system.

Many Ada compilation systems supporting compilation to numerous targets use a special intermediate code to provide a machine-independent representation of Ada modules. Ada library units accepted by the compilation system are thus stored in this intermediate form. It is only when the linker is used to generate executable modules that dependency on a particular type of machine is fixed and the final part of the translation to machine code is performed. The same intermediate representation of an Ada module can therefore be used for many different machine types without recompilation of the original Ada.

When used with such a compilation system, Ada code produced by the translation system can be immediately compiled into the intermediate form. If such a system is not available, however, the Ada cannot be 'compiled' until the mapping to a particular machine type is fixed (by the definition of an executable object) and an appropriately targeted compiler can be used. In this case, Ada is essentially acting as the intermediate code for DRAGOON. In general, the Ada code produced by the translation tool can be immediately compiled to the 'lowest' form maintaining machine independence, which in certain cases may be Ada itself.

9.8   Distribution

The previous sections have described how the 'non-distributed' features of DRAGOON are translated into standard Ada for execution. It is not possible to support the distribution features of DRAGOON entirely in Ada, however, because the language does not have in-built support for distribution. Implementation of the DRAGOON distribution model is bound, to a certain extent, to involve some interaction with the facilities of the supporting environment.

If DRAGOON software is required to execute on a particular type of network operating system or communication system, a translation could be devised to arrange for the necessary interaction with (i.e. system calls to) the services of that type of system. In general, however, it is clearly unsatisfactory to have to develop a different translation, and associated tool, for each different type of network on which DRAGOON software is to run since this entirely defeats the portability advantages of compilation into Ada.

There are two basic approaches for overcoming this problem. One is to *minimize* the dependence of the transformation on the idiosyncrasies of particular operating and communication systems by defining, in the spirit of DIADEM (Atkinson *et al*, 1988), a minimal 'standard' set of primitives which must be supported by any network on which DRAGOON software is to execute. The other approach is, in a sense, to *maximize* the dependence of the translation on the underlying system by developing a distributed run-time system specifically for the execution of DRAGOON software. A dedicated run-time system of this kind can provide much greater efficiency since it is able to support primitives explicitly tailored to the DRAGOON object model and remote communication in terms of method calls. A prototype version of a specialized DRAGOON distributed run-time system, known as the 'DRAGON Distributed Executive' (DDX), has been developed in the DRAGON project. The price of this efficiency, however, is lower portability since the work required to implement the dedicated DRAGOON run-time system for different networks is much greater than that required to reimplement the minimal interface on top of the host operating system.

As the details of the specialized DRAGOON run-time system (DDX) are fully described elsewhere (Bayan *et al*, 1989), the remainder of this chapter will concentrate on the alternative 'standard interface' approach.

9.8.1   Supporting distributed execution

There are two main problems involved in supporting the execution of objects distributed over a network:

- object identification,
- remote communication.

For objects in a system to interact and cooperate effectively, they clearly require some means of uniquely identifying the objects they wish to communicate with. Once they have a means of identifying each other, a mechanism must be provided by which they may synchronize and communicate. If the services provided by the interface to the transport layer of the network are intended to be the minimum necessary, most of these requirements must be handled by the Ada code produced by the translation tool rather than the underlying system.

One project which addressed the problems of supporting remote interactions by automatically generated Ada code interacting with a minimal interface to the underlying communication system was the DIADEM project. This was concerned specifically with supporting the distributed execution of Ada software using the rendezvous protocol. In view of the similarities of this with the method call protocol of DRAGOON, the DIADEM implementation strategy also turns out to be highly suitable for DRAGOON.

To permit remote objects to identify each other in the network, DIADEM introduced the concept of a 'remote access type'. This is simply a record that stores the local reference to an object alongside the unique network address of the machine on which it resides. Together these uniquely identify executable objects in the system. The DIADEM implementation of remote rendezvous transactions is based on the use of dynamically generated tasks to act as the local surrogates for remote callers. These surrogate tasks are generated by a permanent 'port' task which listens at a prearranged communication point for incoming calls.

The fine details of the DIADEM technique for implementing remote communication are explained fully in Atkinson *et al* (1988) and there is little value in reiterating them here. A more important question is how this basic strategy can be integrated with the translation techniques outlined in the previous sections.

Object identification

In DRAGOON, the only objects that may be translated into executable objects for distribution over the machines of a network are 'virtual node' objects conforming to the appropriate construction rules. It is only in the translation of such objects, therefore, that consideration must be given to distribution aspects. In particular, the methods exported by virtual node objects may be called remotely and their *port* variables may refer to remote objects. Since virtual node objects may also be used like any others as private components in the implementation of larger encapsulating objects, the methods of such objects may also be called locally and their variables refer to local objects.

The choice between these two possibilities is made when an executable subclass of a virtual node is defined. Submitting such a class to the compilation system indicates that the methods of the class will be called remotely and that the port variables will refer to remote objects. At the time of *translation* of virtual node classes, however, it is not known whether the implementation of methods and port variables will have to support remote or local transactions, and hence both possibilities must be accommodated in the translation.

To cope with the possibility that the port variables of a virtual node class may refer to remote objects (if inherited by an executable subclass), an extra field is required in the first node of all the state lists – that is, in the record STATE in the predefined package APPLICATION. Strictly speaking, it is only necessary for the state list of virtual node objects to contain this extra field, since only port variables can refer to such objects. However, since it is essential that the first node of *every* object is of the same type, this field, called REMOTE, has to be added to the first node of all state lists.

Like all the other reference fields in this record (e.g. HEIR, MULTIPLE) this record is arbitrarily defined to be of type APPLICATION.OBJECT. In a state list representing a local object (i.e. one in the same executable object),

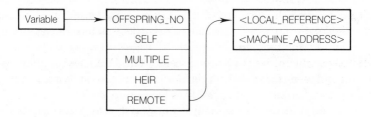

Figure 9.4   Data structure for remote objects.

the REMOTE field has the value 'null' and is essentially redundant. Remote objects, however, are represented by data structures of the form illustrated in Figure 9.4, in which the REMOTE field refers to a record storing the 'remote access type' of the object. In this case the other fields of the APPLICATION.OBJECT record have the value 'null'.

The exact form of the record referenced by the REMOTE field is system dependent, but typically will hold the network address of the machine on which the object resides and the local reference of the object on this machine. Since this record is clearly not of type APPLICATION.STATE, the generic function UNCHECKED_CONVERSION has to be used as for the other fields to change its apparent type to that required.

The port variables of executable objects are thus implemented as normal Ada access values, but refer to 'remote object' structures rather than normal state lists.

Remote communication

The other aspect of distribution that needs to be accommodated in the translation of virtual node classes is support for remote communication. In the DIADEM scheme this requires the definition of special Ada program units – 'port' tasks to listen at prearranged communication points, 'surrogate' tasks to issue local calls, dispatching procedures to translate local calls to the appropriate transport layer messages and special template packages to define the types of the exchanged data structures.

When a virtual node object is translated into Ada, therefore, additional Ada packages are defined containing the necessary program constructs to handle remote and local transactions. These are some of the 'additional' packages referred to in the second 'with' clause in (9.33). Clearly, they are not included in a program that has local instances of the virtual node class.

As well as the additional packages, however, slight modifications have to be made to the 'main' package and selection shell. In addition to the 'implementing' subprograms contained in the inner package SELF, a set of subprograms is defined in another inner package called REMOTE. It is the subprograms in this package that are responsible for implementing remote method calls on the caller's side. In other words, when invoked from a selection shell these subprograms use the object identifier referenced by the REMOTE field to dispatch the appropriate transport layer messages to the remote site. In effect, these subprograms provide a 'remote' implementation of the corresponding methods while the subprograms in SELF provide a 'local' implementation.

Naturally, it is the selection shells corresponding to the methods that are responsible for choosing between these two by checking the value of the remote field of the APPLICATION.STATE record referenced by the access variables. It is this field which is also used to check at run-time that 'ingenerate' references are not exported from executable objects. If one of the subprograms in REMOTE is invoked with an object parameter whose REMOTE field is 'null', the exception REMOTE_ERROR is raised.

Key points

All the characteristic mechanisms of object-oriented languages are exported to a *limited* extent in Ada, including inheritance, polymorphism and dynamic binding. However, these facilities are not compatible.

The simplest representation of an object in Ada is as an *abstract state machine* package, which declares variables in its body to hold the required state. Such objects are unique, however, and may not be defined using any of the important object-oriented features.

Something of the effect of classes can be achieved using generic 'abstract state machine' packages. These can be instantiated to give structurally identical objects, but only at compile time.

Representing objects as tasks and classes as task types facilitates dynamic instantiation, reference semantics, concurrent execution threads and a limited form of dynamic binding. Inheritance is not supported, however.

To have any form of inheritance in Ada it is necessary to model classes as abstract data types and objects as variables of the type. The subtyping and derived type mechanisms of Ada enable a subtype, or new type, to be defined which inherits the existing subprograms and for which new subprograms may be defined. It is not possible to alter or extend the values of the type, however.

Because no feature of Ada *directly* supports all the important mechanisms associated with an object, a uniform lower-level translation strategy is adopted for DRAGOON.

The translation strategy has most in common with the 'abstract data type' approach to modelling classes, but to support the incremental development of class hierarchies using inheritance, and the associated polymorphism, the state of objects is (in general) represented by a linked list of records.

The first node in the state list for every object is of the record type STATE defined in the class APPLICATION. This represents the fact that the root of the DRAGOON class hierarchy is the class APPLICATION_OBJECT. Each additional record in an object's state list stores the state variables added by ancestors of the object's class.

As far as the Ada typing mechanism is concerned, all objects are of type APPLICATION.STATE referenced by access variables of type APPLICA-TION.OBJECT. This provides the polymorphism associated with instance variables.

The HEIR field of each record in the list holds the reference to the next node, should one exist. This field is arbitrarily declared to be of type APPLICATION.OBJECT.

The CREATE function declared in the Ada package corresponding to a class is responsible for appending the record storing the variables introduced by the class on to the linked list of its parent. To do this it must use an appropriate instantiation of UNCHECKED_CONVERSION to change the apparent type of the record to APPLICATION.OBJECT.

The translation strategy relies on the identical representation of record access types in each Ada implementation.

The PART_OF function performs the reverse UNCHECKED_CONVERSION to the CREATE function, changing the apparent type of a state record into the true type.

In order to support dynamic binding, two subprograms are generated for each method of a class. One subprogram, called the *implementing method*, contains the Ada code that actually implements the method, while the other, called the *selection shell*, contains code which dynamically selects which of the various versions of a method should be executed.

To minimize the amount of code that has to be recompiled when a new version of a method is introduced in a subclass, the bodies of selection shells are defined as separate subunits.

To enable a selection shell to determine in which branch of the inheritance tree an object's class resides, each *offspring* of a class is assigned an *offspring number* according to the chronological order of compilation. This number is stored in the OFFSPRING_NO fields of the nodes of the state lists.

Abstract classes are implemented in precisely the same way as concrete classes except that the 'implementing' subprograms corresponding to the deferred methods simply contain a statement that raises the exception CONSTRAINT_ERROR since they should never be called.

Multiple inheritance is supported by combining the linked lists corresponding to the parents of a class into a single data structure corresponding to a 'ring' of linked lists. This enables an object to take on the appearance of any of its parents depending on the type of the instance variable(s) through which it is referenced.

The inheritance of a generic class is supported essentially by instantiating the generic Ada package corresponding to the parent inside the generic Ada package corresponding to the heir, with the actual parameters of the instantiation being the formal parameters of the new package.

Active objects are supported by arranging for one of the fields of the final state record to point to a task that contains the Ada code corresponding to the thread. When this task is started it must be provided with a reference to the state list of the object so that it has access to the appropriate variables.

Behavioured objects are also implemented by appending a task to the object's state list. This task provides entries which the selection shells must invoke before and after the invocation of the corresponding implementing subprograms.

If the behaviour of a task is guarded, the corresponding 'behaviour task type' is defined in a package that is generic with respect to the guard operation. This can then be instantiated with a subprogram, which has access to the state list of the behavioured object, and can thus return the appropriate guard value.

The only executable unit recognized by Ada is the 'main program'. Therefore, one of the things produced in the translation of an executable class is a procedure to act as a main program. This generates an instance of the required state list and also 'withs' all the library units that need to be included in the executable module, including those providing the facilities inherited from the execution support class.

The Ada code corresponding to an executable subclass of a virtual node class must contain the code necessary to implement a method call by message passing over the network. Two 'implementing' subprograms are therefore generated for each method, one providing the true 'local' implementation and the other containing the system calls necessary to arrange for a remote object to service the request.

To enable remote executable (virtual node) objects to be referenced by instance variables, the record type APPLICATION.OBJECT contains an additional field REMOTE which is 'null' for local objects, but for remote objects refers to a data structure containing a 'remote reference'.

Chapter 10
Conclusion

This book has introduced the principal features of the object-oriented language DRAGOON, and by showing how they might be used in a simple case study has described the rationale behind them. This concluding chapter briefly outlines other aspects of the DRAGON project and then summarizes the main design principles embodied in DRAGOON.

10.1   Other DRAGON research

Although much of the effort in the DRAGON project focussed on DRAGOON, particularly the development of the preprocessor into Ada (Genolini and Cardigno, 1989) and the distributed run-time executive (Bayan et al, 1989), the language is actually only one of a number of developments providing a coherent framework for software development (Di Maio et al, 1989).

Reuse toolset

The most crucial part of the design process, and yet the one that is hardest to formalize or define prescriptive rules for, is the very first stage when vague ideas crystalize into a more concrete design. It is at this early stage that the potential for reuse is at its greatest, but also easiest to miss. The project has therefore developed a highly interactive tool, known as the Designer's Notepad (DNP) (Sommerville et al, 1989b), which aims to assist the designer in capturing possible designs with a view to reusing existing components. It has been described as a form of 'electronic paper' replacing the traditional pencil and 'envelope'.

Naturally, to perform its role the DNP requires information about the reusable components available to the designer. The Software Components Catalogue (SCC) has been developed to provide a user friendly interface to the components stored in the Component Information Store (CIS), and can be accessed directly by the DNP. It provides both browsing and retrieval facilities based on the notion of frames which a user 'fills in' to describe the properties of the object required.

Design method

Although it is impossible to define an exhaustive 'cookbook' of prescriptive rules for constructing software, *design methods* are nevertheless useful for providing a general framework to guide the development process. This is particularly so when emphasis is placed on guiding the progress of designs according to the contents of a component library.

There are already a number of so-called 'object-oriented' design methods in existence, such as HOOD (1987), (Berard, 1985) and (Booch, 1987), which use the 'object' or 'class' as the main system building blocks. These, however, all take a compositional approach to design in which new objects are constructed from others by clientship. As pointed out in Chapter 4, object-oriented *languages* support another equally powerful reuse mechanism known as inheritance, which permits classes to be generated by expressing their difference to other classes.

The design method developed in the project, known as DEMON (DEsign Method for an Object-oriented Notation) (Bott *et al*, 1989) recognizes this alternative approach and places equal weight on design using the clientship and inheritance mechanisms. The method first attempts to produce the required 'system' class by modifying existing components in the library by inheritance. If this fails, the required class has to be generated from (possibly modified versions of) smaller classes in the library by clientship. The DEMON design process is therefore inherently recursive. At each point in the dependency hierarchy, attempts are made to derive the required component by inheritance as well as by the usual compositional approach.

Formal aspects

If the many potential advantages of software reuse are to be realized, it must be pursued in a rigorous and controlled fashion. In particular, it is important that reusable components do what they claim to do and are employed in the manner intended by the designer. Formal methods, based on algebraic specification techniques, have been developed in DRAGON to try to ensure that both these criteria are satisfied.

The major effort has centred on the definition of formal semantics for DRAGOON since this provides a basis for reasoning about program correctness. The approach developed extends the traditional denotational style associated with abstract data types to handle the inheritance and concurrency features of DRAGOON (Breu and Zucca, 1989). Formal techniques have also been developed for describing the properties of reusable components in the library (Wirsing, 1988).

10.2   DRAGOON design principles

Accompanied by these tools, it is felt that the DRAGOON language makes two important contributions to the technology of large-scale software systems. Because it is intimately allied to Ada, not only being geared to implementation in the language but also adopting its philosophy and conventions, DRAGOON is a highly practical language 'inheriting' Ada's stability and portability advantages. As well as making the powerful reuse mechanisms of object-oriented programming available to the Ada world, therefore, it brings the advantages of the Ada industry to the object-oriented programming world.

Despite this highly practical side, however, the language also introduces some new ideas for extending object-oriented programming into the domains of concurrency and distribution. Until now no existing language has fully reconciled inheritance-based reuse with the demands of concurrency and distribution. Languages like Eiffel and C++, which exploit the power of inheritance for reuse and extensibility, do not support concurrency and distribution, while those that do, such as POOL and Emerald, do not support inheritance. DRAGOON, however, employs variations on the multiple inheritance theme to support the specification of synchronization constraints and distributability in a manner that is consistent with the normal inheritance mechanism.

Four main principles underlie DRAGOON's approach to these problems.

'Mixed' paradigm

The first principle is the whole-hearted support for a 'mixed' paradigm in which the traditional 'value-oriented' viewpoint is given as much weight as the newer object-oriented approach. Each of these approaches has advantages in certain applications and DRAGOON permits the programmer to adopt the strategy that best fits the problem in hand.

A crucial aspect of this approach is the use of packages as shareable repositories for the declaration of Ada-like types, subprograms and exceptions. In 'pure' DRAGOON these packages must be template packages which cannot contain any variables or subprogram calls that would lead to them having a state. In practice, however, any Ada compilation unit can be included in a DRAGOON program since the preprocessor only operates on classes and ignores any pieces of code that do not require modification.

Unification of abstractions

The second tenet of DRAGOON is the use of classes and objects as a unifying concept for modelling as many different abstractions as possible. Thus, in DRAGOON, classes and/or objects are employed as units of:

- modularity,
- information hiding,
- abstraction,
- compilation,
- typing,
- reuse,
- independent execution (i.e. processes),
- synchronization (c.f. monitors),
- distribution (i.e. virtual node objects),
- reconfiguration (i.e. executable objects).

Many languages support a variety of these ideas, but often by means of distinct and disjoint constructs.

Separation of concerns

By using a single concept to handle all these different requirements, DRAGOON encourages crucial design decisions (i.e. is an object to be active? behavioured? distributable? etc.) to be delayed until the latest possible moment in the design process, thereby minimizing the work required to alter these decisions in other systems and thus increasing the reusability of components. An important principle in DRAGOON is therefore the separation of concerns – separating the description of different aspects of a system so that they may be reused in different combinations.

Full 'lifecycle' support

The fourth principle of DRAGOON, and of the wider DRAGON project, is the use of the object-oriented framework through as much of the software lifecycle as possible. DRAGOON therefore introduces new mechanisms to handle the system integration and execution phases of the lifecycle within the object-oriented framework, while the accompanying DRAGON design method and reuse toolset support these concepts in the early stages of development.

By extending the fledgling object-oriented paradigm in the direction of concurrency and distribution, as well as in the direction of Ada, and conforming to the principles outlined above, it is hoped that DRAGOON will prove to be an important addition to the arsenal of software developers.

Key points

The development of DRAGOON and the associated preprocessor and run-time executive was only one part of the DRAGON project. Other products include a 'reuse toolset', a design method and a formal description of DRAGOON and reusable components in general.

DRAGOON is a 'mixed paradigm' language that supports 'value-oriented' programming in terms of Ada-style types, and object-oriented programming in terms of classes and objects.

So far as possible, features of the language are unified around the notion of classes and objects rather than being added in a disjoint, piecemeal fashion.

An important principle in DRAGOON is the separation of concerns so that the moment of commitment to a particular implementation choice can be delayed as long as possible.

DRAGOON enhances the inheritance mechanism to capture the notion of compilation and linking, and therefore extends the use of object-oriented features to the integration and execution stages of the traditional software lifecycle.

Appendix A
Overview of Ada

This appendix provides an overview of Ada – the origin of many of the ideas discussed in this book, and the language to which DRAGOON is most closely related. The first part of the appendix describes the background to the development of Ada, and the general requirements it was intended to satisfy. The following sections then go on to describe features of the language in more detail.

A.1 Background

Ada was developed in the late '70s in a competitive design effort sponsored by the United States Department of Defense[1]. After several revisions, the final version of the Ada Language Reference Manual (ALRM), which provides the definitive description of the language, was published in 1983 (DoD, 1983).

Motivation for a new language arose from severe shortcomings in the practices used to develop software for embedded systems. These problems essentially stemmed from the lack of standardization and disciplined working practices resulting from the vast number of different programming languages that were being used to develop software for the DoD. The basic goal in the development of Ada was to produce a language that would become a standard for this domain in the same way that FORTRAN is a *de facto* standard for scientific applications, and COBOL for data processing applications.

Embedded software applications share many characteristics with other large-scale, commercial software systems. In particular, they are:

- developed by teams of people,
- long lived, and so must be routinely maintained,

---

[1] Products and publications connected with Ada are usually coloured green because this was the colour used to identify the team which won the contract to produce the final version.

- critical to the safety of life and/or property,
- required to be efficient.

However, the programming of embedded systems also presents several unique problems (Downes and Goldsack, 1982) which require facilities for describing:

- concurrent control of coexisting system components,
- initiation of actions in 'real' time,
- interaction with special-purpose hardware,
- actions to be taken in the event of component failure.

The designers of Ada tried to meet these various (not entirely compatible) needs by embracing the ideas of software engineering. Ada is one of the first languages whose features are designed specifically to support software engineering principles such as:

- modularity,
- data abstraction,
- information hiding,
- component reuse,
- 'readability' rather than 'writeability'.

In fact, it would probably be more accurate to say that Ada was designed to embrace CASE (Computer-Aided Software Engineering) rather than merely software engineering. It was recognized at an early stage that a language is just one of many tools used in software construction, and that the establishment of standard working practices depended also on standardization of the development environment. The Ada design process was therefore paralleled by the design of an accompanying support environment, called an APSE (Ada Program Support Environment), which aimed to define standard protocols and services that should be used in populating such an environment. Although specifications of the APSE were produced around the same time as the language definition, it is only now that the state-of-the-art has reached a stage where it is feasible to implement a practical APSE.

A.2   Frames

Ada is essentially a block-structured procedural language enhanced to support the concepts of software engineering and the requirements of real-time systems. The starting point for the design of Ada was Pascal, and both the block-structuring and data abstraction schemes of Ada are based largely on the Pascal model. However, the notion of a block is generalized in Ada into the notion of a *frame*. In addition to the usual *declarative part* and *sequence of statements* a frame may optionally contain one or more *exception handlers*. The declarative part is also optional, but if present must precede the sequence of statements, which in turn must precede any exception handlers that are present. Although a frame must always possess a sequence of statements, the statement **null**, which indicates that no actions should be performed, is acceptable.

Of the four kinds of frame in Ada, programmers will be most familiar with the *block statement* and the *subprogram*. The other two – the *package body* and the *task body* – will be described later. Blocks differ from the other three kinds in that they are statements, and from part of the sequence of statements of other frames. The other three frames are *declarative items* which appear in the declarative parts of other frames.

Ada offers two kinds of subprograms – procedures and functions. These are similar to procedures and functions in Pascal, but have a more general parameter passing mechanism. The parameters of a procedure may be defined to be of mode '**in**', '**in out**' or '**out**'. Within a procedure '**in**' parameters behave like constants which cannot have a value assigned to them, '**in out**' parameters behave like normal variables (similar to '**var**' parameters in Pascal) and '**out** 'parameters are variables which can only have values assigned to them. Functions are only allowed to have the equivalent of '**in**' parameters and must always return a single value. Function calls are consequently called as (part of) an expression, whereas procedure calls are statements.

The scoping and visibility rules of Ada are similar to those of other typical block-based languages like Pascal, but are complicated by the requirements of separate compilation.

A.3   Flow control

Ada provides all the usual imperative flow-control structures – '**if**', '**case**' and '**loop**' statements. A simple, but important, improvement over the Pascal version of these constructs is the requirement for explicit bracketing (or closing). For example, an '**if**' statement is closed by '**end if**', a '**loop**' statement by '**end loop**' etc. Ada also provides the infamous '**goto**' statement, together with a mechanism for labelling statements, but its use is strongly discouraged.

Under normal circumstances, program execution proceeds according to the typical stack-based execution model of a block-structured imperative language. When a program's thread of control enters a frame, the *declarative part* of the frame is first *elaborated* and then the sequence of *statements* is executed. During the elaboration phase each of the *declarations* in the declarative part is elaborated (i.e. put into effect) in sequence, and during the execution phase each of the statements in the sequence of statements is executed in sequence. If the frame is a subprogram, as soon as each of the statements has been executed, control is returned to the calling frame.

A.3.1   Exceptions

Should an unusual circumstance arise during the execution of a program the usual flow of control may be overridden by the *exception* mechanism. The flow is then controlled by the propagation of an exception *raised* at the point at which the unusual circumstance arrived.

Ada contains several predefined exceptions which are raised automatically by the *run-time system* should certain problems occur in the execution of a program. The most common is CONSTRAINT_ERROR, which is raised when an attempt is made to assign to an object a value outside the range specified by the subtype. Others include NUMERIC_ERROR, raised when an arithmetical operation goes wrong, and STORAGE_ERROR, raised when the program runs out of memory. The applications programmer may declare new exceptions, but these have to be raised explicitly using a 'raise' statement.

When a problem occurs in the execution of a statement, an appropriate exception is raised, and the execution of the rest of the statements in the frame is abandoned. If there is an appropriate *exception handler* in the frame, control passes to that exception handler which is then executed to *handle* the exception. An exception handler may be defined for one specific exception, several specific exceptions or, using the keyword 'others', may be defined to handle any exception.

If an exception is not *handled* by the frame in which it was raised (i.e. there is no corresponding exception handler) then, unless the frame is a task body, the exception is *propagated*. In the case of a subprogram, this has the effect of reraising the exception at the point at which the subprogram was called. The propagation process continues until either the exception is handled, or the program terminates. If the frame is a task body, the task goes *abnormal* (i.e. dies).

A.4   Modularity

The notion of a library of independent modules is central to the Ada philosophy. Logically, a program is composed of a collection of interdependent *program units*, of which there are four kinds: *packages, tasks, subprograms* and *generics*. Program units are all declarative items which have the common characteristic that they are, in general, constructed from two parts: a *specification* and a *body*.

Program units are the main vehicle in Ada for supporting the principle of information hiding. The specification of a program unit represents the visible part which defines, or *exports*, the services made available to users of the unit. The body, in contrast, is hidden from the users of the unit, and contains the implementation details which the users need not, or perhaps even should not, be aware of.

Except in the case of generics, the bodies of program units all conform to the basic frame structure, and the specification is essentially an extension of the declarative part. With the exception of subprograms, program units must have distinct specifications and bodies. The specification of a subprogram – the name, parameter list and, in the case of a function, the result type – must appear in full as the introduction to the body, and so need not (but can) be duplicated in a separate specification. A subprogram body can serve as a specification also.

A.4.1   Separate compilation

An Ada program is hardly ever constructed as a single monolithic block, but is built from a collection of separately compiled units. Except for tasks, the specification and bodies of program units may be combined with a *context clause* to make a *compilation unit* which can be compiled separately. The context clause indicates the dependency of the specification or the body on other previously compiled specifications, or *library units*. Although both parts of a separately compiled program unit must be added to the program library, strictly speaking only the specification of the program unit constitutes a library unit. Separately compiled bodies (together with their context clause) are known as *secondary units*. Note that program units do not have to be part of a library, but may be nested within other library units.

The simplest form of context clause is a **'with'** clause. This names one or more compiled library units which need to be visible to provide the *context* for declaration of the associated specification or body.

Library units support a 'bottom-up' approach to program construction in which a new application is generated by combined smaller, predefined components. Ada also supports the alternative strategy – 'top-down design' – through the notion of subunits. A subunit is the separately compiled body of a program unit declared within another library unit or secondary unit. The program unit logically belongs to the encapsulating *parent* unit, but for convenience its body is physically separated from the text of the parent unit, and defined in another compilation unit. Not only does this facility enable the volume of text in the body of a program unit to be reduced, but it means that the full definition of the parent unit can be *deferred*. This enables the programmer to compile and check some parts of program unit's implementation while other parts are still to be defined.

The body of a program is defined to be a subunit by putting a body *stub* in the place where the unit body would normally go. A stub is constructed from the normal introductory part of the body followed by the keyword '**separate**'. To provide the context in which the corresponding subunit should be compiled (once it has been defined) the body has to preceded by the name of the library unit in which the program unit is declared.

A.4.2   Packages

An important building block in Ada is the package. A package is a program unit which may be declared within the declarative part of another unit, or as a separate library unit. The body of a package has the general form of a *frame*; in addition to a declarative part it may contain a sequence of statements, and some exception handlers. These statements are used only for initialization purposes, however, and are executed once when the package is elaborated.

Packages are used to group together declarations which are related in some way. Sometimes the relationship is merely that the declarations need to be shared by the same set of program units, but usually it is that the declarations are components of some higher-level abstraction. Two such abstractions are common. A package may be used to group together declarations forming an *abstract data type*, or may itself represent an *abstract state machine*, or object (Section 9.1). In the first scenario the package exports a set of subprograms, and a *type* on which they operate, whereas in the second scenario, the subprograms have a side-effect on 'persistent state' declared in the package (usually in its body).

The specification of a package contains those declarations that are visible to clients, while the body contains the details of the implementation. Moreover, the separate parts of program units declared in a package may be separated between the package's body and specification – the unit bodies appearing in the package's body, and the unit specifications in its specification. Thus packages provide a powerful way of controlling the visibility that other units have of a particular abstraction.

Packages lie at the heart of Ada's approach to extensibility. Very few 'standard' operations and types are defined in the language itself, but are provided in 'predefined' packages. For example, whereas most languages (e.g. Pascal, Algol, FORTRAN) include the definition of standard input/output operations as part of the language, in Ada these are specified in predefined packages called TEXT_IO, SEQUENTIAL_IO and DIRECT_IO.

Even the most primitive data types and operations, such as INTEGER, FLOAT, BOOLEAN, CHARACTER and their operations, are declared in a special predefined package called STANDARD. However, programmers can relieve themselves of the burden of having to use the full name of such entities declared in library packages (the package name followed by the entity name) by means of a '**use**' clause. Such a clause may be included in the context clause of a compilation unit, or may appear in the declarative part of a program, and indicates that the programmer wishes to identify the entities declared in a package without having to provide the package name prefix in the full name.

By defining these 'standard' facilities in packages, rather than in the language itself, Ada enables programmers to provide alternative versions, and to add new facilities in a consistent style. The hope is that over a period of time programmers and organizations will build up libraries of 'reusable' packages, which can be employed in different applications.

The notion of extensibility through packages is reinforced by the mechanism of *overloading*. The definition of an alternative input/output package, for example, would be an extremely arduous task if a programmer was forced to think of a new set of operation names completely different from those used in TEXT_IO or other packages. Therefore, Ada enables the same name to apply to more than one subprogram at the same time, provided the subprogram specifications can be distinguished in some way. This means that their parameter profiles must differ in some way. Subprograms with the same name must either have a different number of parameters, or different types of parameters, or different result types (or a combination of these), so that the compiler can determine, by the form of a subprogram call, which subprogram needs to be executed. Overloading is not limited to subprogram names. It is possible, for example, to overload a literal of an enumeration type by using it to refer to a subprogram.

A.5   Data abstraction

The data modelling features of Ada are another area of the language which is based on the Pascal model. Like Pascal, Ada is strongly and statically typed – every data value is associated with a type that defines the operations which may be performed on it and the contexts in which it may be used. Moreover, each new type must be explicitly declared, and operations are checked for the type correctness of their operands at compile time. Although this tends to make Ada more verbose than equivalent programs written in other languages, it also reduces the chances of errors and makes the program more understandable to other programmers. This is a manifestation of Ada's philosophy of maximizing the readability of a program at the expense of writer's convenience.

Type compatibility in Ada is based on *named equivalence* rather than *structural equivalence*. An assignment from one variable to another is only valid if they are both declared using the same type identifier. Each type declaration therefore defines a new type, even if it is textually identical to another type declaration (apart from the type name).

Ada provides all the usual facilities for declaring user-defined types that have become customary in high-level languages. Three main categories of types are available for building data structures: scalar types, composite types and access types. *Scalar* types are those with primitive values without components, and are divided into two categories – *discrete* and *real*. Each of these, in turn, is divided into two categories: discrete types are divided into enumeration and integer types, while real types are divided into floating-point and fixed-point types. The package STANDARD contains predefined instances of most of these types. INTEGER and LONG_INTEGER, for example, are predefined integer types, BOOLEAN and CHARACTER are predefined enumeration types, and FLOAT is a predefined floating-point type.

Composite types, whose values are composed of several components, also come in two forms: *array* types and *record* types. These offer similar facilities to arrays and records found in Pascal, but provide some important enhancements. Array types may be defined to be *unconstrained*, which means that the number of elements in the array is left unspecified until a variable of the type is defined, or an actual parameter is matched to an unconstrained formal parameter in a subprogram call. Record types, on the other hand, may be defined to have one or more discriminants. A discriminant is essentially a parameter which can affect the form of other components in the record. A variant record, for example, has a discriminant whose value determines which other fields are present in a value of the type.

Access types correspond to pointer types in other languages. They enable values of a composite or discrete type to be identified indirectly through an internal name (i.e. pointer) rather than by an explicit identifier. Objects referenced through an access type are generated 'dynamically' by the execution of an 'allocator'. Such types are essential for constructing recursive structures such as lists and trees.

Apart from task types, which are discussed later, these are all the different forms of data structure available to the Ada programmer. However, there are several ways for defining the way in which these types may be related, and for controlling the way in which they may be used.

A.5.1   Subtypes and derived types

Every data value used in a program belongs to one, and only one, type. However, *objects*[2] (i.e. variables and constants), which are the entities that store (or possess) values, may be constrained to containing only a subset of the values of a type by means of subtype constraints. A *subtype* does not define a new type, but rather defines a subset of the values of an existing *base* type. An object has both a type and a subtype, therefore. Subtyping constraints are checked dynamically (i.e. at run-time) where necessary, and may be applied directly at the point at which an object is

---

[2]In Ada the term 'object' refers to a variable or constant that may possess a value of a certain type. In contrast with object-oriented languages, it does not imply a structured entity encapsulating associated operations.

declared, or indirectly through the use of a *subtype declaration*. Subtypes greatly increase the expressive power of the Ada typing systems, since they enable many more logical errors to be identified. The exception which tends to occur most frequently – CONSTRAINED_ERROR – is raised when subtyping constraints are violated in an assignment or in the passing of parameters.

The subtyping mechanism is used when objects or parameters need to be of the same base type, but are designed to handle different subsets of the type's values. Sometimes, however, it is useful to be able to define objects which handle identical sets of values, but which are nevertheless regarded as being of different types. This can be achieved using the *derived type* mechanism. When a type is declared to be *derived* from another – the *parent type* – it 'inherits' an identical set of values and all the subprograms declared in the same package specification as the parent, but is nevertheless regarded as a distinct type. In essence, therefore, a derived type is a copy of the parent type; values of a derived type may not be assigned to variables of the parent type, and vice versa. Although values of a derived type are of different types to values of the parent type, type conversions are permitted.

A.5.2   Private types

Subtypes essentially define constraints on the way in which a type may be used. Another form of constraint is provided by the notion of private types. Declaring a type as *private* is a way of restricting the knowledge that a programmer may have about the type in use. A private type is thus a type upon which only a certain limited set of operations may be performed. More specifically, users of a private type only have available assignments, equality tests and operations defined by the programmer of the package exporting the private type declaration.

The restricted set of operations provided by private types is an important element in Ada's support for abstract data types, and is closely related to packages. By making the type exported to the user of a data abstraction 'private', and hiding details of the real data structure that is used to implement it, the user of the abstract type is forced to use the operation intended by the designer of the component.

Unfortunately, in order to enable compilers to allocate storage efficiently when making space for variables of a type declared in the specification of a package, it is not possible to hide all the implementation details in the body. For this reason, package specifications containing the declaration of a private type must have a *private part* in which the details necessary for allocating space for variables of the type are made known to the compiler[3]. Although physically part of the specification, the private

---

[3] If the type is an access type, the definition of the accessed type can be defined in the body.

part is not regarded as part of the visible part imported by clients of the package.

Sometimes even the limited operations available on a private type are too liberal, and the designer of an abstract data type wishes to control also the way in which assignment operations and equality tests are implemented. This can be achieved using a *limited private type*. A limited private type has all the properties of a private type, but does not have automatically defined assignment and equality testing operations. If required, these operations have to be defined by the user in the package exporting the limited private type. An important use of private types is in the definition of the parameters of generic units.

A.6   Generics

Strong typing provides important benefits with regard to readability and reliability of programs. However, it has the drawback that it conflicts to a certain extent with the goal of a reuse. A subprogram defined to operate on one type cannot be reused with another type, regardless of whether or not the algorithm would work or how similar the types may be. Most sorting algorithms, for example, will operate on any type for which an ordering relation is defined. However, if ordinary procedures were used to implement a sorting routine, a different copy of the routine would have to be defined for each different type upon which a sort was required.

Ada introduces the notion of generic units to address this problem. A generic unit is a template for a program unit which can be parameterized in certain ways, and can be statically *instantiated* to generate a new program unit. There are, in fact, two kinds of generic unit: generic subprograms and generic packages. Generic units are themselves program units which may added to the library, or declared within another unit (possibly also generic).

Instances of generic subprograms are normal subprograms that can be called in the usual way, and instances of generic packages are normal packages. Both the generic unit and its instances may be library units, or may be nested within other program units. A generic program unit has precisely the same form as the corresponding base unit, except that it has an additional generic formal part. This precedes the specification of the program unit, and in general contains the definition of the various *generic formal parameters*.

Three different kinds of generic formal parameters may be defined: types, subprograms and objects. The first form of parameter is used to overcome the problem caused by strong typing mentioned above. It enables the algorithm of a subprogram or package to be decoupled from a particular type. Various different forms of generic formal type parameters enable the generic unit to define the precise properties required of a type on which it is able to operate. A generic formal type parameter defined to be 'private', for example, could be matched to any actual type which provides an assignment and equality operation, whereas a limited private generic formal type could be matched to any actual type since it assumes that no operations are available. Different syntax is available to indicate that the actual type matched to a formal type should belong to any one of the different type categories outlined earlier (e.g. a discrete type, an integer type, a floating-point type, a fixed-point type, an array type and access type).

The second kind of generic formal parameter completes the type parameterization capabilities by enabling the requirement to be expressed that additional operations be available on an actual type. A generic sorting routine, for example, would have, in addition to a generic formal type parameter, a boolean generic formal function parameter through which an actual type's ordering operation would be provided. To avoid having to pass every operation on a type in this manner, facilities are available for expressing default options.

The final form of generic formal parameter complements the first two forms in that it enables constant values of an abstract data type to be provided when a generic unit is instantiated. Good examples are the values corresponding to 'zero' and 'one' in an abstract data type representing a group in algebra. Like generic formal subprograms, generic formal objects do not have to be accompanied by a generic formal type, but can be used for other purposes.

In fact, it is not necessary for the generic formal part of a generic unit to contain any parameters at all. Such a generic unit corresponds simply to a template from which several structurally identical program units can be instantiated. This is not particularly useful in the case of subprograms, but in the case of packages provides a way of achieving something of the effect of a class as understood in object-oriented languages.

A.7   Concurrency

The program unit which remains to be considered in detail is the *task* – the unit of concurrency in Ada. A task defines a 'process' whose body executes in parallel with other tasks. It has several characteristics not shared by the other program units. First, a task cannot be declared as a separate library unit, but must always be encapsulated within another. Second, tasks are regarded as 'first-class citizens' of the language – it is possible to define task types, and to pass tasks as subprogram parameters.

As with the other categories of types, Ada supports the definition of access types to task types. This means that tasks can be generated in two ways. They can be declared in the declarative part of another program unit, or can be generated dynamically through the execution of an allocator.

Tasks of the first kind may either be declared directly (so that their task type remains anonymous) or may be instantiated from a task type.

All tasks depend on another program unit. Declared tasks depend on the unit in which they were declared, whereas allocated tasks depend on the units in which the access type was declared. Tasks of the first kind begin parallel execution at the same time as the sequence of statements of the unit on which they depend begins execution, whereas allocated tasks being execution at the moment they are generated. An important rule resulting from task dependency is that a program unit (including a task) cannot terminate until all the tasks which depend upon it have terminated. This means, for example, that a procedure which has declared several tasks cannot terminate until all the tasks have also terminated.

Tasks may be assigned a *priority* by means of a *pragma*. These are compile time directives which 'assist' the compiler in determining how best to compile a program. Several pragmas are predefined in the ALRM, but implementations are free to add their own. Since pragmas are not meant to affect the logical properties of a program, merely its performance, a compiler is not obliged to act upon a pragma. Priorities in Ada are static; a task is assigned a priority at compile time and this cannot be changed.

A.7.1   The rendezvous

Tasks communicate and synchronize through entries. Entries are the only declarations which can appear in the specifications of tasks, and define the operations which may be invoked by other tasks or procedures. From the point of view of the caller, entries are very similar to procedures, and in fact, an entry may even be renamed as a procedure. However, there is a big difference in the way in which they are executed.

The sequence of statements executed in response to an entry call is not defined in a distinct body, as with procedure calls, but instead is defined in an 'accept' statement contained in the body of the task to which the entry belongs. There may be more than one 'accept' statement corresponding to a given entry, and each 'accept' statement may be executed only when there is an outstanding call to the entry, and the flow of control of the called task reaches the 'accept' statement. In other words, the calling and called task must synchronize for the 'accept' statement to be executed. The task which reaches the synchronization point first must wait until the other arrives. The two tasks are then said to 'rendezvous', and the two threads of control are locked together while the statements in the 'accept' statement are executed. Only when the rendezvous is complete are the two tasks able to continue executing concurrently.

Intertask communication in Ada is asymmetric. A calling task must explicitly name the entry and the task it wishes to call, and can only issue one call at a time. If there are several outstanding calls to the same entry the calls are queued in FIFO order until they can be accepted. Called tasks, on the other hand, are unaware of which task they are communicating with.

It is possible for a task to exert a fairly fine degree of control over the entry calls to be accepted using 'select' statements. A 'select' statement enables a task to wait on a call to one of several entries, to determine which 'accept' statement should be executed depending on the state of variables, to specify an alternative course of action if an entry call does not arrive within a certain period of time (possibly zero), or even to terminate if the prevailing circumstances are appropriate.

A.8   Real-time features

Concurrency is, of course, one of the major requirements of a language for embedded systems. There are, however, several other features which are important for real-time programming, the first being a notion of time. There are two notions of time recognized by Ada. The first is absolute time, which is represented by values of type TIME defined in the predefined package CALENDAR. This package also exports a function CLOCK which uses the system clock to return the absolute time at the moment when it was invoked.

The other notion is that of a period of time, or duration, and is represented by the predefined fixed-point type DURATION. Values of type DURATION can be used in a 'delay' statement to arrange for the execution of a task to be suspended for the specified time, or can be used in a timed entry call to indicate that an entry call should be abandoned should the rendezvous not start within the specified time.

A.8.1   Representation clauses

As mentioned earlier, another important requirement when programming real-time systems is to be able to define interaction with hardware devices. This is achieved in Ada by means of representation specifications, which are used to inform the compiler how entities in a program should be implemented in terms of the low-level system properties. There are several different types of representation clause but the important ones as far as interacting with external devices are concerned are the *address clause* and the *length clause*. The first specifies the (start) address of a particular entity (e.g. an object, subprogram, task, package) in memory, while the second is used to indicate how much space the entity should occupy.

Interrupts are handled in Ada by using an address clause to associate an address with an entry. When the interrupt occurs, the corresponding 'accept' statement is executed as if it had been called by a task with a priority higher than any in the program. This ensures that the interrupt handler cannot be pre-empted by another task.

Interaction with an external device is achieved by using an address clause and length clause to identify the region of memory which is used by the device to deposit data or to read commands. By arranging for an object of the appropriate type to occupy this particular region of memory, these values can be written and read by the components of an Ada program.

A.9 Execution

Execution of Ada software is achieved through the notion of a 'main program'. Although an application may be designed in terms of separately compiled program units, and may contain several concurrent tasks, the 'program' is the only vehicle for the execution of Ada software.

A 'main program' is denoted by a library subprogram. Although the ALRM permits any library subprogram to be used as a main program, most implementations permit only parameterless procedures to be used. In general, a library subprogram chosen as a main program will depend on (i.e. have context clauses for) several other library units, but this is not necessary. In either case, implementations of Ada invariably require a 'linking' operation to be performed before a program may be executed. During this operation the compilation system identifies all the library units on which the specified subprogram depends, and combines them in an executable image.

The execution of the program proceeds as if the main subprogram was called by an imaginary 'environment' task. First the units on which the main subprogram depends are *elaborated* according to a partial ordering defined by the language, and then the main subprogram is elaborated and executed.

A.10   The future

Since its introduction in the early '80s Ada has had a significant influence on the practice of software engineering in most areas of software development, not merely in the domain of embedded systems. Unfortunately, it has not been as successful as was envisaged and hoped. This is mainly due to the fact that complexity of the language has caused a significant delay in the appearance of high-quality, efficient compilers. Many early experiments with the language have failed due to the lack of suitable compilers.

Over the last few years, however, compilers have been released of comparable efficiency to those in most other languages. Nevertheless, the language does have some features which are inherently inefficient, particularly in connection with tasking. It is hoped that the next version of Ada, which is under development at the time of writing, will tackle some of these problems. One of the central proposals for Ada9X (the temporary name for the language) is the introduction of *protected* records, which offer a much more efficient way of achieving exclusion synchronization than tasking.

While Ada was experiencing these 'teething' difficulties other technologies emerged with alternative strategies for software engineering, and some of these are beginning to displace Ada outside the immediate domain of embedded systems. The most important of these is, of course, object-oriented programming. Not surprisingly, many of the proposals for Ada9X aim to introduce more 'object-oriented' features into the language.

From the point of view of DRAGOON, the features proposed for the new version of Ada will facilitate a much neater and more efficient implementation of the language. Given that there is likely to be a similar delay in the emergence of high-quality Ada9X compilers, an important role for object-oriented Ada enhancements like DRAGOON, implemented through a preprocessor, may well be to provide a bridge between Ada83 and Ada9X. Code written in DRAGOON can be implemented by translation into Ada83 until high quality Ada9X compilers emerge, and it becomes beneficial to translate the code (without modification) into Ada9X.

Appendix B
Glossary

Abstract class A class that has one or more 'deferred' methods, and thus does not have a fully defined implementation. The deferred methods are intended to be 'concreted' by subclasses. It is possible to define instance variables of an abstract class type, but it is not possible to create objects of such a class.

Active object An object which possesses a thread.

Actualization The step by which a generic class is 'instantiated' to generate a normal (non-generic) class. When a generic class is actualized the generic formal parameters must be matched with actual parameters satisfying the specified requirements.

Ancestor A class higher up in the inheritance hierarchy from which a class inherits properties. An ancestor of a class does not have to be an immediate parent.

Behaviour A set of synchronization constraints which define how the methods of an object may execute in relation to one another (i.e. how their execution may be temporally interleaved).

Behavioural class A construct which describes an abstract behaviour in terms of boolean expressions over 'history' functions. A behavioural class is not a class in the normal sense, since it cannot be directly instantiated, but is called a class to emphasize the fact that it may serve as a parent.

Behavioured class A class that has one parent which is a behavioural class, and one or more parents which are conventional (i.e. unbehavioured) classes. The class inherits its functionality from its 'sequential parents' and its behaviour from its behavioural parent.

Class The basic structuring module used to describe components of a system. Classes have three distinct facets; they represent object templates, object types, and object sets.

Clientship The fundamental relationship between objects and classes in a system. Clientship is used when instances of one class need to 'use' the services (i.e. methods) exported by instances of other.

Conferred behaviour The behaviour which a class/object obtains through interaction with behavioured clients.

Conformance A relationship between classes, based solely on the form of their interfaces, which guarantees that instances of one class will be able to service all the method calls that instances of another will. Conformance is a necessary, but not sufficient, condition for type compatibility.

Deferred method A method of an abstract class whose implementation is to be provided by subclasses. A deferred method may have a partial body defining pre and post-conditions that future implementations must satisfy.

Descendent A class lower down in the inheritance hierarchy which inherits properties from a class. Descendents of a class need not be its immediate heirs.

Executable class A class that has one parent which is an 'execution support' class, and one or more parents which are normal (non- execution support) classes. The class inherits its functionality from its normal parents, and the ability to execute on a particular type of machine from its execution support parent. An executable class corresponds to a fully-linked, executable object module.

Execution support class A class which exports methods providing services idiosyncratic of a particular kind of execution environment, and endows its subclasses with the ability to execute in that kind of environment.

Generic class A class which is parameterized with respect to one or more types. The generic formal types may be Ada-style type parameters, or may be classes. Generic classes must be 'actualized' to generate instances from which objects can be created. An actualization of a generic class is not type compatible with any other class.

Heir An immediate descendent of another class in an inheritance hierarchy.

History functions Predefined functions (sometimes called synchronization counters) used in the definition of behaviours. They return information about the calls to, and execution of, methods in a set since system initialization time: 'req' returns the number of calls to methods in the set, 'act' the number of activations, and 'fin' the number of completions.

Imported reference A reference stored in an object's instance variable which was not generated by the object itself through invocation of a CREATE method.

Ingenerate reference A reference stored in an object's instance variable which was generated by the object itself through invocation of a CREATE method.

Inheritance A relationship between classes in which one class – the heir – automatically obtains the properties of another class – the parent. Inheritance is therefore a powerful mechanism for reusing class implementations. It is also a necessary condition for a subclass (i.e. subtype) relationship between classes.

Instance variable A variable, analogous to an access variable in Ada or pointer in other languages, which stores a reference to an object. An instance variable has two associated types: the 'static' type with which it was declared and the 'dynamic' type associated with the object it refers to at a given moment.

Instantiation The act of generating an object (class instance) from a class. It is achieved through activation of the special method CREATE.

Method The fundamental construct in object-oriented languages for defining actions (corresponding to the subprogram in Ada). Every method is intimately associated with one object, and can only directly affect the state of that object.

Multiple inheritance An enhancement of the inheritance mechanism in which a class may have more than one parent.

Object The fundamental structuring unit of object-oriented systems. In its simplest form an object is composed of a data structure combined with the operations that manipulate it. The object is the abstraction through which many mechanisms that are often separated in other languages are unified in DRAGOON.

Parent An immediate ancestor of another class in an inheritance hierarchy.

Passive object An object which possesses no thread, and which therefore lacks an independent execution thread (thread of control).

Physical node class A class which exports methods providing services idiosyncratic of a particular kind of processor. Instances of the class model processors in a network.

Port variable An instance variable designed to hold imported references, and thus to refer to 'external' objects.

Safe method A method which has no parameters of a class type or an access type. All the parameters of the method are thus of a static type.

State variable An instance variable designed to hold ingenerate references, and thus to refer to 'internal' objects.

Subclass A class which is both a descendent and a subtype of (i.e. conformant with) another class by the virtue of the fact that it does not remove any methods from the inherited interface.

Superclass The inverse of the subclass relationship.

Template package An Ada-style package which is subject to the restriction that it may not contain any declarations that would give it a state, or may not 'with' another package which breaks this rule.

Thread The execution thread (or process part) of an object which executes asynchronously with the object's methods and the threads of other objects.

Type compatibility A relationship between two classes which indicates that instances of one class may be used wherever instances of another are expected. More specifically, it means that instances of one class may be assigned to instances variables of another class, or may be matched to formal parameters of another class. Inheritance and conformance are both necessary for type compatibility.

Unsafe method A method which contains one or more parameters of a class or access type, and may thus be used to exchange references.

Virtual node class A class which conforms to a set of rules designed to ensure that its instances do not communicate with other objects by exchanging references. Virtual node classes are therefore suitable for execution on the separate nodes of a loosely-coupled network.

References

Agha, G., 1986,
"An Overview of Actor Languages", *SIGPLAN Notices*, vol. 21, no. 10, pp. 58–67.

Almes, G.T., Black, A.P., Lazowska, E.D. and Noe, J.D., 1985,
"The Eden System: A Technical Review", *IEEE Transactions on Software Engineering*, vol. SE–11, no. 1, pp. 43–59.

Andrews, G.R. and Schneider, F.B., 1983,
"Concepts and Notations for Concurrent Programming", *Computing Surveys*, vol. 15, no. 1, March, pp. 3–43.

Andrews, G.R. and Olson, R., 1986,
"The Evolution of the SR Programming Language", *Distributed Computing*, no. 1, July, pp. 133–149.

America, P., 1987,
"POOL-T: A Parallel Object-Oriented Language", in *Object Oriented Concurrent Programming*, MIT Press, pp. 199–220.

America, P., 1989,
"Issues in the Design of Parallel Object-Oriented Languages", *Esprit Project 415 Document 452*, Philips Research Laboratories, Eindhoven, March.

Atkinson, C., 1988,
"Programming Distributed Systems in Ada", in *Proc. IFIP Conf. on Hardware and Software for Real-Time Process Control*, Warsaw, (ed. Zalewski and Ehrenberger), North-Holland Publishing Company, pp. 45–53.

Atkinson, C., Moreton, T. and Natali, A., 1988,
Ada for Distributed Systems, The Ada Companion Series, Cambridge University Press.

Atkinson, C. and Di Maio, A., 1989,
"From DIADEM to DRAGOON", in *Proc. Distributed Ada Symposium 1989 (DA'89)*, Dec., The Ada Companion Series, Cambridge University Press, pp. 109–139.

Atkinson, C., Goldsack, S.J., Di Maio, A. and Bayan, R., 1990,
"Object-Oriented Concurrency and Distribution in DRAGOON",
Journal of Object-Oriented Programming, vol. 4, no. 1, March/April,
pp. 11–19.

Bach, W.W., 1989,
"Is Ada Really an Object-Oriented Programming Language?", *The
Journal of Pascal, Ada and Modula-2*, March/April, pp. 19–25.

Banerjee, J., Chou, H., Garza, J.F., Kim, W., Woelk, D., Ballou, N. and
Kim, H., 1987,
"Data Model Issues for Object-Oriented Applications", *ACM Trans-
actions on Office Information Systems*, vol. 5, no. 1, pp. 3–26.

Barnes, J.G.P., 1989,
Programming in Ada – Third Edition, Addison-Wesley Publishing
Company.

Bayan, R., Destombes, C. and Kaag, F., 1989,
"DDX Distributed Executive Interface for MOTOROLA 68020
Multiprocessor DRAGOON Applications", *Project Report, DRA-
GON/WP2.T5/TECSI/1*.

Bayan, R., Crespi-Reghizzi, S. and Di Maio, A., 1989,
"DRAGOON: Distribution and Reconfiguration of Ada Programs",
*Workshop on Communication Networks and Distributed Operating
Systems within the Space Environment*, ESA ESTEC, Noordwijk,
Netherlands, Oct.

Ben-Gershon, M.Y., 1990,
"A Library of Reusable Components for DRAGOON", MSc Thesis,
Dept. of Computing, Imperial College, London.

Bennet, J.K., 1987,
"The Design and Implementation of Distributed Smalltalk", *OOP-
SLA'87 Conference Proceedings, SIGPLAN Notices (Special Issue)*,
vol. 22, no. 12, pp. 318–329.

Berard, E., 1985,
Object-Oriented Design Handbook for Ada Software, EVB Software
Engineering Inc.

Birtwistle, G., Dahl, O., Myrhaug, B. and Nygaard, K., 1983,
Simula Begin, Studentliteratur (Lund) and Auerbach Publishers Inc.

Black, A., Hutchinson, N., Jul, E. and Levy, H., 1986,
"Object Structure in the Emerald System", *OOPSLA'86 Conference Proceedings, SIGPLAN Notices (Special Issue)*, vol. 21, no. 11,
pp. 78–86.

Black, A., Hutchinson, N., Jul, E., Levy, H. and Carter, L., 1987,
"Distribution and Abstract Types in Emerald", *IEEE Transactions
on Software Engineering*, vol. SE13, no. 1, Jan., pp. 65–76.

Blair, S.G., Gallagher, J.J. and Malik, J., 1989,
"Genericity vs Inheritance vs Delegation vs Conformance vs ...",
Journal of Object-Oriented Programming, vol. 2, no. 3, Sept/Oct,
pp. 11–17.

Boari, M., Crespi-Reghizzi, S., Dapra, A., Maderna, F. and Natali, A.,
1984,
"Multi-Microprocessor Programming Techniques: MML a New Set of
Tools", *IEEE Computer*, Jan., pp. 47–59.

Booch, G., 1983,
Software Engineering with Ada, Benjamin/Cummings Publishing
Company.

Booch, G., 1987,
Software Components with Ada, Benjamin/Cummings Publishing
Company.

Borning, A., 1986,
"Classes versus Prototypes in Object-Oriented Languages", *Fall Joint
Computer Conference*, ACM/IEEE, Dallas, Texas.

Bott, F., Higgs, C. and Ormsby, A., 1989,
"DEMON User Manual: Version 3.0", *Project Report, DRA-
GON/WP2.T3/UCW/5*.

Breu, R. and Zucca, E., 1989,
"An Algebraic Compositional Semantics of an Object Notation with
Concurrency", *Project Report, DRAGON/WP2.T1/D2*.

Brinch Hansen, P., 1973,
"Concurrent Programming Concepts", *ACM Computing Surveys*,
vol. 5, no. 4, pp. 223–245.

Bobrow, D.G. and Stefik, M.J., 1982,
LOOPS: an Object-Oriented Programming System for Interlisp, Technical Report, Xerox PARC.

Burns, A., 1985,
Concurrent Programming in Ada, The Ada Companion Series, Cambridge University Press, pp. 34–36.

Burns, A., Lister, A.M. and Wellings, A.J., 1985,
"A Review of Ada Tasking", *York Computer Science Report No. 78*,
Dept. of Computer Science, University of York.

Campbell, R.H. and Habermann, A.N., 1974,
"The Specification of Process Synchronisation by Path Expressions",
Lecture Notes in Computer Science, vol. 16, Springer-Verlag, pp. 89–
102.

Cardelli, L. and Wegner, P., 1985,
"On Understanding Types, Data Abstraction and Polymorphism",
ACM Computing Surveys, vol. 17, no. 4, pp. 471–522.

Cardelli, L., Donahue, J., Glassman, L., Jordan, M., Kalsow, B. and Nelson, G., 1988,
Modula-3 Report, Systems Research Center, Palo Alto, California.

Chikayana, T., 1984,
"ESP Reference Manual", *ICOT Technical Report: TR-044* Tokyo, Japan.

Coad, P. and Yourdon, E., 1990,
Object-Oriented Analysis, Yourdon Press.

Comandos, 1987,
"Comandos Object Oriented Architecture", *Intermediate Report on Global Architecture*, Feb.

Conway, M.E., 1963,
"A Multiprocessor System Design", in *Proc. AFIPS Fall Jt. Computer Conf.*, vol. 24, Spartan Books, Maryland, pp. 139–146.

Cook, W.R., 1989,
"A Proposal for Making Eiffel Type-Safe", in *ECOOP'89 Conference Proceedings* (ed. Cook), BCS Workshop Series, Cambridge University Press, pp. 57–70.

Cox, B., 1986,
Object-Oriented Programming – An Evolutionary Approach, Addison-Wesley Publishing Company.

Crowl, L.A., 1988,
"A Uniform Object Model for Parallel Programming", position paper for *Proc. ACM Sigplan Workshop on Object-Based Concurrent Programming, SIGPLAN Notices*, vol. 24, no. 4, pp. 79–80.

Davison, A., 1989,
Polka: A Parlog Object-Oriented Language, PhD Thesis, Dept. of Computing, Imperial College, London.

Dasgupta, P., 1986,
"A Probe Based Monitoring Scheme for an Object-Oriented Distributed Operating System", *OOPSLA'86 Conference Proceedings, SIGPLAN Notices (Special Issue)*, vol. 21, no. 11, pp. 57–66.

Decouchant, D., Le Dot, P., Riveill, M., Roisin, C. and Rousset de Pina, X., 1990,
"A Synchronization Mechanism for an Object-Oriented Distributed System", Bull - IMAG / Systèmes, Z.I. de Mayencin - 2, rue Vignate, 38610 Gières, France.

Dijkstra, E.W., 1968,
"Cooperating Sequential Processes", in *Programming Languages*, (ed. Genuys), Academic Press.

Di Maio, A., Bott, F., Sommerville, I., Bayan, R. and Wirsing, M., 1989,
"The DRAGON Project", *1989 Esprit Conference*, Brussels, pp. 554–567.

Di Maio, A., Cardigno, C., Bayan, R., Destombes, C. and Atkinson, C., 1989,
"DRAGOON: An Ada-based Object-Oriented Language for Concurrent, Real-Time, Distributed Systems", *Proc. Ada-Europe International Conference 1989*, Madrid, The Ada Companion Series.

Di Maio, A., Cardigno, C., Genolini, S., Crespi-Reghizzi, S., Bayan, R., Destombes, C., Atkinson, C. and Goldsack, S.J., 1988,
"DRAGOON: The Language and its Implementation", *Project Report DRAGON/WP1.T6/TXT/11*.

DoD, 1983,
Reference Manual for the Ada Programming Language, Ada Joint Program Office, Department of Defense, ANSI/MIL-STD-1815A.

Downes, V.A. and Goldsack, S. J., 1982,
Programming Embedded Systems with Ada, Prentice-Hall International.

Dulay, N., Kramer, J., Magee, J., Sloman, S. and Twidle, K., 1987,
"Distributed System Construction: Experience with the CONIC Toolkit", *Experiences with Distributed Systems: Proc. Int. Workshop*, Kaiserslautern, FRG, pp. 189–212.

Forestier, J.P., Forarino, C. and Franchi-Zannettacci, P., 1989,
"Ada++: A Class and Inheritance Extension for Ada", *Proc. of the Ada Europe Int. Conf.*, Madrid, June, pp. 189–212.

Gautier, R.J., Bott, F. and Elliott, A., 1989,
"Ada Reuse Guidelines", in *Software Reuse with Ada*, (ed. Gautier and Wallis), Peter Peregrinus Ltd.

Genolini, S., Di Maio, A., Cardigno, C., Goldsack, S. and Atkinson, C., 1989,
"Specifying Synchronisation Constraints in a Concurrent Object-Oriented Language", *Proc. First Int. Conf. on Technology of Object-Oriented Languages and Systems (TOOLS'89)*, Paris – La Defense, Nov.

Genolini, S. and Cardigno, C., 1989,
"Detailed Design of the DRAGOON Compilation System", *Project Report, DRAGON/WP2.T4/TXT/6*.

Goldsack, S.J., 1989,
Specifying Requirements: An Introduction to the FOREST Approach, Imperial College Research Report, Dept. of Computing, London.

Goldsack, S.J., Atkinson, C., Natali, A., Di Maio, A., Maderna, F. and Moreton, T., 1987,
"Ada for Distributed Systems: A Library of Virtual Nodes", *Ada Components: Libraries and Tools, Proc. Ada-Europe Int. Conf.*, The Ada Companion Series, Cambridge University Press, pp. 253–265.

Goldsack, S.J. and Atkinson, C., 1989,
"An Object-Oriented Approach to Virtual Nodes: Are Package Types an Answer?", *Proc. 3rd Int. Workshop on Real-Time Ada Issues*, Nemacolin Woodlands, Farmington, PA, June, pp. 95–101.

Goldberg, A. and Robson, D., 1983,
Smalltalk-80: The Language and its Implementation, Addison-Wesley Publishing Company.

Gregory, S., 1987,
Parallel Logic Programming in PARLOG, Addison-Wesley Publishing Company.

Hoare, C.A.R., 1974,
"Monitors: An Operating System Structuring Concept", *Communications of the ACM*, vol. 17, no. 10, pp. 549–557.

Hoare, C.A.R., 1978,
"Communicating Sequential Processes", *Communications of the ACM*, vol. 21, no. 8, pp. 666–677.

HOOD, 1987,
The HOOD Manual, Issue 2.1. The European Space Agency, Postbus 299 AG Noordwijk, The Netherlands.

Hutcheon, A.D. and Wellings, A.J., 1987,
"Ada for Distributed Systems", *Computer Standards and Interfaces*, vol. 6, no. 1, pp. 71–82.

Hutcheon, A.D. and Wellings, A.J., 1988,
"The Virtual Node Approach to Designing Distributed Ada Programs", *Proc. 7th Ada UK International Conference*, Ada User, vol. 9 (supplement), pp. 35–42.

Ichbiah, J.D, Barnes, J.G.P., Firth, R.J. and Woodger, M., 1986,
Rationale for the Design of the Ada Programming Language, Honeywell Systems and Research Center, Minneapolis, and ALSYS, France.

Ishikawa, Y. and Tokoro, M., 1987,
"Orient84/K: An Object-Oriented Concurrent Programming Language for Knowledge Representation", in *Object-Oriented Concurrent Programming*, (ed. Yonezawa and Tokoro), MIT Press, pp. 159–198.

Jackson, M.A., 1975,
Principles of Program Design, Academic Press.

Kafura, D.G., 1988,
Concurrent Object-Oriented Real-Time Systems, Technical Report, TR 88-47, Dept. of Computer Science, Virginia Tech.

Kafura, D.G. and Lee, K.H., 1989,
"Inheritance in Actor Based Concurrent Object-Oriented Languages", *ECOOP'89 Conference Proceedings* (ed. Cook), BCS Workshop Series, Cambridge University Press, pp. 131–145.

Kaiser, G.E., Popovich, S.S., Hseush, W. and Wu, S.F., 1989,
  "MELDing Multiple Granularities of Parallelism", *ECOOP'89 Conference Proceedings* (ed. Cook), BCS Workshop Series, Cambridge University Press, pp. 147–166.

Khosla, S., 1988,
  System Specification: A Deontic Approach, PhD Thesis, Dept. of Computing, Imperial College, London.

Krakowiak, S., Meysembourg, M., Nguyen, H., Riveill, M., Roisin, C. and Rousset de Pina, X., 1990,
  "Design and Implementation of an Object-Oriented, Strongly Typed Language for Distributed Applications", *Journal of Object-Oriented Programming*, vol. 3, no. 3, Sept./Oct., pp. 11–22.

Kristensen, B.B, Madsen, O.L., Moller-Pederson, B. and Nygaard, K., 1985,
  "Multisequential Execution for the BETA Programming Language", *SIGPLAN Notices*, vol. 20, no. 4, April, pp. 57–70.

Kramer, J. and Magee, J., 1985,
  "Dynamic Configuration for Distributed Systems", *IEEE Transactions on Software Engineering*, vol. 11, no. 4, pp. 424–435.

Kramer, J. and Magee, J., 1988,
  "A Model for Change Management", *IEEE Workshop on Future Trends in Distributed Computing Systems in the 1990s*, Hong Kong, Sept., pp. 286–295.

Lieberman, H., 1986,
  "Using Prototypical Objects to Implement Shared Behaviour in Object-Oriented Systems", *OOPSLA'86 Proceedings, SIGPLAN Notices*, vol. 21, no. 11, pp. 214–223.

Liskov, B., 1982,
  "On Linguistic Support for Distributed Programs", *IEEE Transactions*, vol. SE-8, no. 3, pp. 203–210.

Liskov, B., Atkinson, R., Bloom, T., Moss, E., Schaffert, J.C., Scheifler, R. and Snyder, A., 1981,
  CLU Reference Manual, Springer-Verlag.

McHale, C., Walsh, B., Baker, S., Donnelly, A. and Harris, N., 1990
  "Extending Synchronisation Counters", Dept. of Computer Science, University of Dublin, Trinity College, Dublin, Ireland.

McIlroy, M.D., 1969,
  "Mass Produced Software Components", in *Software Engineering*, report on a conference sponsored by the NATO Science Committee, Garmisch, Germany, 1968, pp. 138–150.

MacLennan, B.J., 1982,
  "Values and Objects in Programming Languages", *SIGPLAN Notices*, vol. 17, no. 12, pp. 70–79.

May, D. and Shepherd, R., 1985,
"Occam and the Transputer", in *Concurrent Languages in Distributed Systems*, North-Holland.

Matsumoto, Y., 1984,
"Some Experiences in Promoting Reusable Software Presentation in Higher Abstract Level", *IEEE Transactions on Software Engineering*, vol. SE-10, no. 5, pp. 502–513.

Meyer, B., 1986,
"Genericity versus Inheritance", *OOPSLA '86 Proceedings, SIGPLAN Notices*, vol. 21, no. 11, pp. 391–405.

Meyer, B., 1988,
Object-Oriented Software Construction, Prentice-Hall.

Meyer, B. and Nerson, J., 1989,
Eiffel Release 2.2 Overview, Interactive Software Engineering Inc.

Milner, R., 1984,
"A Proposal for Standard ML", *Proc. of the Symp. on LISP and Functional Programming*, ACM, pp. 184–197.

Moon, D.A., 1986,
"Object-Oriented Programming with Flavors", *OOPSLA '86 Proceedings, SIGPLAN Notices*, vol. 21, no. 11, pp. 1–8.

Mullery, G., 1976,
"CORE – A Method for Controlled Requirement Specification", *Proc. 4th Int. Conf. Software Engineering*, Munich, IEEE Computer Society Press.

Nierstraz, O.M., 1987,
"Active Objects in Hybrid", *OOPSLA '87 Conference Proceedings, SIGPLAN Notices (Special Issue)*, vol. 22, no. 12, pp. 243–253.

Ormsby, A., 1990,
"Object-Oriented Design Methods", chapter to appear in *Object-Oriented Languages, Systems and Applications* (ed. Blair, Gallagher, Hutchinson and Shepherd), Pitman Publishing.

Perez, E. P., 1988,
"Simulating Inheritance with Ada", *Ada Letters*, vol. VIII, no. 5, Sept./Oct., pp. 37–46.

Peterson, G. L., 1981,
"Myths about the Mutual Exclusion Problem", *Information Processing Letters*, vol. 12, no. 3., pp. 115–126.

Potts, C., Finkelstein, A., Aslett, M. and Booth, J., 1986,
"Structured Common Sense: A Requirements Elicitation and Formalisation Method for Modal Action Logic", *FOREST Deliverable Report 2*.

Schaffert, C., Cooper, T., Bullis, B. and Killian, M., 1986,
"An Introduction to Trellis/Owl", *OOPSLA '86 Conference Proceedings, SIGPLAN Notices (Special Issue)*, vol. 21, no. 11, pp. 9–16.

Seidewitz, E., 1987,
"Object-Oriented Programming in Smalltalk and Ada", *OOPSLA '87 Conference Proceedings, SIGPLAN Notices (Special Issue)*, vol. 22, no. 12, pp. 202–213.

Shepherd, D., Coote, S., Gallagher, J., Lea, R., Mariani, J. and Scott, A., 1988,
"An Object-Oriented Approach to the High Level Programming of Distributed Process Control Applications", *Proc. 3rd Int. Conf. on Computer-Aided Production Engineering*, Michigan, June, pp. 235–342.

Simonian, R. and Crone, M., 1988,
"Innovada: True Object-Oriented Programming in Ada", *Journal of Object-Oriented Programming*, Nov./Dec., pp. 14–21.

Sloman, M. and Kramer, J., 1987,
Distributed Systems and Computer Networks, Prentice-Hall International.

Sommerville, I., Mariani, J., Haddley, N. and Thomson, R., 1989a,
"Software Design With Reuse", *Internal Report*, Dept. of Computing, Lancaster University, Bailrigg, Lancaster.

Sommerville, I., Haddley, N., Mariani, J. and Thomson, R., 1989b,
"The Designer's Notepad – A Hypertext System Tailored for Design", *Proc. Hypertext II Conference*, York, June.

Snodgrass, R., 1983,
"An Object-Oriented Command Language", *IEEE Transactions on Software Engineering*, vol. SE-9, no. 1, Jan., pp. 1–8.

Snyder, A., 1986,
"Encapsulation and Inheritance", *OOPSLA '87 Conference Proceedings, SIGPLAN Notices (Special Issue)*, vol. 22, no. 12, pp. 38–45.

Stroustrup, B., 1986,
The C++ Programming Language, Addison-Wesley Publishing Company.

Tedd, M., Crespi-Reghizzi, S. and Natali, A.,1984,
Ada for Multi-Microprocessors, The Ada Companion Series, Cambridge University Press.

Tomlinson, C. and Singh, V., 1989,
"Inheritance and Synchronisation with Enabled-Sets" *OOPSLA '89 Conference Proceedings, SIGPLAN Notices (Special Issue)*, vol. 24, no. 10, pp. 103–112.

Vishnubhotta, P., 1988,
"Synchronisation and Scheduling in ALPS Objects", *Proc. 8th In-*

ternational Conf. on Distributed Computer Systems, San Jose, CA, June, IEEE Computer Society Press, pp. 256–264.

von Wright, G.H., 1951,
An Essay in Modal Logic, North-Holland Publishing Company.

von Wright, G.H., 1980,
"Problems and Prospects of Deontic Logic: A Survey", in *Modern Logic – A Survey: Historical, Philosophical and Mathematical Aspects of Modern Logic and its Applications* (ed. Agazzi), D. Reidel Publishing Company, pp. 399–423.

Wegner, P., 1987,
"Dimensions of Object-Based Language Design", *OOPSLA'87 Conference Proceedings, SIGPLAN Notices (Special Issue)*, vol. 22, no. 12, pp. 168–182.

Wegner, P. and Zdonik, S.B., 1988,
"Inheritance as an Incremental Modification Mechanism or What Like Is and Isn't Like", *Proc. ECOOP'88, Lecture Notes in Computer Science 322*, Springer-Verlag, pp. 55–77.

Wirsing, M., 1988,
"Algebraic Description of Reusable Software Components", *Proc. of COMPEURO '88*, Apr., (ed. Milgrom and Wodon), IEEE Computer Society Press, pp. 300–312.

Wirth, N., 1982,
Programming in Modula-2, Springer-Verlag.

Yokote, Y. and Tokoro, M., 1986,
"The Design and Implementation of Concurrent Smalltalk", *OOPSLA'86 Proceedings, SIGPLAN Notices*, vol. 21, no. 11, pp. 331–340.

Yonezawa, Y., Briot, J. and Shibayama, E., 1986,
"Object-Oriented Concurrent Programming in ABCL/1", *OOPSLA'86 Proceedings, SIGPLAN Notices*, vol. 21, no. 11, pp. 258–268.

Program Unit Index

ALTERNATION (6.4)   102
ALTERNATIVE_CASH_REGISTER_PHYSICAL_NODE (8.9)   165

BOUNDED_BUFFER (6.11)   117
BOUNDED_QUEUE (4.6)   64
BOUNDED_SIMPLE_QUEUE (4.3)   60

CALLABLE_DISTRIBUTED_SUPERMARKET (8.14)   176
CASH_REGISTER_PHYSICAL_NODE (8.5)   162
CENTRAL_CONTROLLER (6.9)   109
CHECKOUT_POINT (8.6)   163
CHRONO_QUEUE (5.5)   76
COLOUR (3.1)   25

DATA_BASE (5.15)   85
DATED_DESCRIPTOR (3.13)   40
DATED_ITEM (3.12)   40
DATED_LIBRARY_BOOK (3.14)   41
DESCRIPTOR (7.1)   143
DESCRIPTOR_CHRONO_QUEUE (5.10)   78
DISTRIBUTED_SUPERMARKET (8.12)   172
DYNAMIC_QUEUE (4.8)   65

ELECTRICAL_DESCRIPTOR (3.8)   37
EXTENDED_CHRONO_QUEUE (5.14)   84

FORWARDER (6.10)   115
FORWARDER_CONTROLLER (8.16)   177
FULL_CENTRAL_CONTROLLER(8.15)   177
FUSE (7.2)   145

GUARDED_QUEUE (6.12)   118

LIBRARY_CHRONO_QUEUE (5.9)   78

MC_68000_EXECUTION_SUPPORT (8.10)   167
MC_68000_PHYSICAL_NODE (8.4)   162
MUTEX (6.2)   102
MUTEX_UNI_BUFFER (6.3)   102

PAR_CHRONO_QUEUE (5.8)   78
PARTIAL_CENTRAL_CONTROLLER (8.13)   176
PERISHABLE_DESCRIPTOR (3.6)   35
PRIORITIES (6.13)   121
PRIORITY_CONTROL (6.14)   122
PRODUCT (3.2)   30
PRODUCT_DESCRIPTOR (3.4)   31
PRODUCT_TYPE   25

QUEUE (4.4)   62

READERS_PRIORITY (6.7)   105
READERS_WRITERS (6.5)   103
RECONF_CENTRAL_CONTROLLER (6.17)   126
REDEFINED_DESCRIPTOR (3.9)   38
REGISTER_HARDWARE_INTERFACE (8.8)   165
RENAMED_DESCRIPTOR (3.10)   39
RESTRICTED_DESCRIPTOR (3.11)   39

SIMPLE_CALENDAR (3.3)   30
SIMPLE_ITERATOR_QUEUE (4.2)   59
SIMPLE_QUEUE (4.1)   57
STACK (3.15)   49
SUPERMARKET (6.15)   123
SUPERMARKET_NETWORK (8.11)   169

UNBOUNDED_QUEUE (4.5)   64
UNI_BUFFER (6.1)   101
UNMANAGED_QUEUE (4.7)   64

VAX_EXECUTABLE_DATA_BASE (8.1)   153
VAX_VMS_EXECUTION_SUPPORT (8.2)   153
VAX_VMS_PHYSICAL_NODE (8.3)   156

WRITERS_PRIORITY (6.6)   104

Index

abstract classes 14
abstract data types 9, 26, 77, 185
accept statement 119, 166
access functions 31
ACTIVATE method 156, 159
active
    – iterator 58
    – objects 94, 108
actor model 93
actors 110
actualization 78, 82
ad hoc polymorphism 85
Ada 2, 235
    – translation into 183
agents 110
ancestor 36
anchor 80
application object 83
APPLICATION_OBJECT 190
Aspect project 133
asynchronous
    – message passing 91
    – methods 93

balking queue 56
behaviour 98
    – conferred 113
    – indexed 121
behavioural
    – class libraries 106
    – inheritance 98
    – deficiencies 120
behavioural classes 99, 101
behavioured classes 99, 101, 214

Booch, G. 10, 106
bounded component 55
bounded queue 60

CALENDAR – Ada package 30
canonical class pairs 161
Cardelli, L. 85
checkout points 4
chronological queue 76
class 9, 30
    – abstract 17
    – body 31
    – canonical pairs 161
    – implementation 31
    – interface 31
    – representation in Ada 183
    – specification 31
    – types 43
clientship 13
CLU clusters 150
communication transparency 134
completes 65
component
    – bounded 55
    – concurrent 106
    – engineering 53, 70
    – hierarchy 56
    – managed 55
Component Information Store 229
condition
    – synchronization 91
    – variables 92
CONDITION_ERROR 63

conferred behaviour 113
configuration phases 113
conformance 45
CONIC 133, 153
constrained genericity 75
contravariance 45
copy semantics 137
CREATE method 32, 192
    – redefinition 61
critical region 91

data abstraction 26
database object 4, 85
dates 25
declaration by association 79
default form 206
deferred 62
delegation 17
DEMON 27, 230
descendant 36
design
    – for reuse 53
    – with reuse 53
Designers Notepad 229
DIADEM project 4, 29, 133, 222
discrete type 82
discriminant 188
distribution 129
    – language approach 132
    – operating system approach
       132
DRAGON
    – design method 230
    – distributed executive 222
    – formal methods 230
    – project 27, 229
    – reuse toolset 229
DRAGOON 3
    – design principles 231
dynamic binding 14, 66
    – implementation 198
dynamic typing 42

Eiffel 23, 81
    – genericity 79
elaboration 158

embedded systems 1
Emerald 152
entry 166
enumeration types 25
exceptions 31
exclusion
    – symbol 104
    – synchronization 91
executable
    – class 153
    – objects 219
execution
    – model 1149, 158
    – support classes 152
    – threads 89
extensibility 67

fault tolerance 130
fixed-point type 82
floating-point type 82
FOREST project 100
forking 90

generality 54
generic
    – classes 82
       – implementation of 209
    – formal parameters 82
    – instantiation 74
    – units 2
guard 92
    – evaluation 118
    – implementation of 214
guarded
    – component 106
    – permissions 117
Guardian – in Argus 133, 151

hardware specification 168
heavyweight objects 150, 153
heir 16, 35
HEIR field 191
history functions 99
HOOD 10, 23
host 129
HOST pseudo-variable 170

hybrid language 11

immutable objects 24
implementing subprograms 200
imported reference 138
in 50
include relationship 138
inclusion polymorphism 73
indexed behaviours 121
ingenerate reference 138
inheritance 15
– Ada support for 187
– behavioural 98
– linear 194
– multiple 39, 205
– of execution support 152
– of genericity 83
instance variable 32
instantiation 78
interrupt 161
– methods 166
iterator queue 58

lightweight objects 150
limited private types 82
linear inheritance 194
LOAD_ONTO method 154
loosely coupled systems 129

MacLennan, B. J. 24
main program 150
managed component 55
MASCOT 10
memory management 55
message passing 90, 129
method 31
– modification 38
– overloading 85
– redefinition 38
– renaming 38
– restriction 39
– selection shells 199
Meyer, B. 23, 74
mixed paradigm 25, 231
monitor 92, 95
multiple component 106

MULTIPLE field 191
multiple inheritance 40, 205
multiple offspring 202

name clashes 41

object 8, 30
– active 94, 108
– in Ada 183, 190
– passive 110
– state list 190
object-oriented
– analysis 19
– design 10, 19
– environments 19, 131
– languages 11
– programming 7, 19
OFFSPRING_NO field 191, 203
open and closed principle 71
ORIGIN field 208
overloading 85

parameterization contract 81
parametric polymorphism 74
parent 16, 35
PART_OF function 194
passive objects 110
path expressions 99
per operator 100
persistence 18
physical node classes 156
polymorphism 14, 66
– Ada support for 187
– *ad hoc* 85
– inclusion 73
– parametric 74
POOL 95, 111
port
– task 223
– variables 139
postconditions 63
preconditions 63
priority queue 56
private 138
private types 75, 82
product descriptors 5

program partitioning phase 133
programming by difference 70
prototypical objects 17

queue
    – balking 56
    – bounded 60
    – chronological 76
    – iterator 58

reconfiguration 1, 125
    – environment driven 174
    – system driven 175
redefines 38
reference-free communication 136
remote
    – communication 224
    – procedure call 95
REMOTE_ERROR – exception 142
removes 39
renames 38
resource – in SR 1233
reuse 53
root class 123
ruled 102, 118
ruled by 102

safe methods 140
select 111
    – statement 119
semaphore 91
sequence – in MML 133
sequential component 106
servers 110
shared variables 90
Simula 11
software
    – compilation 149
    – Component Catalogue 229
    – execution 149
spatial form 55
START_ERROR exception 110
START method 109, 158
state variables 140
static
    – inheritance 16

– types 43
strong typing 42
subclass 47
superclass 47
Supermarket Control System 4
surrogate tasks 223
synchronization 91, 95
synchronous message passing 90
system
    – calls 156, 161
    – configuration 149

task module – in CONIC 133
taxonomy of components 55
template packages 29
temporal forms 55, 106
thread 108
type 41
    – compatibility 44, 80, 85
    – conversion 48
    – dynamic 42
    – enumeration 25
    – limited private 82
    – private 75, 82
    – redefinition 79

unconstrained genericity 74
unsafe methods 140
update operations 31
using 'old' methods 61

value
    – abstractions 25
    – oriented paradigm 25
virtual node 133
    – characteristics 134
    – objects 137

Wegner, P. 19, 85
where 102